D0001178

"In elevating the voices of people who struggle every day for understanding, accommodation, and equal treatment, Pia Justesen has made an important contribution to the movement to end the 'invisibility of disability.' This moving and highly engaging collection demonstrates the many ways in which society imposes institutional, physical, and attitudinal barriers that prevent people with disabilities from enjoying true equality and freedom. A beautiful work of nonfiction."

—Nadine Strossen, former president of the ACLU

"These extraordinarily moving narratives put us in contact with a set of vivid individuals who know more about the realities of life than many of us, and who testify to their experience with insight, warmth, fury, and humor. Pia Justesen has done a remarkable job in eliciting these candid self-portraits and then crafting them into powerful, evocative stories. The result is a compelling book we very much need at the present moment—or maybe always."

—Phillip Lopate, author of *To Show and to Tell: The Craft of Literary Nonfiction*

"This book takes the reader on a loving and respectful journey into the hearts and minds of ordinary persons with disabilities with extraordinary tales to tell. It takes the reader into their kitchens and all the 'small places' that Eleanor Roosevelt so cherished. It really takes the reader into their souls. Through their heartfelt testimony, it reveals deep hurt as well as the beauty of the human spirit even in dire circumstances. It touches on the intergenerational effects of disability—the love and loneliness of parents and sometimes the distance of siblings. It powerfully reminds us that to be human is to be loved and to feel a sense of belonging. The stories it tells are universal. The right to 'pursue happiness'—and love and value—belongs to all."

—Gerard Quinn, Wallenberg chair, Raoul Wallenberg Institute of Human Rights

"Unless you are disabled, it is difficult to understand how it feels to be disempowered and excluded by barriers, prejudice, and the false assumptions of others. This book makes painful reading, because it throws light on disabling barriers and shows how deeply they penetrate and effect the life of every person who has an impairment. It helps to give voice to the individuals interviewed and to the wider community of persons with disabilities."

—Lisa Waddington, professor and chair in
European disability law at Maastricht University

From the
PERIPHERY

From the PERIPHERY

REAL-LIFE STORIES *of* DISABILITY

PIA JUSTESEN

Lawrence Hill Books

Chicago

Published by Lawrence Hill Books
an imprint of Chicago Review Press Incorporated
814 North Franklin Street
Chicago, Illinois 60610
978-1-64160-158-0

Library of Congress Cataloging-in-Publication Data
Is available from the Library of Congress.

Photos by Pia Justesen. Taken in Chicago, these photographs illustrate disability life and culture. They also illustrate places that can be difficult to access for people with disabilities and some of the barriers in the environment.

Cover design: Preston Pisellini
Typesetting: Nord Compo

Printed in the United States of America
5 4 3 2 1

CONTENTS

FOREWORD

by Senator Tom Harkin

DURING MY FORTY-PLUS YEARS of working to advance the cause of full inclusion for persons with disabilities in all aspects of society, I have learned that the most powerful arguments for pursuing this goal come from the voices and stories of real people with disabilities.

This, then, is a powerful book. Pia Justesen has captured these voices and stories in a compelling narrative about the struggles against barriers, both physical and attitudinal, that prevent full inclusion. There are certain themes that weave through most of the stories: anger, isolation, rejection, frustration, and loneliness; pity, patronization, and low expectations.

It is appropriate that the author starts with Marca Bristo. Marca, a personal friend of mine for many years, is one of the pioneers of the independent living movement. Marca has an acquired mobility impairment as the result of a diving accident when she was twenty-three years old. She initially thought the burden was on her "to adjust to the world. It never dawned on me that the world had to change." Marca speaks of her "anger," how her "world shrank," and how "my friends would go places that I couldn't go. And I just had to stay home." These are sentiments echoed by many throughout this book. But Marca also talks about how she came to understand that the inability to do certain things—like going to the grocery store—was not inherent in her or her disability but part of a world of built-in discriminatory practices and structures.

This, in essence, is what the Americans with Disabilities Act (ADA) began to change—to shift the focus from a "medical" view of disability, which had existed for centuries, to a system in which changes would be made in the "built" environment: in transportation, housing, public spaces, and private businesses that catered to the general public. These changes would permit individuals with disabilities to be free from artificial barriers—to allow them to "go to the grocery store."

Another burden that has been like a heavy weight preventing so many disabled youth from dreaming big and pursuing those dreams has been the culture of low expectations. We meet Kiel, whose parents were told they were "not being realistic about what [Kiel] was capable of." I have confronted this fear of failure, not on the part of the young person with a disability but on the part of the parents or guardians or the general public. Before I retired from the Senate, I made changes in federal law to keep young persons with disabilities who are graduating from an individualized education program (IEP) from being piped blindly into dead-end, sub-minimum-wage jobs, mainly in what are called "sheltered workshops." Now they would first be directed toward competitive integrated employment—real jobs in the workforce. During committee hearings on this initiative, one parent, well meaning and understandably protective of his child, said, "Senator, you are setting these kids up for failure." I replied, "And what is your point? Are you saying that kids with disabilities shouldn't face failure? But failure is a part of life, of growing up. All kids try things and find out they don't like that type of work or are not suited for it, until they find something they both like and are capable of doing. Why should kids with disabilities be any different? Let them experience life!" The burden of low expectations is repeated in other stories throughout the book. I am sad to say it is still very prevalent in general society today.

Kiel's discussions also focus on his loneliness and on being ostracized during his school years. This sense of rejection and isolation, and even bullying in school, is repeated by several other interviewees. Jennifer Wheeler talks about her son eating lunch "by himself in the lunchroom every day." Candace Coleman recalls how she "wanted to be in a relationship, have fun after school, and socialize with peers," but bullying "penetrated my whole life." Curtis Harris remembers that "other students treated me like crap. . . . They called me . . . 'retarded.'" Susan Aarup was isolated in high school and not invited to school dances. Gary Arnold's dwarfism brought bullying, ridicule, and embarrassing encounters in school. Mary Rosenberg was "picked on" in school and says it "affects you for longer than you're probably even aware of."

And Julie Schrager has an observation that cuts to the core of what is happening in America today when she says, "There's a change in the American culture in our society. The idea that it's OK to be hateful is appalling." Witness a candidate for president of the United States, who is afterward successful, mocking a person with a disability in front of a large crowd—as Alissa Chung observes in her interview.

An antidote to such attitudes can be found in another of the author's keen observations: the fact that "people with disabilities do not constitute a homogenous group." For much of history, that's how people with disabilities were seen, not as individuals but as part of a "disability group" suffering from a "medical condition." The notion of disability as a pitiful medical condition has been replaced under the ADA by a new construct of disability as a *social* condition, defined mainly by the obstacles, both structural and attitudinal, that turn an impairment into a "disability." By focusing on breaking down barriers in the built environment, the ADA also helps to dismantle the "attitudinal barriers" held by the general public.

Yet as we move toward seeing disability as a social construct, the one form of disability that remains widely, intractably misunderstood is mental disability. We still refer to it as "mental illness," as though the person is somehow "sick." It should simply be called a "mental disability." Fred Friedman's story of his lifetime of struggle with mental disability is so sad: his attempted suicide at age thirteen, his loss of everything—his wife, his home, his profession—and the years he spent in nursing homes and homeless shelters. But he also displays his determination to live and cope with his disability and to help others who struggle with mental "illness."

From the Periphery also dares to examine a subject that is treated almost as taboo in talking about persons with disabilities—that is, the view held by much of the nondisabled populace that those with disabilities are "asexual . . . incapable of being lovers and partners." For many, the author explains, "it is controversial to imagine people with disabilities having sex." This, again, is part of the view that people with disabilities are "less than human." The author adds, "Young people with disabilities are often not taught about sexuality and healthy sexual practices." To this I might add that "raging hormones" are not limited only to young people without disabilities!

The author correctly observes that "most people with disabilities do not want to be pitied or admired; they simply want to get on with their lives without being stared at." This reminded me of a young woman with cerebral palsy I met during the drafting of the ADA. We were talking about various things, and I was going on about how things would change for persons with disabilities if we could get this bill passed. She replied, "That's all fine, but all I want is to be able to go out and buy a pair of shoes like any other person."

In the final chapter the author explores the psychological internalization of feelings of inferiority by persons with disabilities—but also how more and more of them "refuse to accept perceptions of inferiority." I believe this has a lot to do with what I called the "ADA generation." These are the young people who have been raised since the passage of the ADA, which banned discrimination on the basis of disability, began to change the physical structures, and empowered individuals with disabilities to assert their rights in court. Members of the ADA generation are not going to just sit back and accept anything less than full inclusion. They see, as the author states, "that the way they are treated has more to do with their surroundings than with their individual impairments and capabilities. The problem is the attitudinal, structural, and physical barriers in society."

As I said, this is a powerful book. The author has distilled what must have been hundreds of hours of conversations into a wonderful narrative that speaks to our hearts, our souls, our intellect, and our hopes for a more inclusive society.

SENATOR TOM HARKIN (RET.),
SENATE AUTHOR, AMERICANS
WITH DISABILITIES ACT (1990)

PROLOGUE

"We as a society get cheated. People who could give an amazing gift of their own abilities to the world don't get to do it."

—Kathiana, chapter 11

THIS BOOK IS ABOUT disability oppression. It is about discrimination against individual people with disabilities and about exclusion of the group. It is about a quest for equality. It is about emotions more than it is about facts. It includes narratives about anger, school, work, independence, bigotry, solidarity, and love. Like the great author Studs Terkel, I call the persons I have interviewed "oral historians."

The law represents the crucial foundation of the fight against disability oppression. But laws cannot stand on their own. Awareness must be promoted and attitudes need to change. Although legislation and court rulings send powerful signals of basic values, they do not necessarily foster changed attitudes and awareness. Something more and something deeper is needed to really change social patterns toward genuine equality. It is my firm belief that understanding, love, and empathy must complement the law.

People with disabilities make up the largest minority in the world, and disability is an issue that concerns every one of us. Most of us either have a disability ourselves or know a close friend or family member who has a disability. And if we do not, aging and impairments will catch up with us sooner or later in life. According to the US Census Bureau, the number of Americans sixty-five and older will more than double over the next forty years. So we need to put an end to the invisibility of disability. It is pertinent to have a conversation about disability oppression and how to break down social barriers, whether physical, structural, or attitudinal. True equality will benefit all of us.

My Journey

The first time I met Torben was at a job interview in his home. He lived in a small town house in a suburb of the Danish city of Århus. He interviewed me for a position as one of his personal assistants. I was nervous. I had no experience and had difficulties understanding his questions because of his speech impairment. I had taken a year off law school and wanted to do something different. I also wanted to travel and really needed the money.

As a child, Torben had been in a fire and had scars from burns all over his body. He used a wheelchair and needed assistance twenty-four hours a day. I got the job and I started working seventy-two-hour shifts. I did not get any training but Torben instructed me. Because of my eagerness to do well, I initially wanted to do and say everything for him. I soon learned what should have been obvious: Torben knew what was best for himself and I only needed to help when he asked me to. I stopped worrying when I lay in bed at night; I knew that Torben would wake me if he needed help. In the daytime, we did ordinary household chores, had meals, and talked. Sometimes I would suggest places to go or things to do, but Torben made the decisions. We became friends and I respected him deeply as a person and as my employer. It became a matter of course to me that Torben had choices and control. He lived an independent life.

Today, more than twenty-five years later, I am an international human rights lawyer. I am from Denmark and have lived in the Chicago area since 2014. Before coming to Chicago, I researched and worked on issues of human rights, discrimination, and disability, both in Denmark and internationally. I know what discrimination and exclusion look like on paper and have written books and articles about the protection of human rights.

I have tried to understand the complex nature of discrimination and exclusion, as well as their underlying causes. Still, I have not been able to fully appreciate the experience of being oppressed, the consequences for the individual, or the journey to find a way to cope and act. I have searched for answers. But even though the work of a lawyer is full of emotional situations, I have realized that I never truly researched the emotions of oppression. So when I read *The Unwomanly Face of War* by Svetlana Alexievich,* I knew

---

* See Svetlana Alexievich, *The Unwomanly Face of War: An Oral History of Women in World War II*, trans. Richard Pevear and Larissa Volokhonsky (New York: Random House, 2017).

that I had found my teacher. I knew what I needed to do. In her Nobel Prize lecture from 2015, Alexievich described her nonfiction prose writing: "I collect the everyday life of feelings, thoughts, and words. I collect the life of my time. I'm interested in the history of the soul. The everyday life of the soul, the things that the big picture of history usually omits, or disdains. I work with missing history."

I wanted to embark on a similar route on the topic of disability oppression. I wanted to be a microphone for the voices of the oppressed and to hear how people with disabilities and their relatives experience and survive the physical, structural, and attitudinal barriers of their surroundings. I wanted to become more knowledgeable about the effects of discrimination and exclusion on the individual, about the ways in which disability oppression works on different groups and classes in society. I wanted to facilitate a dialogue with the majority population to increase awareness and contribute to a kinder world.

So instead of the law and the overall societal structures, I wanted to focus on the individual. What does discrimination and exclusion look like for the person who experiences it? How does it feel? What does it do to the soul? How does the person cope? In order to better understand disability oppression in society, I wanted to listen to the emotions of oppression.

I interviewed nearly fifty individuals over a two-year period between 2016 and 2018. The majority have disabilities themselves, but I also interviewed parents of children with disabilities. I started interviewing people with disabilities whom I met through my work for the independent living organization Access Living in Chicago and also through my teaching in disability studies at the University of Illinois at Chicago. One person would refer me to the next. One life was threaded to another. A majority are activists in various disability movements. When I started the project, I expected opinions to be more contradictory. But they were not. And this is probably explained by the number of activist voices in this book.

Most of the oral historians in this book live in and around Chicago, but their experiences and underlying emotions are universal. I listened to their voices. For hours and days. There was always a new voice.

My in-depth interviews had questions and answers. They were long interviews. I strived to do like Studs Terkel—to have casual and fluent conversations with people: "The talk was idiomatic rather than academic. In short, it was conversation. In time, the sluice gates of dammed up hurts and dreams were opened."*

On one occasion, a person said, "I don't think that I have ever talked to anybody with all of these details laid out. I don't think anybody wanted to hear. And I haven't wanted to myself." I, too, was overwhelmed.

I was constantly amazed at the details of personal life that people would share with me. I was taking much and giving little, but I was grateful. At the same time, I knew that some people got relief and empowerment from telling their stories to me, from letting their stories go.

I'm a white woman belonging to the privileged majority, and I don't have a disability myself. I know that stories in this book would be different if they had been told to a person with a disability because of a mutual understanding and recognition, whereas experiences have to be explained in more detail when told to an outsider like me. However, my intention with this book is for other outsiders to understand the physical, structural, and attitudinal barriers that we as the majority knowingly and unknowingly place around persons with disabilities in most communities today. All the oral historians that I have interviewed for this book have found it important to visualize and talk about discrimination and exclusion in this way.

The Disabling World

This is a book of voices and lived experiences of people with disabilities. The participants have various visible and invisible physical, mental, or developmental disabilities themselves or are parents of children who have them. They are all disabled by their surroundings. The book is about harmful effects of discrimination and exclusion. It is about powerful individuals, their responses and coping strategies. It is the history that I have found in the participants' narratives.

My intention with this book is to facilitate a broader conversation about exclusion and about discrimination against people with disabilities. Traditionally, disability has been seen as deserving pity, aid, and special treatment. But my aim is not for the outsider to feel pity. This is not a project of charity. The problem is not the individual with a disability. The problem is the disabling

---

* Studs Terkel, *Working: People Talk About What They Do All Day and How They Feel About What They Do* (orig. publ. 1974; New York: New Press, 1997), xx–xxi.

world. My hope is to win hearts and minds. My purpose is to change attitudes and behavior in the majority population and improve genuine equality.

Love

Meeting people with disabilities and hearing their individual stories and emotional responses to oppression, I was moved and motivated to explore new places and depths of understanding. I was constantly astonished. When I told my friends and family about some of these experiences, they got tears in their eyes and became thoughtful.

I learned. The individual voices gave me awareness and a deeper realization of barriers in society and how people with disabilities cope with them. I felt love for and empathy with those whom I spoke with. I realized that I needed love in order to understand and empathy in order to act. My hope is that other outsiders in the majority population will hear and feel the voices of this book, just as I have.

So I felt more deeply what I already knew: we cannot save the world with facts and laws alone. We need to try out each other's shoes and take longer walks with one another. We need to feel. We need to show empathy. And we need the voices of oppression in order to find the kindness in our hearts to fully understand, love, and act. In Toni Morrison's words, "Narrative . . . provides a controlled wilderness, an opportunity to be and to become the Other. The stranger. With sympathy, clarity, and the risk of self-examination."*

Power

The reasons for disability oppression, for inequality, for discrimination and exclusion do not lie with the individual person with a disability. The reasons are social; the others, the world, are to blame. As stressed by one of the oral historians of this book, Gary Arnold, "You know that you're not alone. You know there are plenty of other people out there that have similar experiences. And you know that you're not to blame for the negative stuff that happens."

When people with disabilities realize that they are not responsible for the discrimination and destruction that they experience, it empowers them to be

---

* Toni Morrison, *The Origin of Others* (Cambridge, MA: Harvard University Press, 2017), 91.

free from intimidation, anxiety, and fear of exclusion. I hope that people with disabilities, as well as their families and friends, will also hear the voices in this book.

To the Reader

This book embraces experiences of being discriminated against and excluded in various areas and aspects of life. People with different kinds of physical, mental, or developmental disabilities explain how the barriers in their surroundings make them disabled. They describe how the world around them, more than their actual impairments, creates their disabilities.

The participants tell stories of disability oppression and its consequences and describe their responses. Anger and rage is the focus of chapter 1. The meaning of disability as a social construct is elaborated upon in chapter 2. Invisibility, embracing disability as an identity, school, love, work, being out in public, independent living, inspiration porn, and internalization are the topics of chapters 3 to 11. Intersectionality and coping mechanisms are the final themes in the epilogue.

Two notes about language: First, in line with international human rights, I have chosen people-first language to emphasize the importance of putting the person before the disability. In other words, I talk about people with disabilities instead of disabled people. With this language, I also strive to focus on the social, meaning the barriers and the world around the person, instead of the individual disability. In no way does my choice of language constitute a disregard for disability-first language, which is preferred by some people with disabilities in the United States. Even more people in Europe—particularly in England—prefer the term *disabled persons.* They find that person-first language implies that their differences are undesirable and separate from them.

Second, I want to warn readers that some language in this book may be construed as very offensive. The people I interviewed used this language to accurately portray the taunts that they have received, as well as the ableism, racism, and sexism that they have experienced.

From the
PERIPHERY

1 | I GOT ANGRY

When Torben hired me as his personal assistant, I had already been engaged as a human rights activist in Amnesty International for several years. Working for Torben gave me a sense of the everyday exclusion that persons with disabilities experience. Many places were inaccessible to a wheelchair user like Torben. He was left out, and I was left out with him.

Nevertheless, I did not think of the inaccessibility and exclusion as a violation of human rights. At that time, it was not illegal to discriminate because of disability in Denmark. It was not until many years later, when I became involved in the implementation of the UN Convention on the Rights of Persons with Disabilities into Danish law, that I understood how disability—just like race, ethnicity, and gender—should be acknowledged as a human rights issue.

THERE ARE AROUND ONE billion persons with disabilities on the planet. That is about 15 percent of the world's population. In other words, persons with disabilities represent the largest minority in the world. In the United States, the US Census Bureau estimates that nearly one in five persons has a disability.

Even though people with disabilities constitute a large minority, until recently most societies have not regarded disability as a human rights issue. People with disabilities are poor, marginalized, and invisible. They are still among the most oppressed minorities of the world. Exclusion has historically been—and remains—a central feature of disability oppression. As a group, people with disabilities have been excluded for hundreds of years. And individuals still experience such exclusion based on their disability. In this chapter, Kiel

Moses describes how he experienced loneliness when he was in middle school. He didn't have that many friends: "I was the outcast already."

Some people with disabilities have resigned themselves to exclusion and internalized a sense of being less valuable. Some can never get angry enough. Some suppress their anger and do nothing against the injustice. Renee Moses talks about the exclusion of her son some thirty years ago. She says that if there had been a different kind of cultural awareness at the time, if she had known about equality and the language of human rights, she would not have felt like a lone voice in the woods. She would have felt not only enraged but also outraged and would have been more empowered. If her surroundings had been different, she might not have put her head down. She might have acted more forcefully against her and her son's surroundings. Also in this chapter, Julie Schrager, who has a daughter with a disability, explains how she internalized the intentional exclusion. She says that she gets angry, but only sometimes, because "What's the point?"

For some, the poverty, exclusion, degradation, and frustration come to a breaking point. It has made people with disabilities furious. It has provoked new ways of thinking. Getting by no longer seems viable for many people with disabilities. Anger has fueled politicized rage and consciousness and produced activism. In this chapter, Jacky Dorantes explains how she "learned that the best way to cope is by being angry."

Disability rights organizations and disabled peoples organizations have evolved all over the world during the last couple of decades. These organizations work to undermine the status quo and to increase control over the things people with disabilities need to survive. They organize the individual and the community. They fight back and insist on gaining control over the necessities of life. They struggle to advance social change.

In this chapter, Marca Bristo explains how she became a disability rights activist: "The emotion that I did have was anger. And that served me well." Marca turned her rage into power.

I FELT THIS RAGE

MARCA BRISTO

Marca helped launch Access Living*—Chicago's center for independent living—in 1980 and has been the president and chief executive officer ever since. Marca was one of the first disability rights advocates I met after I moved to Chicago. I am forever grateful that she guided me in my search for a better understanding of discrimination and exclusion because of disability. For this book, I interviewed Marca in her sunny meeting room at Access Living. We had Marca's favorite drink, Diet Coke, while we talked. There was much smiling and laughter in between Marca's stern criticism of the stigma and the discrimination against people with disabilities.

I Couldn't Cross the Street

I was young and out with some friends. They were all musicians. We went to a party, and it was boring. So we left and went out to the lake. I dove into Lake Michigan in water that looked deep. And it wasn't! So I broke my neck at the C7-8 level, which has caused paralysis in my legs, no sensation below the level of my breast, and some weakness in my arms. I've been using a wheelchair since then.

I'm a registered nurse and the first thing that happened was that I lost my job. There really was no initial effort to see whether I'd recuperate.

---

* Access Living is committed to fostering an inclusive society that enables Chicagoans with disabilities to live fully engaged and self-directed lives. Access Living challenges stereotypes, protects civil rights, and champions social reform.

There was no talk of putting me on medical leave. It was just, "You're fired."

That was probably my very first concrete experience of really clear discrimination. The story changed later, but I lost my job. I lost my income. So at least initially, I experienced that commingling of poverty and disability. It was sudden for me. And I did not know whether I'd be able to work again.

I acquired my disability when I was twenty-three, but I had a good education growing up. I had finished college. I was socially acclimated to the world. I had all those skills that were already inherent and, through that, a certain degree of self-confidence. And also, I was shaped by the world around me, because I had been living in the world, so to speak. But pretty quickly, I experienced all the messages that form the basis of discrimination, the stigma or the attitudes that people had toward disabled people, which are still to this day so carefully woven into our culture. They started to descend over me. But I didn't have any words for it. I just felt, *OK, my life's gonna shrink.*

I can't say I saw it as discrimination when I was going through it. And of course, that's part of it. The story line for people with disabilities is so deeply entrenched in our culture that you tend to look at certain behavior and just think that it's normal rather than discriminatory.

From the get-go, when I was in the hospital, they would take me out in the community to practice pushing my wheelchair. Right around the rehab institute where I was a patient, there were a handful of curb cuts, but not too many. So just realizing the limits placed on my mobility because I couldn't cross the street was really shocking. *That* I started to feel immediately in the hospital.

I had to find a place to live. My house had seven stairs. I didn't see this as discrimination. I didn't have a word for it. All I knew was that I was being excluded from where I used to live. And finding a place to live that I could afford was like finding a needle in a haystack. This was before the Fair Housing Amendments Act. My injury occurred in 1977 and the Fair Housing Amendments Act would not come along until 1988. My grandmother ended up giving me enough money for a down payment for the first month's rent. I got a roommate and we moved into a very expensive two-bedroom high-rise condominium. But even in that apartment, I couldn't get into the bathroom. We had to take the bathroom door away and hang curtains instead. So finding a place to live was experience number two of discrimination. But again, I thought, I was just having to make do. That was how I experienced it: having to make do. Having to adjust to all of this. The burden is on you to adjust to the world. It never dawned on me that the world had to change. Never dawned on me.

Before the accident, I didn't drive. I always used the bus. In a wheelchair, there was no way you could get around the city. After I got out of the hospital, Medicaid paid for transportation to get to and from the hospital doctors. So number one, you're riding like in an ambulance. Number two, the only time you can use it is to go back and forth to medical appointments. So my world shrank. Entirely shrank.

I was in my apartment on the Near North Side. There was a grocery store one and a quarter blocks away. But the building with the grocery store was in between two alleys. The alleys had curbs. It was a busy Chicago street. So the first day, I went to push to the grocery store, I pushed and realized the curb. So I went all the way around the block, which at that time was hard for me to do physically. And then I realized there was a curb on the other side. I could not get to my grocery store without going into the street. Again, I just saw these as things that I had to adjust to.

So you can see how my world shrank. I had been a foreign exchange student when I was in high school. So I really had been practically around the world. I was a world traveler. And now I couldn't get around the block. I was completely dependent upon my friends to come and take me places.

I got angry. But I internalized it. I just shrank in. At the rehab institute, they would do classes for doctors and others. I would get invited to come in on panels. There would be presentations about attitudes toward people with disabilities. So there was an acknowledgment on the part of that teaching hospital that attitudes had to change. But there was an equal amount of attention focused on helping people with disabilities to accept their disabilities. The focus was on you having to accept these conditions and figure out ways to do the work-around. So of course your relationships with people change because of those dynamics. You need the help. A ride. It influenced everything. But you just figure that you have to make do. Your world shrank. You don't go to as many places as you used to.

Like I Was Invisible

My friends were musicians, so I would go out in the evenings to some of the clubs. I'd get a pass from the rehab institute and go out to listen to my friends play music. I could get in the clubs but I couldn't get in the bathrooms. So I'd have to either go out in the alley and pee [*laughs*] or time my comings and goings to when I'd have to go to the bathroom.

I remember going to those clubs. I was twenty-three—not unattractive. But the men who used to flirt with me would look right through me—like I was invisible. Literally invisible. I'd be sitting there with one of my girlfriends and the very same guys that used to hit on me a month prior would walk right over and ignore that I was even there. Or I would get that paternalistic talk, like, "Hey, does that thing . . . ?" [*Points to her wheelchair.*] They'd wanna push my chair and make sound effects with it like I was a little kid in a truck. So the infantilization or paternalism or invisibility, these were the kind of themes that I experienced. And they still run through the collective unconscious of America about people with disability.

I felt dehumanized. I felt like I was never gonna have a boyfriend again. I started second-guessing my sexuality.

It was a shock to my system to have that experience. But I'm a fighting woman. I had a strong sense of self. I was confident enough that I would overcome that stuff somehow. But it was depressing, I guess. I didn't get depressed. This is interesting. I got angry. So my reaction to all the loss that I was experiencing was that I felt grief. I went through the different stages of grief. I jumped over depression. I never really felt depressed. I had great friends, and they stuck with me. My family stuck with me. I was gonna push through somehow. But the emotion that I did have was anger. And that served me well.

I remember one time while I was still in the hospital, my friends came over and we were going out for a drink. We went to a bar on Lincoln Avenue, accessible bar. I pulled in to the bar with two of my girlfriends and we went up to order a drink. And the bartender said to them, "You and you can stay. She has to leave." He didn't even talk to me.

And my friends said to him, "What are you talking about?"

He said, "I don't have insurance. She's an insurance liability."

I was furious and just stormed out. I went outside and burst into tears. I'm not a crier generally, but I could not take it. That rejection. I was so angry.

And there was nothing I could do about it. Nothing I could do. There was no law prohibiting it. My friends were still arguing with the bartender, and I was outside on the sidewalk in my wheelchair crying. And this Chicago policeman came up to me and said, "Are you OK?"

And I said, "Actually, no! I'm not." And I told him what had happened. He said, "Come with me."

And we walked back into the bar. He went up to the bartender and said to me, "What would you like?"

And I told him, "A glass of white wine."

And he turned to the bartender and said, "This lady would like a glass of white wine."

The bartender just looked at him . . .

But the policeman goes, "Oh, on second thought, give her a bottle." And then he said, "On third thought, it's on the house." [*Laughs.*]

Isn't that great? Chicago's finest. So we ended up walking out. We didn't even have to stay there with our bottle of wine.

What I took out of that was that the policeman validated that what was going on was wrong. But had I not run into that guy, there was nothing that I could have done.

I sucked it up. That's the best way I can describe it. And inside, I felt things were slipping away. Like, my friends would go places that I couldn't go. And I just had to stay home. I felt some sadness. But I just internalized it. I think you know this: I'm a recovering alcoholic. I believe I was an alcoholic already by the time I had my accident. But I did not know it yet. I think I have the genetic makeup. I have a strong family history. But I wasn't in touch with my alcoholism then. So part of what I did was that I used alcohol and drugs to make things more fun and easier. I extinguished some of the feelings through partying. That also fixed some practical issue because my home became sort of a center for people to come over and listen to music and have parties. I think my accident actually fueled my alcoholism because I started to use alcohol as a vehicle to cope with some of the feelings. Again, I only have this with the benefit of hindsight. While I was in it, I thought I was just living out life as best I could. Making do.

In Those Charts, I Saw Unequal Care

The director of nursing at Prentice Hospital saw an article about me. I think of her as my fairy godmother. She picked up the phone and called me up at home and said, "How would you like to come back to work?"

So this was the same place that had fired me. Something in this person just caused her to do that. Was it charity? I don't know what it was. What remarkably hit me at this point was to say to her, "I can't work."

I had just been told that I wasn't gonna be able to work as a nurse. It had already settled in.

But I did go back to work. I was in the sexuality and family planning clinic and I was doing counseling. What happened was that I started to have the paradigm shift. I bring this up because it happened to me as a woman who'd been raised in the era of the women's rights movement, the civil rights movement, and the antiwar movement. So you might think that I was steeped in all this. Right? My older brother was gay and had been involved in the early, early gay stuff. So I had been raised in that civil rights climate. In some respect, it was remarkable that I never saw my own experiences as discrimination. Until . . . Until I started to see it happening to others.

So here I am, a feminist, now working in this women's health clinic. What happened was the staff started to refer women with disabilities to me. Keep in mind that this was a family planning and abortion clinic. A sexual health clinic. I was there to do primarily the family planning and abortion counseling. I wasn't there to do the basic gyne stuff. I began having all these women referred to me and I was like, "Why is this seventy-two-year-old woman referred to me?"

A lot of the women were no longer sexually active. But something told me to write their names down. So I did that on my desk calendar. I just kept their names. And then on a particularly boring day when I didn't have much to do, I pulled all their charts and sat down in a room and just read them all—back to back, everybody's. And that was when I had—I would say—my first transformational moment. Because in those charts, I saw unequal care. I saw page after page of questions not asked. Questions about sex and illness: "Are you sexually active?" "Have you ever had an abortion?" "Have you ever had a sexually transmitted disease?" That was what we were there for. Right? These were not immaterial questions. But the charts were blank. And the pattern was so . . . There were twenty-six charts. And probably twenty of them looked like this. Then I started to read more on the notes. And I read a note saying, "The woman left because her Medi-Van came before we saw her." I had this realization: *Oh my God! That's happened so many times.* Their Medi-Van would arrive. And we hadn't seen them yet. But if they didn't get the ride, they weren't gonna get home. So we'd send them home unseen. And then I was wondering why they would be waiting all day without being seen. And I sort of put it together that we didn't have the staff to lift them onto the inaccessible table. So these little pieces started to come through for me.

I remember counseling this one woman who was a seventy-two-year-old woman. She was there for a postop check on a bilateral mastectomy. Why was she referred to me? There's a good and a bad side to that. Right? The bad was that they had no business medically referring her to me. The good was that they must have thought that there was something I could connect with these women on; something that would be of value. Which today, of course, we call "peer support." What I remember about that woman was that she started to cry when I was interviewing her. And I said, "What's wrong?"

And she was nonverbal. She had a Ouija board, which is how she communicated. We didn't have any tech back then. So she pointed the letters out. What she pointed out was "I didn't want the surgery."

And I said, "Why did you have it?"

And she pointed, "No one would listen."

That was the thing. I felt this rage. This sense of injustice. Again, I didn't have the word *discrimination*. But just an intuition, *This isn't right!*

So I took the charts to my supervisor's office.

The lesson in this was that I was not really self-identifying with injustice until I saw it in others. It was the nurse in me who was professionally insulted. These women weren't getting good care. That triggered my activism. Only then—only then did I have this sense of *That could have been me!*

Nothing in my experience up to this point had told me that I was a member of a protected class that was having my rights violated. I didn't get it until I saw it in somebody else. And what was so important about that for me was that I was able to then tap into why I was so angry. But only a little. Only enough to say, "We have to fix this."

I Didn't Have to Sit on the Sidelines Anymore

I was sent to a conference in Berkeley on sexuality and disability. It was my very first airplane ride after the accident. And that opened me up to a whole new set of barriers. It wasn't smooth. But once I got to Berkeley, there were curb cuts everywhere. Right! There were people with disabilities out in restaurants. And some of the restaurants had accessible bathrooms. There was a woman on the faculty of the program who had a spinal cord injury. She was a specialist on sexuality and disability. Not only was she a speaker, she was on the faculty of this whole conference and helped shape it. She was in a leadership role. I was just like, *Wow!*

I remember the airplane flight going home like it was yesterday. I was sitting on that airplane riding home and what flashed into my head were all the barriers that I'd been experiencing. I couldn't go around the block. I couldn't get on the bus. I couldn't . . . And how they'd figured that shit out in Berkeley. They had curb cuts in the neighborhood. There were toilets I could use. There was a public vehicle that had a wheelchair lift. All this stuff shifted. And I started to realize that the world needed to change.

Also on that airplane, I read this little pamphlet on sexuality and birth control and disability. In the back of it, there was an appendix with section 504 of the Rehab Act. I love to tell people that I discovered that I had rights in the appendix of a birth control pamphlet. For real! The minute I saw that, everything changed. I had a paradigm shift. I had a framework that was flipped around. It was no longer my problem. I was a member of a protected group like my big brother, like African American women who fought for law change. The world needed to change.

Instantaneously, I started thinking, *If there's a curb at the driveway, all I need is a sledgehammer.* That was my experience of how it all shifted. It was a complete worldview change. The old saying about the glass half-full or half-empty. You know, you look at the very same thing, but all of a sudden you see it completely different. That was so empowering. Because I didn't have to sit on the sidelines anymore. And not only did I have rights, I also felt that I had some responsibility.

The second transformational moment was finding out that once I took responsibility, once I had this new lens, I also got to have some power. It was a moment of empowerment when I realized that I had something to offer that the rest of the world didn't have. I realized that things couldn't be changed without the worldview that we now know as *Nothing about us without us*.

I JUST NEVER COULD GET ANGRY ENOUGH

KIEL, RENEE, AND KEN MOSES

I met Kiel's parents, Renee and Ken, in their large house in Evanston. The house had a warm feel and was full of modern design. It reminded me of homes in Denmark. I talked to Renee and Ken individually on different days. We drank hot tea and spoke about baseball and the excitement of being a Chicago Cubs fan. When I met with Ken, rain was pouring down in Evanston. There was a continuous soft drumming on the wooden porch outside the window.

Kiel and I talked for several hours on FaceTime. I was on my computer, and he was on his phone. He walked me around his apartment in Portland, Oregon. It felt like I was right there with him.

Even though I met separately with Kiel, Renee, and Ken at different times, I built their individual narratives into one comprehensive family story.

Deaf, Blind, Retarded

Renee

When I was in the hospital after delivering Kiel, I looked at him and I said to myself, *There's something wrong with his eyes.*

Everybody said, "Oh, that's so silly. He's an infant."

Well, within a short amount of time, I realized that there was reason to be concerned. He was highly allergic. Indeed he did have problems with his eyes. And he had a right-sided hemiparesis. The initial diagnosis on him from the children's hospital was that he was deaf, blind, retarded! Which turned out not to be true!

He does have some difficulty with his vision. His right eye . . . I get confused, I have to try to visualize . . . His right eye has limited vision. His left eye was paralyzed and turned outward. He ultimately had surgeries to bring the left eye into the center, but he cannot move that eye. The other eye that he has less vision in does move. But he tends to keep that eyelid down so that he doesn't get double vision. And he uses his right arm as a functional assist. He still has allergies but way more under control.

Kiel

I was born in 1978. There's some confusion about how this all went down. But the reality for me was that I lost some valuable time with oxygen. It created some learning disabilities, a visual impairment, and a weakened right side. My parents never wanted to say [laughs] that I have cerebral palsy. But in more colloquial terms, that's what I have.

I was born into a German Jewish home. My dad is German Jewish. My mom is Jewish. I have a sister who's six years older than I am. My dad dealt with loss and grieving issues as a psychologist. So he wasn't so far off in terms of having me. But he was also a career man, and he was in and out a lot of the time. So most of the parenting fell on my mom.

Ken

The impact of Kiel's birth on me was just so traumatic and so incomprehensible that I not only went into denial, I threw myself into my work. Which is not atypical of a lot of fathers of kids with special needs. For me, it was more dramatic, I believe.

When Kiel was born, I had already established a national reputation as a psychologist who worked with parents of kids with special needs. So all of a sudden, I got a kid with special needs myself. My whole identity felt threatened. A flashback of the history that I had as a child and what my parents went through. So when that happened, something just short-circuited inside me and . . . I . . . couldn't . . . deal. And I didn't know I couldn't deal. So I became an outrageous workaholic. I never said no. And my phone was ringing off the hook to do workshops. I had two full-time jobs. One was faculty at Northwestern University. One was a full-time private practice, which had about 20 percent parents of kids with special needs. The others were people who were traumatized by death, dying issues, and those things. I would get all these calls to do workshops all over the place. And I never said no.

So when you ask a question that says, "So what was it like for Kiel when he first went to school?" it . . . it touches me in a bad way . . . I have to say . . . [*weeps*] I don't know . . . I wasn't there . . . [*Whispers:*] Renee took all the burden . . . Because I couldn't. I just couldn't.

Renee

I took Kiel to work with me. I was a full-time principal at a school for children who had severe disabilities and had been excluded from the public school. In the school, I had several highly trained staff people who happened to be women. Many of them were getting pregnant, and I had been able to convince the board to set up a baby room and hire someone to take care of the babies. That was how I had agreed to become pregnant the second time. Because I didn't want to stop working. And the deal was that I would take Kiel to work with me and Ken, who was working in the house, would oversee our daughter being in kindergarten, coming home, having friends. So I went back to work almost immediately.

The Gate Was Opening

Renee

Kiel was enrolled in a Montessori preschool here in Evanston. They were willing to accommodate when he couldn't keep up with the children if they went on a walking trip. So they had a little red wagon that they would put him in. But other than that, he did quite wonderfully. So when he was about to turn five, I called the school district—the psychologist there was someone we knew professionally—and I said that we wanted him evaluated for public school placement. There was a *loooong* silence on the phone. And all I could think was, *She thinks that we're totally out of our minds.*

Because apparently the community here in Evanston had talked about our child and his limitations. I think the word on the street was that we had this severely handicapped child, and we were not being realistic about what he was capable of. And this call to the public school about getting him into kindergarten was the front end of that train coming down the tracks. But the psychologist came out with a team and they observed him at the Montessori school. I got a phone call from her, and she was all excited. She said, "Not only is he going to be able to go to the public schools. I'm not even recommending that he goes into the orthopedic special class."

She thought that he was perfectly able to be mainstreamed into the kindergarten. And that felt to me like a real break in the feelings that I had started to develop about needing to hide or keep a low profile. I mean, it felt like the gate was opening and we were gonna be able to walk through—just like every other family. That we were gonna be able to take advantage of the community and the school system.

So Kiel started kindergarten. We had to keep in touch with the teachers. But things seemed to be going well enough. And academically he was doing just fine. Cognitively, he was right on target. The physical limitations, or the differences that he had, seemed to be in the background rather than in the foreground. There were kids who would come over and he would go to other kids' houses.

Ken

When did I become more involved in Kiel's life? It was gradual. Maybe when he was six or seven. I started to come to my senses because it caused tremendous challenge in our marriage. So that seemed to be the focus that I had. Much of the time I was just very unhappy and very angry, as Renee was very unhappy and very angry about how we were with each other. Strangely, as very skilled as I am in helping other families and couples in these kinds of circumstances, I was clueless about myself. It's embarrassing to look back and recognize how absolutely clueless I was. But I was.

I do remember something happening with Kiel at that time. It was deeply disturbing to me. Kiel was still in preschool. He was a little guy, and he was as cute as could be. He was wearing these big dark glasses on his tiny nose. He was a cutie. And people would stop, and even though he was cosmetically different because of his eyes, he was a little boy—a cute little boy. And a little character.

We'd gone to the farmer's market. I was gonna make zucchini, and I was picking out the different vegetables. Kiel was sort of running around and all of a sudden, I hear, "*Daad.*"

And I go, "Oh. I don't think I wanna hear this . . ."

"*Daaad.*"

And I turn around and there's this woman, and she's kind of got a hold on him. And she says, "Is this your boy?"

"Yeah. What did you do, Kiel?"

"I didn't do anything."

And she said—she points into his face and she said, "There is no reason for this to be the way it is. My son is an optic surgeon and this can be corrected. There is no reason for this not to be attended to." She said, "This can be cured. This can be cured."

She picked the right person in some ways, because I'm flippant and I'm bright and I'm fast on my feet. I was used to being in front of audiences doing stuff when people would be throwing comments at me. I said, "Well, I find you to be one of the more inappropriate and rude people that I have ever met, to say such a thing—and to say it in front of my son. But I want you to know, I'm a psychotherapist and that could be cured. But it would take an awful lot of years."

I could later tell the story in front of audiences, and of course they always loved it. But I have to say that was the first time that . . . It just cut me so deeply. What I especially felt was Kiel's vulnerability. That people could be so stupidly cruel and . . . That's the memory that comes back to me.

It got worse as he got older. But that was the first time.

My Parents Say I Can't Play with You Anymore
Kiel

I was in the special ed crew. My friends either had physical disabilities or emotional disabilities. I had a teacher that was so worried that I was lonely that she ended up connecting me with a friend who turned out to be my best friend for a long time. Because he was lonely too.

Renee

As he started to go a little further along in the grades, things got more complex socially. That's when things started to fall apart. It's hard for me to remember exactly when, but I think third grade, fourth grade. Because things that the other boys were doing, he couldn't do.

The problem for Kiel became more that he looked different. Because with his eyes being off, his disability showed. And before he was even given a chance to participate socially, kids would give him a once-over and dismiss him. He wound up sort of being alone most of the time. He didn't have people to eat lunch with. When they would go on field trips, nobody would sit with him. He just became more and more resigned. He didn't talk a lot about it. But sometimes he would come home from school and I would look out the window and watch him coming off the school bus walking home. I could just look at his face and I would know that he had had a bad day. And what invariably would happen, if he had a bad day in school, was that it wouldn't take much for him to come into the house and find some reason to blow up. Or to be difficult or somehow let it out on me. I used to dread those afternoons. I mean . . . *aah* . . . I would want to go out the back door while he was coming in the front door.

Kiel

I spent a lot of time by myself. Being by yourself takes its psychological toll on you, for sure. I spent a lot of time reading and trying to do things by myself. But you can only do that for so many hours in a day.

Ken

Kiel was mostly at home. He didn't have that many kids that he got together with. And those that he did have were rare. There was a deaf child that he was friendly with. There was a child who tended to be more feminine and turned out to be a ballet dancer ultimately. I think he was also excluded. Kiel was friendly with him. But his family were religiously fundamentalist Christian people, and when they figured out that Kiel was Jewish, that was the end of that relationship. The parents cut it off.

Renee

Kiel had a friend that he really liked. He and this boy loved to laugh together. They just had the best time. Happened to be a black family living here in Evanston. The young boy came over here a few times and Kiel went over there a few times. The father came here and sat with me in the living room, and we talked. We just talked. I mean, it was parent to parent. And the next time Kiel invited this boy over, the boy said to him, "My parents say I can't play with you anymore."

Kiel was bereft. And I all could think was *Here's a black father, who himself must have experienced some discrimination, must be concerned about his own son being discriminated against in the school system.* And he's telling his son that he can't play with Kiel anymore. Because why? Kiel's not a good influence? Kiel's gonna drag him down socially? Kiel's gonna make his son into a pariah because Kiel's not a desirable friend?

And I *couldn't* call that parent up and say anything to him. I couldn't have that conversation with him, where I basically would say, "Are you serious? You're really gonna pull these two kids apart that really like each other?"

I let it go. I couldn't bring myself to confront the unkindness of this man. I don't know if it was because I felt some sense of shame or embarrassment or vulnerability. I just couldn't do it! And when I look at the way Kiel dealt with some of the meanness of kids . . . kids he would invite to his birthday party and they wouldn't show up. They wouldn't RSVP. I don't believe he ever said anything to those kids.

And I never said anything to that parent. It was as though Kiel and I both felt that we had to take what was given to us and be grateful and not expect or ask for more. I'm surprised when I think back on myself being like that. But I think there was something in the fabric of my experiences with the school and with the families that basically said, *Don't go there. Don't go there.*

And I'm not proud of that. I used to tell Kiel to be braver. But I'm not sure that I was as brave as I'd hoped he would be. And I'm not by any means a shrinking violet. But there was something about this experience that altered my basic self in a way that to this day I struggle to understand.

Kiel

I was picked on a lot. I started karate when I was eleven because I was being picked on. I've done martial arts for twenty-five years now—on and off. That helped in some ways to kind of curb the bullying. It gave me a sense of fearlessness in some ways and a sense of confidence. It sort of made me feel from the inside out that I was worthwhile. It also gave me body control. It was an internal focal point.

There were a few kids on the bus that would pick fights with me or pick on me. They would say that I was different, or stupid. It was typical in some ways. It was sort of differentiating between the us versus the them. Or the me versus the you. And I was not worthy and everyone else was. They said that I was retarded! That I was stupid!

Renee

Kiel and I became sort of a team. I certainly relied on him to let me know how he felt about things. Because I just felt that I was making all these decisions alone. Ken was really preoccupied with his work. I think that Ken would admit in this day and age that he really believed that the mother's job was to take care of the children. I was only working part-time at that time. I was working at night. So my job was the household and the children, and he pretty much left all those decisions and activities to me. I would hope that he and I would both do it differently if we could rerun the tape now. But that was then. That was the way it was.

Kiel was bullied. It was subtle. The boys didn't beat him up. It wasn't that kind of thing. But he was emotionally and psychologically bullied. When I would talk to Kiel about something that he was explaining about the kids or the school, I would ask him, "Do you want me to do something?"

He almost always said no.

Because he believed that if we made more of a fuss, if we blew it up, then things would get harder for him—not better. He never believed that anything like that would make things better for him. That was his concern. And I think I believed him. What's the point of trying to do something for your child, when your child is saying, "Don't! Please don't." He didn't want more attention. Certainly not negative attention.

Ken

High school was a nightmare. Hard, hard worker. Bright. Good student in spite of the visual impairment and learning disabilities. Teachers tended to like him. The special teachers or the resource teachers loved him. Loved him. And he loved them. He really had that.

Kids would target him. To the point where he could barely walk down the hall without kids shouting at him. It could be like a ten-second thing. But it was like, "Hey man. Pimp walk. Wow."

And they'd walk behind him and do his walk. That was like a surface kind of thing as to what kind of stuff he suffered there. Nightmare.

Kiel

Studying was a coping mechanism. I dove into my books because no one else was really willing to take what I could do. The socializing was so awful and destructive and not helpful, so I was just like, *If this is the way it's gonna be, then I guess that's why books were invented. I can dive into them.*

I'd come home. I'd had like a fifteen-minute break from school after being in school for seven hours. And then I'd go straight to work. I'd work pretty much until ten o'clock with a dinner break. And I'd do it again the next day. High school was me and myself mostly. There were only a few friends that I had in my resource room that I could really talk to. High school was not positive for me. Lots of sadness.

At lunch I was sitting with the same couple of friends from special ed. We always felt like we were the outsiders. It was never that thing, you know, *You're OK. You're one of us.* We were seen as the outcasts. We were our support group. That was what we could do in the special ed classes. It was so sad that it was reduced to that point. But all of us had been hurt in different ways and we ended up finding each other just for that particular purpose. To sort of be with each other as best as we could. Just so that we didn't do anything that was destructive. We were very passive in those times. Because we were so neutered in so many ways. About who we were. We were so disempowered and so disenfranchised. We just kind of sat there for those fifteen minutes.

We Have to Disarm Everyone Else
Kiel

As I got older, I not only learned that I was different but I also started to feel that I was treated differently. The fear is a common experience for a lot of people with disabilities. It's like we create a psychological discomfort. We have to disarm everyone else. We can't just be ourselves. So we spend a lot of time code-switching, which is basically saying, *Oh well, I'm this able-bodied person like everybody else. I can do what everybody else can do.* When in reality, everybody else is treating you like an alien. So there's a sensibility that allows you to say certain things. But then when you get attracted to people, they can't handle it. [*Laughs.*] Because it feels so unusual to them. There's a sense of asexuality that comes up: "Oh, how could you ever think that I would be interested? What's wrong with you?" [*Laughs.*] There's a feeling of disconnect. You're just cast out.

Loneliness is a really hard part of life. And I think disability accentuates that tremendously. There's such a psychological, unknown fear that people aren't even aware of. It's like when I walk into a room, the whole dynamic changes: *Oh my God! He's disabled. What's going on?* And it's about the fear. *What if that happens to me?*

When I was a child, people would react in a very odd ways when I walked in. They'd kind of look at me as if I had five eyes. So there was a certain sensibility. [*Laughs.*] They didn't know how to approach me. They didn't know what to do with me exactly. I think that's part of why it's so difficult for me to engage in the world sometimes. Because I feel I have to take care of everyone else. There's like a certain inability to just be and have that be OK. Without having everyone else being taken care of by me. It's what I call disarming others from their own psychological hang-ups. I've spent a lot of time doing that. Sadly.

I Was Lonely

Renee

In eighth grade, Kiel's homeroom teacher ran sessions where the kids would talk. In that milieu, Kiel apparently began to talk about some of his feelings and some of his issues. And there was a girl who according to Kiel responded very compassionately. She said something like "Boy, it really has been hard for you."

He decided that that young woman was someone he could have a relationship with, because he'd become aware of girls. He was certainly not being very successful. But he began calling her, and they would talk on the phone. He was like a typical teenager. He'd be laughing. He'd be telling jokes. He'd be talking to her about school, and one night on the phone she said to him—again—"My parents say you can't call me anymore. I can't talk to you anymore."

He was bereft. And when he tried to talk about it in school, in the same milieu where he had originally made some kind of contact with this girl, she wouldn't engage with him. She started complaining to the teachers that he was looking at her. Well, the way I understood the story was that his eye came out on the side. She was making an issue around this. It became pretty ugly and pretty tense.

Kiel

My first quote/unquote "love" was a girl in eighth grade. I had really strong feelings, and I was really excited. All the hormones were flying. But then she forbade me from going around her locker. That was my first indication that I was not welcome in terms of having those feelings. And if I had those feelings, I'd have to sort of hide them and not express them overtly or even covertly. So I was basically made to be a robot. I was lonely. I didn't have that many friends. I was the outcast already. I tried to use her friends to see if she was interested in me. I came out too strongly.

Renee

Then Kiel and this girl started high school, and it turned out that their lockers were in the same hallway. Kiel told me that the girls were hanging around her locker and saying nasty things to him when he went by. So I made an appointment with the social worker at the high school. I went in and talked to him about what was going on, and I was basically saying, "He's being harassed."

And this young man said to me, "Well, he should go around the hall the other way so he doesn't have to go by her locker."

And I said to him, "That's not a solution. You're not dealing with the issue. You're avoiding the issue."

He then told me that the father of this girl was a high-powered lawyer and that he had come in to the school. He had told the social worker that if Kiel continued to harass his daughter, he was going to file a sexual harassment lawsuit.

So I screwed up my courage and I went to see the mother. I went to see her in her office. I made an appointment. She knew who I was. And I said to her, "You're a mother. You bleed for your children like I bleed for my children." . . . I think I'm emotional . . . [*Weeps.*]

I said to her, "This is not right. Kiel is not doing anything to your daughter. And to have your husband bulldoze the school to the point that they won't do anything about this because he's threatening to take legal action, I don't know where else to turn. But I am coming to you mother to mother—person to person—and saying, 'You gotta do something.'"

And she said, "I can't. My husband is very strong and I can't go up against him. And I'm sorry."

That was the end of our conversation. And that was how things stood. Nothing happened. Not at the school. And not with the family. And not with this girl. To this day, when Kiel talks about trauma, he talks about this girl. I think it was another time where I really felt like I'd had my hands slapped. And I just never could get angry enough, indignant enough.

Ken

It took four years or something for the school to admit that they were completely wrong. To apologize, to acknowledge that they were terrified of the father and that they mishandled the case. But in the meantime, Kiel was ostracized and all the kids in the school knew about it. They knew what had gone on. This was the popular clique of girls. I mean, it was horrifying. And we just had to bear witness to it. We did not know what to do.

I felt humiliated and powerless. Because of my upbringing, I'm a very compliant person when it comes to rules, the law, or whatever. If the principal says it, that's the way it is! I'm much, much better at this point in my life. But I'm a post-Holocaust child. I'm German Jewish. My parents both came from Germany in 1938 just before all hell broke loose. After Kristallnacht. There were twenty-five thousand Jews that got out in the nine months from Kristallnacht until the borders were sealed for the Jews. My parents were two of the twenty-five thousand that got out during that time. The survivors of the family came and lived with us after the war and I bore witness to all of that. So I'm extremely compliant, or certainly was when Kiel was in high school. I was easily shamed or embarrassed or humiliated, which absolutely was the wrong thing at that time. But that was just in my character. So I couldn't . . . didn't . . .

Renee has a different kind of character. She's a fighter. You can't humiliate or intimidate her. She goes out there. But she was as ineffective as I. There was no going up against it.

Kiel

No. No. I didn't date in high school. I tried to date a few times. But the whole situation with that girl really sparked, like, a certain sense of asexuality in me. I tried to date a few people through my dojo but that didn't work very well. I mean, to this day . . . I've been on just a handful of dates. It's been really hard because I'm starting at such a deficit. It's like the things that people started to learn much earlier on, I didn't learn. I feel like I'm kind of in a trapped time war. I'm almost thirty-nine, and I have a feeling that I'm trapped in a ten-year-old's body in that regard. It's kind of a fucked-up way of being . . . Again I live in a world of paradoxes. My chronological age does not match a lot of the experiences that I've had—for better or for worse.

It's always really hard to know how I'm feeling. The outside world wants me to be happy. Most of my life has not been very happy. And even though there have been happyish parts, I think that a lot of it has just been unhappy.

I had more friends in college. But it was still difficult not knowing how to engage properly. My previous experiences were so bad. So I would still be attracted to women but I couldn't read the signals because of my nonverbal learning disability, which affects the nonverbal me picking up nonverbal clues. That doesn't lead to a whole lot of positive reinforcement. It leads to a lot of self-doubt and self-isolation. I kept thinking that I was probably gonna run into another wall of rejection and I'd had enough of that already. So I basically stayed in my room again and studied.

I went to the University of Arizona to become a rehab counselor, and I had another run-in with a female. I was twenty-three at that point. She was my counseling partner. I went into some troubles with her. I was stupid, naive in that regard. And there was an Islamic woman in the program. I touched her shoulder because I was having trouble with my vision at that point. And she flipped out on me. At that point, I knew that this was not the right place for me. I was unceremoniously let go, basically, from the university.

That was another horrible change because I knew that I would have been a good rehab counselor. It was another experience where my disability played havoc on me and on people around me. It was a shit storm and I ended up coming back home just in a terrible state. I didn't know what to study, didn't know what to do. Didn't care anymore. It was another experience where I was shamed. I was told that what I was doing was completely inappropriate. That put me in a real negative place. And sad . . .

Renee

He came home here. And he was devastated. He was emotionally fragile. He was psychologically traumatized again. We were stuck with it. We had no recourse, it seemed. Once again.

It's hard to take back those kinds of moments in someone's growing-up time. It becomes very profoundly shaping. I think that's probably my sense of helplessness.

Ken

So when you ask how all of this has affected his self-esteem . . . Kiel has such outrageous hypervigilance and hyperarousal around the potential of rejection but also, more important, the possibility of being identified as some kind of pervert or bad person or wrong person or . . . It's horrifying. And as a psychotherapist who very successfully works with people with all these kinds of things, I'm helpless. I mean, I do the best I can. We have a great relationship. He shares with me his most personal stuff and calls me all the time. I was on the phone with him just before you came. But he has never been on more than two or three dates with someone. And the women he's been on two or three dates with are very few. But he wants to. He gets so anxious in circumstances where he wants to approach particular women.

He's still struggling. So that's the effect of what's happened to his self-esteem. He has to keep reminding himself that he's a good person. He's a kind person. And he's hardworking and bright. And would be an asset to anybody who would have him, whether it's career-wise or whatever. He has to keep reminding himself because he keeps running into this wall. That's the best that I can describe it. Horrifying.

Noodling a little more with the idea of how this all affected Kiel's self-concept or his self-confidence and whatever else goes with it . . . it hasn't broken him. It scared him. But it has not broken him. His sense of dignity, his sense of worth, and his sense of goodness as a human has not been broken. It has not! He's still hopeful.

Pushed on Through

Kiel

I pushed on through. I studied hard. And I think a lot of the psychological energy was spent on just getting through without getting too many more bruises psychologically, so to speak. So I got through high school, went to college, where I did fairly well. I have two master's degrees.

But I know this might sound bizarre. Over time, I think I've disconnected a lot with the world. I just . . . I don't know what else to do. As for a coping mechanism, it's too unpleasant overall to keep saying "Oh no. That's gonna be fine. No problem at all."

And I know just damn well. That's not what it is. There's such an emphasis on just being happy. Like that's the cure for everything. I just don't see it that way. I'm not saying that happiness doesn't exist. It's kind of a fleeting experience. Especially when you're a person with a disability who's been kind of trampled on—over and over and over. You just have to disconnect on some level. For me, mostly—I turn all that in as internalized oppression.

Renee

I think . . . I think what I started to do was not that dissimilar from Kiel. I just sort of put my head down. And continued to not make waves. The best analogy that I have used over the years with him and for myself is this: We never sat down at the table for a full meal. We always felt that we got the crumbs that fell off the table, and we should be grateful. Grateful that they'd allowed him into the school. Grateful that they saw him as a competent student for as long as they did. Grateful for the kids that were willing to invite him over or to come over here. Just grateful!

Even though I advocated for him and I think I did a good job, I had that feeling of: *Don't rock the boat. Don't expose your vulnerability. Don't ask for too much. Don't show that you're hurting. Don't talk to other parents about your concerns.* I think that that was pretty much the way I got through those years.

The thing that affected me early on and carried me for a long time was fear. You know: *Who's this child gonna be?* Having worked with all kinds of kids before he was ever born, I've watched children being either institutionalized or marginalized or put into special programs or special schools. Is that what's gonna happen here? Or was I really gonna be able to save him?

I think that was the foundation of a lot of my struggle at the beginning. I believed I could plug in with Kiel and make it work. I think it became sort of my life mission to save him. If I got angry, I might lose the thread of the optimism. Or I might alienate the wrong people. Or I might add an additional burden to my life, or his life. And I think that all sort of pressured me into being much more compliant or complacent or . . . I don't know what the right word is. I didn't wanna come across as combative. I think, through it all, there was this sense of optimism. I wasn't willing to give up! My worst moments were lying in bed at night when I couldn't fall asleep. That's when the anxiety would come up. That's when the fear would come up. That's when the tears would come up. But during the daytime, I was a soldier. And nothing was too hard. Nothing was impossible.

But again . . . At night, when it was dark and I couldn't do anything except feel what I was feeling, that's when I dissolved. I felt little and ineffectual and frightened. And the other thing, characteristically, I kept my own counsel. Didn't talk to other people. Ken was not available to listen because he had his own difficulty. I just learned to keep it all inside until night, when I couldn't. Then I'd cry myself to sleep. When I hear myself saying that, there's a critical part of me that says, *That's pretty pathetic.*

But I just couldn't let myself get into that kind of a place in the daylight, where it mattered. I was afraid I would never pick myself up again and be able to carry on. And I felt like I needed to do the hard lifting. Because I was the one that was in charge.

I think I didn't give myself permission to feel entitled to my rage. I think that, just like Kiel, on some level I believed, *Well, if we're nice, if we're reasonable, if we're pleasant, everybody will just like us.* And I could not get over that hump for the longest time to not only feel rage but to feel outraged.

I've thought recently that if the language of today's culture was available back then, I would have felt more empowered. If Kiel and I just could have felt, *We're not the lone voice out in the woods. There is a cultural awareness about human rights, equal rights, and bullying.*

Ken

Sorry . . . Again . . . Renee with all her skills and all her stuff with child rearing and work with children with special needs . . . And me with all my skills . . . What to do? [*Weeps.*] It breaks our hearts.

Part of my coping mechanism is that I become very philosophic. I become very psychological. And I contain things. I work with what's here right now. That's what I do. I work with Renee, and I mean, it's been years for us to really put together what I'd consider to be a wonderful marriage at this point. Hard . . . hard won. We've been together over fifty years.

My coping system is really my beliefs. It's not so much religious as it is philosophic and human nature. It's really talking about the things we can't change that give us pain. How to listen to it and how to work it changes everything. And that's definitely now my primary coping mechanism. Don't need to run anymore. Don't need to become a workaholic. Don't need to drink. I don't . . . But I did have to retire.

Renee

My reactions have always been intimately tied to Kiel's reactions. When he bleeds, I bleed. When he's disappointed, I'm disappointed. When he feels devastated, I feel devastated. I've gotten better at this point to disentangle myself from his emotional state. Because there's only so long that you can be so tied in with someone else that every moment like that in life goes to your core. I mean, that's been a struggle of mine, to differentiate and have some objectivity. I suspect that it's been made easier by the fact that he's had a lot of successes. But it doesn't take much to keep me on the edge of that precipice. When he's really bleeding or hurting. But I am better. I am better . . .

Assumptions That People Made

Renee

I always wanted to make him look more acceptable to try to avoid the fallout that was there. Because his disability showed. If he simply had limited use of his right hand but his eye was fine, his life would have been different. I'm positive of it. And that may be the mother in me talking. But his personality got altered and formed around how people looked at him . . . assumptions that people made and then acted on, and some of the traumatic stuff that we've talked about.

I even had a reaction—it's interesting—I had a reaction when I heard that he was gonna Skype with you. I thought, *No, let him talk to you on the telephone. You'll like him. You'll have a very nice conversation with him on the telephone.*

I don't like to Skype with him because I don't like the visuals in general on Skype. But I also don't like to Skype with him because it's right in front of me in a way that I would rather not have be part of my psychological experience. So you know, there are parts of me that in some ways are all too aware of my feelings and how I cope or compensate—things that, as a mother, I shouldn't feel. That I think, as a human being, I ought not to feel. But it's all part of the fabric of the relationship and of the struggle. It's all interwoven, and I'm very aware. I don't know how it sounds to you. Because I don't think that I have ever talked to anybody and laid out all these details. I don't think anybody wanted to hear. And I haven't wanted to myself. But for your purposes, I'm happy to do it. Particularly if somebody else reading this—another mother—can grab on to some of my experiences and have it matter. Then it's all worthwhile.

So Uncomfortable That She Had to Withdraw

Renee

I was working. Most mothers were not working. Ken was on the road a lot on the weekends in particular. So in effect, I was a single parent. I don't know whether I was defensive and self-protective and messaged that out to the other mothers so that they kept their distance. But there was a distance. I mean, it was complicated and multilayered, and it wasn't an experience that you get any road maps for. So I just put one foot in front of the other. I just dealt with the things that I felt I could deal with and manage. But it was a hard time. And I can't say that I had any close friends to really confide in or take guidance from. I don't know if that's an outgrowth of who I was at that time—separate and apart from Kiel and his difficulties—or whether that became the mitigating circumstance. I don't know. I don't know how to pull that apart.

Just as Kiel has had his own sensibility and sensitivity develop about people's reactions to him, I almost immediately developed the same kind of sense that people didn't wanna hear. They didn't want me to be public with them about being in any kind of pain. The best example I can give you of that comes from my sister. I have two younger sisters, one of whom was living up the street from where we lived when Kiel was born. She and her husband came over a few times, and I felt tremendously bereft and scared. I think it made her so uncomfortable that she had to withdraw. And the withdrawal came under the guise of her calling me and telling me that her husband couldn't stand the noise here at the house of a young baby and another child. And that they weren't gonna be able to come over here anymore to visit. To this day, I believe that my initial pain, which was so palpable, was so frightening to some of the people who were in my life that, just like in

Kiel's experience, they would withdraw. They would disappear. There was no going to them and having a conversation. There was no way of testing it out. It's a hypothesis on my part. But to not believe that there was some kind of cause and effect between my state of mind and these people little by little pulling away, I just have to stay with my sense of reality that that was part of what was going on. I think that in part that was the early lesson of learning to not be too emotional, not share my feelings, not go to these people and say, "Help, help, help, help."

It's like you just develop a sense. And in talking with you, it seems to me that my talking doesn't scare you. Of course, it's a lot of years later, but it's something I've learned. I've learned who can listen and who's available and who's gonna be put off by me talking about real stuff in a real way. I just didn't have any people like that in my life. Including my parents. My parents never heard the truth of what was going on and how scared I was, or the diagnosis, or any of those medical things early on. I wound up feeling like I had to protect them, so that they wouldn't fall apart. That became part of my MO. To take care of the people around me, rather than letting them take care of me.

A Real, Functioning, Autonomous Person
Kiel

There is a huge disconnect between who I am, what I'm doing, and how I'm viewed in society. I think that there's such a massive disconnect there. I don't know how else to say it. Between what I can do and what society allows me to do. So it's just a very complex and difficult and fairly unpleasant reality. Like why did I go to grad school if I thought that I was going to be on the outskirts of society?

Almost every facet of my life, whether it's been socially, educationally, psychologically, or emotionally, it's just been a massive paradox. I feel sort of like the king of paradoxes at this point. Nothing has ever really added up—ever. I'm an empowered disabled person and yet so much of the system doesn't wanna include me. It doesn't wanna have me being a real, functioning, autonomous person.

It's fascinating to me that I'm still alive. In all honesty, I really cannot believe all this stuff that I've been through in this very, very short amount of time, relatively speaking. I feel like I'm a thousand years old. You know what

I mean. I feel sort of in a strange position right now. I have a lot of privilege. I'm very aware of that. And yet, I'm often seen in a very devalued way. And then people ask me why I'm not happy all the time. It's like, *OK, I don't know what to say to that.* There are too many disconnects. That's what I'm saying. There're just too many things that don't equate.

Am I hopeful? I guess in some ways. It's part of the makeup. My mom put up a sign that said CAN'T with a big line through it. You know, it was about being aware of who you were and, in essence, not letting the bastards get you down. And of course, when you're younger, it's much easier to go into that and be like, *Oh, sure. They're never gonna get me down. No problem.*

But when you get worn down, it's a lot harder to do that. At least on a consistent basis. I've kind of . . . Do I feel hopeful? On some level, I guess.

THE BEST WAY TO COPE IS BY BEING ANGRY

JACKY DORANTES

When I worked at Access Living, Jacky was in the cubicle on the other side of the room. We never communicated much except for the occasional lunchroom chat. She seemed quiet. I was quiet. Yet finding words was not difficult for Jacky when we finally sat down together and talked.

I Wasn't Fit to Go to College

I grew up on the Northwest Side of Chicago in Irving Park. My family is all Mexican. I'm first-generation Mexican American and a daughter of two factory workers. I have two older brothers and one older sister, so I'm the youngest. I'm the only one who was born here.

I acquired my disability when I was thirteen. I was hit by a car on my way to school. Before, I had perfect vision, so transitioning into being blind was really difficult. A lot of the trauma came along with the accident. It wasn't just the actual bodily trauma. I also had PTSD. It was me and my nephew in the accident. He ended up with some fractures, but for the most part he's OK.

In the beginning, my family was scared and anxious. They were also really hungry for information. They wanted to get as many resources and as much information as possible so that I could go back to school. I was in seventh grade. When I did go back to school, my family was exposed to other children who had visual disabilities and were blind. Seeing students who were blind in a classroom really motivated all of us. It gave us a real-life point of view. It was possible. There was support and technology that would make transitioning easier. So acceptance came slowly.

After the accident I went to a school that had a separate VI program for visually impaired children. But it was still an integrated school. Everyone in school was really great. They didn't see my disability as a deficit. They only saw something that I needed accommodation for or extra support.

But in high school I was struggling. I remember being upset because when it came to the time of having ACT tests, everyone would get prep books and prep materials. We didn't have that option in the VI program. It really pissed me off. Because if there's something that's challenging it's doing math and plotting graphs in Braille. I feel that in my VI class we were really excluded. I felt like we were shit on because we didn't have that prep material. We weren't able to get a grasp of what the ACT would look like for us. I'm sure I would have had higher scores if I'd had that prep material.

Socially, it wasn't as bad. In the VI program we would have our own cliques. We huddled together and gave each other support and helped each other with homework. We still talked to and hung out with people who weren't visually impaired. It seemed to me that the culture was pretty welcoming. No one was bullying me. I didn't have a feeling of being excluded. I just hung out with my friends.

After high school I applied to Northeastern Illinois University. The special education department in my high school told me that I wasn't fit to go to college. The VI teacher at the time and my high school adviser told me that we were just wasting our time applying because I wasn't going to be accepted anywhere. I don't know why. I had good grades. I don't know if it was because I gave off the impression that I was the bimbo type. [*Laughs.*] I don't know if it was because of the fact that I had a low ACT score. I always had a good GPA, so it wasn't that my grades weren't there. It was the testing that really screwed me over.

It hurt. I could see the way that I was being treated in comparison with other students. Other people would be encouraged to go to school. Other people would get offered opportunities to get letters of recommendation. So it hurt. But most of all it pissed me off and it gave me motivation to apply. It really fueled me to do good in school. At that time my whole purpose was to prove them wrong. It made me work harder.

My cousin helped me do the application step by step. My family was really supportive and wanted me to go to school. So I was accepted and started at Northeastern. College was scary. I'm the first one in my family to go to college, so I didn't really have an understanding of what college looked like or what was required of you. I knew it was going to be hard. I knew I had to be a dedicated student. I knew there would be different opportunities for me. But I didn't know what simple things looked like . . . like getting financial aid documents. I didn't know that I had to register for classes. I didn't know that I could talk with an adviser to figure out my major. I didn't know that there were, like, college clubs and other things that you could do on campus. So a lot was really overwhelming.

College had a students with disabilities office. My cousin helped me figure out what kind of accommodation I needed. I remember coming into the office and being given a lot of forms to fill out. I had no idea how to do this. I didn't know what kind of support that I needed. I didn't know what kind of accommodations that I needed. I didn't know what it would look like. My cousin helped me to figure what type of support that I really needed, and she helped me fill out those forms. From there, it was basically a trial and error type thing. At first I would have note-takers. But then I realized that even though I'm blind, I'm still a visual learner. I still need to have something in front of me to look at in order for me to understand it and retain it. So note-taking didn't work for me. I needed to sit down and take my own notes. So I ended up getting this machine—a Braille note-taker. That was something that I had used in elementary school, and because of the accident I had some settlement money that I could use. So I purchased the machine myself.

People Just Cannot Stop Looking at Me

I had an Uber driver who refused to allow me into the car with my guide dog, Archie. He wanted me to put her in his trunk. [*Laughs*.] There was no way that was going to happen. It was summer and ninety-five degrees outside. He was going to kill my dog. I told the driver that he wasn't going to put my dog in the trunk. She had to be by my side. Then the driver said that he couldn't take me. I told him that he was basically discriminating against me. We argued for a while, and he finally agreed to let me in. I still filed a complaint.

People look at me. People just cannot stop looking at me. I sense it. Sometimes I don't care. Sometimes I get really annoyed. I turn in another direction. I stick my middle finger out and ask them what they want. Most times I try not to pick up on it, because it's just going to bother the crap out of me.

I remember being younger and going to the store. I would be in line, and when I came up to the cashier I would give her money. Instead of giving the change back to me, she would give it to the person that I was with. Growing older I've gone shopping with my niece. Often cashiers refer to my niece or ask my niece questions that should have been asked to me. I'm the adult in the situation and not my ten-year-old niece. Today they are still talking over my head. When I'm shopping and asking for a special thing in a store, they'll ask the person that I'm with if I would like such and such. Well, I'm right here—I'm the one who's buying it, and I'm the one who's going to wear it. So how the hell would the person I'm with know if I like it?

I get annoyed and angry. It makes me feel like I'm being infantilized. I feel like I'm being treated like a child—like I cannot make decisions on my own by myself. I even feel less than human sometimes. My voice isn't even being given a choice to be considered.

The Only Way That I've Been Able to Cope

Because of the accident, I had to go through different stages to accept my blindness. But I learned that the best way to cope is by being angry. So when things happen to me, instead of getting sad and pitying myself, I feel really, really pissed off. And sometimes it's good because it motivates me. But sometimes it's bad because I don't know what to do with this anger. I don't know how to deal with being so pissed off about things.

I also feel that I represent people who are blind. That I have to be a role model. It might not be very often that people in the general population see a blind person. So I don't want to give a shitty impression. I don't want them to think that all blind people are angry, that all blind people have really bad attitudes.

Sometimes the feelings of being hurt stay with me. I'm not going to say that it doesn't affect me. Because it does. Sometimes I feel that I need to be more assertive the next time something happens. Or I just need to make it clear to people that I'm the one who's in charge and not the person who's with me.

I feel like the times that I've experienced these situations, I tell my friends. They understand, and they will be there for me. They will basically be supportive and make me feel better about myself. They will point out how stupid or ignorant other people are. With my family, it depends on whom I'm talking to. If it's my mom, who's a lot more emotional, I tend not to tell her a lot of things that happen to me. She'll get extremely anxious. I'd rather not burden her with my things. So I won't keep my mom in the loop as much. I feel like I can talk to my dad about these things. He will feel bad for me about whatever has happened. But he'll also just be supportive at the end of it all. My mom will just feel bad.

I think even in high school the whole anger as a coping thing started. I had a grandmother who wasn't the nicest. She wasn't an understanding person. She would tell me, "You lost your sight because you're like the devil and full of sin." She basically told me that I had my accident because God was punishing me. I was still trying to accept everything that was going on at that time. I was still trying to gather my self-esteem. I was very young and she would say these things . . . Finally, I got pissed off. I had enough. I told her not to say these things to me. I knew that God wasn't doing this to punish me. I started getting angry. She also said, "No one is going to marry you because you're blind, and no one wants to be with you. Your life's over."

So that was when the whole anger started. I was sure that I could do this life, and I was going to go off and do it. I wanted to piss her off and prove her wrong.

So far, getting angry has been working. It's the only way that I've been able to cope. There are times when I do stay quiet. If I meet someone who annoys me on the bus, I might want to come off as a bit nicer or just ignore it. It's weird. That's more the kind of situation where I won't say anything. But then my frustration stays longer. [Sighs.] So afterward I talk to people. I tell my boyfriend or call my good friend. We process it together.

You Inspire Me

I have had people come up to me and say, "You inspire me." And I'm like, *I don't fucking know you. I don't know you. You don't know me. How the hell's that inspiring?* It's the same thing as if I told some girl that she inspires me because she's wearing heels.

So really what you're telling me is that you expect me to do a lot less because I'm disabled. The mere fact that I'm doing what everyone else is doing impresses you. That's just really shitty, and it's not a compliment. I'm seen as someone who's supposed to have a shitty life!

My boyfriend. He has never been weird about anything. Sometimes he will tell me that people ask him, "Oh, how does she cook and what does she do?" And he will just turn around and say, "What do you mean? How do you not expect her to know how to cook? You should feel stupid just asking this question now." [*Laughs.*]

I Feel That I'm Responsible for Her Anxiety

Early on, when I first acquired my disability, my mom was in denial. She would take me to different churches. She would say that I could get healed and that I would be OK and I would be able to see again. People held prayers for me. They would hold out their hands and pray on top of me. [*Sighs.*] I hated it. In the beginning—I'm not going to lie to you—part of me was hopeful. Maybe I would get healed. I wasn't accepting it yet. But more than anything, I grew to hate it. It made me feel really angry. It got to the point that I didn't want to go to church anymore. I would tell my mom that I didn't want to go. I was crying and screaming at that point. She was asking me if I didn't believe in God. And I said, "I don't, because he's not doing anything for me."

My mom still holds on to that hope. A part of her still feels that way. I don't think she ever will accept. Honestly. The accident was such a traumatic experience for everyone. She's always going to hold on to the hope. It's not like she doesn't accept me. She defends me. She talks about me a lot. But there's still part of her that hopes that maybe one day I will . . .

I don't talk about my disability. Even when it comes to the time of the anniversary of the accident, I don't talk about it. I don't bring it up. I don't talk to my family about it. My nephew and I make jokes about it. We call each other and say happy anniversary. [*Laughs.*] We make fun of it. But with my mom I tend not to bring it up. Because it gets her sad. If she forgets the date, it's better for me because then I don't have to worry about consoling her. I learned early on when I was in rehab that I can't overcommunicate my feelings with people and with my family because they take it upon themselves. It's the whole burden thing—they take it on. Especially my mom. There are many things I will not tell her about. I feel that I'm responsible for her anxiety.

I'M ASKED TO FIGHT ALL THE TIME

JULIE SCHRAGER

I met Julie through a very good friend of mine. I visited her one early November morning and found her house on a quiet sunny block in Wilmette—a village in the North Shore region of Chicago. The house looked petite compared to the other homes on the block. Her daughter Claire had been picked up by the school bus already. We had a cup of tea in Julie's living room, where we talked.

An Amazing Smile

My daughter Claire is almost sixteen and a half years old. She was born after a pretty uneventful pregnancy. But she was really small at birth and started missing developmental milestones early on. We spent about a year or two searching for a diagnosis but were largely unsuccessful. There were a couple of hypotheses, one of which turned out fifteen years later to be correct.

In the meantime, she wasn't able to walk, she wasn't able to talk, she wasn't able to feed herself. She wasn't able to do really any self-care and she couldn't be left alone. So we started out very young with a number of physical, occupational, and speech therapies every week. We kept wondering what was going on with her. She seemed stable, and her skills have improved over time—not dramatically, but she definitely hasn't degenerated. And then a year ago, she was diagnosed definitively through the use of a genetic test with something called Aicardi-Goutières syndrome, type 5. It's a degenerative white matter disease. Characteristics are inflammation in the brain and usually in the skin. So these kids have chilblains on their hands and feet, and they have a lack of

39

white matter in their brain. Their disability ranges from moderate to severe, depending on which genetic type they have.

Every morning I get her up at the same time, which is 6:15 . . . seven days a week. She does a lot better sleeping if she has an absolutely regular schedule. I always pay for it the day after if we stay out late. I'll change her diaper, brush her teeth, get her dressed, fix her hair, get all of her things ready to take her to school, feed her breakfast. She can't do any of it herself. Then I'll get her on the school bus.

She has a full-time person with her in school. Claire is driving a 250-pound wheelchair, and she's a good driver. But the hallways at the high school are crowded; she needs to get in and out of an elevator. She could never do anything like that by herself.

She'll come home in the afternoon either right after school or a little bit later if she does a club. And we sort of repeat the pattern in reverse. She'll have a snack. Maybe we'll go to the supermarket. Maybe I'll have her watch a show. She'll have dinner. Meals take a longer time. I have to be careful feeding her because there's a danger of aspiration. Always. Which you don't wanna have happen.

And then I get her ready for bed. I can't give her a bath by myself anymore. So I have a babysitter coming in once or twice a week to help give her a bath and wash her hair. I can take her in and out of the house. As long as it's not winter, we're better off. She has a really strong reaction to the cold. And when there's snow around and so few places are accessible, she doesn't tend to go out as much.

Claire is a master of nonverbal communication. She has an amazing smile. Sometimes I'll get her to come over here and use the assisting communicative device. I'd say, "What are you feeling?" "Why are you feeling mad?" "What do you want?"

She can also talk about other things. She can ask me questions. But more often, on a typical school day, her communication is nonverbal. Like, *I'm driving to the door if I'm ready to go to school. I'm smiling if you're saying that we're doing something after school that I'm excited about.*

I have a nineteen-year-old daughter as well. Emily is a sophomore in college. So it's only Claire and I living here now.

We Knew You Couldn't Come Because of Claire

At the outset, many members of my family had a really hard time getting their arms around what had happened to Claire. My sister didn't touch her for two years. It was almost like it was contagious or something . . . whatever it was that she had. She didn't even touch her! It was like she had cooties. That was so hurtful. It has been hard to ever get past that. My family. That's definitely been one of the hardest things. You think you get over it, and then you don't get over it. You think that it's fine, and they are who they are. And then you revisit it again.

It's hard to know who excludes you and whom you exclude. It's a complicated dynamic. There are definitely people that I'm not friends with anymore. Either because they were uncomfortable or I perceived them to be uncomfortable with the situation. And then there are numerous people that I'm friends with—I don't wanna say because of the situation—but because I met them through Claire or through people who knew Claire. So Claire's situation certainly changed who I spend time with and who I care to spend time with.

Less directly, there are often times when somebody would say, "Oh, we just didn't even think to invite you. We knew you couldn't come because of Claire." And it's complicated. Are they being sensitive to you? Or are they not including you? Sometimes it's hurtful.

But it was even more hurtful when I felt it affected my older daughter, Emily. You know, when we wouldn't be included as a family because people knew that we couldn't do it. I remember girl's night out for moms, where I wouldn't be included. They didn't invite me.

I don't think about all these things as discrimination. I'm sort of this ferocious fighter on behalf of my kid. I just think about being an advocate for her. There's this club at New Trier High School that makes periodic social events for typical kids and for kids with disabilities. Claire is a sophomore at New Trier and was invited last year, as she's invited this year. Last year they had a holiday party in the club. I got the invitation and the party was at somebody's private house. I e-mailed the person at New Trier and asked, "Is the house accessible?"

The staff member at New Trier who was organizing the event hadn't checked at all whether the house was accessible. She wrote back to me, and it wasn't. But there were only two stairs and it was OK to manage. Same thing happened this year. I got the invitation for the party on Monday. This year it's in a house that I know isn't accessible in any way. You sort of think, *OK. This is a program for kids with disabilities and they don't even consider my daughter with her disability.*

But I don't wanna make everybody unhappy. I'm not gonna make them move. I'm not gonna shut down the party. I'm just gonna not tell Claire. But you feel that these are the people that should understand you. This is awful! But she's in a minority of a minority.

I think, for me, exclusion has more been the issue than discrimination. Some of the exclusion has been intentional and some of it unintentional. Not inviting me to things, or my family not being hospitable to Claire is intentional. I think that's my big message. Exclusion.

Mostly, I've internalized the intentional exclusion. Sometimes I get angry. But often I just say, *What's the point?* You can't really give up!

I mean, it's hard. I certainly have a lot of anger. I think everybody in the disability community has a lot of anger.

By Connection, You Have a Disability

It's interesting not being disabled myself, but being connected with somebody with a disability. I'll be in a handicap parking space and I get out of the car, and I've experienced people say, "You don't belong there," "You shouldn't be parking in that space." Until they see me getting Claire out of the back end of the van. It's a little weird that people don't think you have a disability when you so acutely identify with people with disabilities. You feel like, by connection, you have a disability, even though you're not perceived to.

My reaction to such people totally depends on my mood. I will sometimes be rude. Most of the time, I'll just say that I have a daughter with a disability. But I'm asked to fight all the time. It's so wearing every day to be doing this. It's just so draining. All the time, I feel like I have to beg for something special. All the time.

I always saw in myself this danger of measuring yourself by how your children are doing. That's not healthy for any mom. We all know people whose worth is defined by what college their kid is at or how much money they're earning. That never made sense to me. But when you have a kid with a disability . . . How could it? I can devote myself 24-7 to Claire and she's never gonna be able to walk. She'll never be independent . . . There's nothing within my power . . . Nothing . . . [*Weeps a little.*] I guess the hard thing is that I can't give up. I don't want to do nothing. But I can't make it everything either.

I Insist on Living a Typical Life

My marriage fell apart soon after Claire was born. In part, that was because of my ex-husband's anger about the situation and definitely blame toward me—for wanting to have a second child. So it has probably made me defensive. I just feel like I'm an advocate. I'm all about that. I was thinking about it because we're all formed by our experiences. And I'm sure that I'm affected by being a typical parent too. But nowhere near the amount that I am by having a kid like Claire.

So after she was born, I was much more conscious about what I needed—for me. I started seeing the importance of exercise and sleep. Those had always been things that I did, but I don't think I knew why they were important before. Exercise, sleep, friendships, and work—that makes me feel really good about myself and my contributions. I never let any of them go for any length of time. And you know what? Reading is the fifth thing. I read a lot. Books are really important to me. And that's a continuity thing. That's one of the things I've always done in my life.

And then, I gotta tell you. People with disabilities do what they do, just because they have to do it. There are no other alternatives. You know, stay home and cry? Not live a life? There are sacrifices you make, but you have to be able to do something. I don't think any human being can cut off all want and need.

Another thing has just been being satisfied with a smaller life. This is such a first world problem, but we don't travel. As a family we took no vacation except for a visit to my parents in Florida. They have a three-bedroom condo on the first floor, and the weather makes it easy there. But that's pretty much all the travel we've done for the last sixteen years. I haven't left Claire for more than two nights in sixteen years. I haven't been away from her for a month for the past sixteen years—a month altogether.

Sometimes I get my energy from anger. But there's also just, you know, the show must go on. The way we have made it through these sixteen years has been to normalize as much of our lives as we can. It's not a crisis unless it's a crisis. These are just little things that you have to deal with. We live a normal life. I insist on living a typical life.

Claire Will Always Be at the Mercy of Strangers

The hardest thing is not knowing what the future will bring. The key to that is that you have to plan to the extent that you can. And you have to save as much money as you can, without thinking about it all the time. Because there's nothing you can really do. Claire will always be at the mercy of strangers. As people with severe disabilities always are. Just so vulnerable.

There's a change in the American culture in our society. The idea that it's OK to be hateful is appalling. People with disabilities are just one of many groups that are subject to that. I also feel there's gonna be a change in the law. And whether it's gonna be health care or education, it's terrifying. The interesting part is that as a parent of a child with special needs, you always know that you can't count on anybody besides yourself to take care of your kid. In some ways the current developments are just further proof of that for me. It's completely terrifying, and I don't think we're wrong to be that scared. I am grateful that Claire doesn't understand politics.

2 | WHAT I MEAN WHEN I TALK ABOUT DISABILITY

PEOPLE WITH DISABILITIES DO not constitute a homogenous group. They may live in urban areas. They may live in the countryside. They may be young or old. They may be black or white or brown. They may be male or female. They may be rich or, more likely, poor. They may have been born with a disability. They may have acquired a disability suddenly—by way of accident, natural disaster, or war—or gradually because of disease. They may have disabilities that come and go in their lives. Their disabilities may be visible or invisible. There is no "one size fits all" for people with disabilities. Disability should be seen as an aspect of human variation.

Throughout history, and often still today, disability has been seen exclusively as a personal medical problem. The medicalization of disability has been dominant for generations and has focused on what is considered wrong in the person. This medical model is preoccupied with the individual person. It strives to help or cure the individual or to ameliorate the impairment through medical interventions. In short, it is about fixing the individual.

Today, disability advocates look at disability through a more complex social lens. Disability is seen as a social construct and not as a medical category. The focus is moved from the individual person to the social, and disability is viewed as a condition largely imposed on individuals by society. Many persons with disabilities do not frequently think about their impairment. It is simply part of who they are and not a focus of consciousness. However, impairment is often the center of other people's attention, illustrating that disability is still seen as an illness or a medical issue by many.

The social model approach is reflected in the Americans with Disabilities Act (ADA) of 1990. The idea of a social model emanates from a distinction between impairment and disability. Whereas impairment should be understood as a variation in body function or structure, including mental ones, disability should be considered a limitation that results from physical and attitudinal barriers in the surroundings, including social oppression and discrimination. In other words, disability results from social context, from the interaction between the impairment and the environment.

A vast literature about disability rights underscores this distinction between impairment and disability. Not being able to use your legs, for example, is an impairment, but being unable to get into your local cinema is a disability. So if there are ramps, curb cuts, and physical accessibility everywhere, a person using a wheelchair may have an impairment. But that person has equal opportunities and therefore does not have a disability in these contexts. The example illustrates that it is the barriers more than the actual impairment that disable a person, whether these barriers are physical, structural, or attitudinal.

Today, the approach of most groups in the disability and human rights community is to focus is on the barriers that a person meets in society instead of the individual impairment. The foundation is the social model and there is no striving to fix the person. The aim is to change disabling structures and attitudes in society. The fact that many persons with disabilities face difficult lives has much more to do with the social environments they live in than their individual impairments.

Considering disability as a social construct rather than a medical diagnosis does not imply that individuals with impairments should not get the medical treatment and services that they need. Generally, the disability and human rights community accepts medical research and treatment. Decisions to maximize health and avoid illnesses do not devalue those who are sick or otherwise different.*

The UN Convention on the Rights of Persons with Disabilities is an international human rights convention on disability rights from 2007. Most of the countries of the world have ratified the convention, but not the United States. Like the ADA, the convention is based on the social model and clarifies that

---

* Andrew Solomon, *Far from the Tree: Parents, Children, and the Search for Identity* (New York: Scribner, 2012), 31.

disability results from the interaction between persons with impairments and external barriers that hinder their participation in society.

Many of the individuals who have shared their stories with me for this book are proud members of the disability rights movement in Chicago. They speak about oppression and being excluded as a group. They speak about being discriminated against as individuals. They speak about self-awareness and a change in consciousness whereby the notion of disability as a pitiful medical condition has been replaced by an understanding of disability as a social condition. They speak about this consciousness as profoundly liberating. They are no longer interested in charity and help but in the fundamental human rights of people with disabilities.

In this chapter, James Charlton and Heather Gabel share their knowledge and lay out the basis for understanding what it actually means to be a person with a disability.

WE ARE LESS

JAMES CHARLTON

I visited Jim in the neighborhood of South Shore in Chicago. The day was hot and humid. We were sitting in his sunroom facing the street. The breeze came through the mosquito net and scattered my notes on the floor. Every so often cars and people passed by the house and a police siren sounded in the distance. Children were laughing in the street. A gardener was blowing leaves with a loud and smelly gasoline engine in the neighbor's yard. I stopped noticing. Jim shared his many years of thinking about disability, oppression, and empowerment. His compelling book Nothing About Us Without Us *details these thoughts.* He was eager to help me in my endeavor.*

I Don't Think They Really Knew What to Do with Me

I grew up in rural Wisconsin, went to college in Iowa, and then to graduate school at University of Chicago. I've been in Chicago ever since. I was in grad school when I was injured in a car accident. It happened in 1977 and I was twenty-five.

I was out of school for six months after the accident. Coming back was different. The University of Chicago is really old, and I think I was the first student with a wheelchair. I don't think they really knew what to do with me. Somebody in the dean's office called me and asked me what I wanted. And I just didn't know yet. I started up again in the winter, and that was really a headache. Anyway, there's not a lot more to tell.

---

* James I. Charlton, *Nothing About Us Without Us: Disability Oppression and Empowerment* (Berkeley: University of California Press, 2000).

The other students . . . I think I was oblivious to them. And uninterested. My recollection is pretty foggy about that. There's no doubt that I was a very odd-looking person on campus. There was nobody else using a chair. I was just trying to survive. And trying to figure out about my spinal cord injury. I really had no personal experiences with disability. I had a political view about it. I was a political person, and I had a political conscience about oppression and discrimination. So the fact that I couldn't get into buildings, this wasn't at all shocking to me. I expected that. My reaction to all of this was much more intellectual than emotional. In some ways, a lot of it just confirmed what I'd already assumed. But my goal really was to just get a degree and get out of there.

I was very lucky. After my accident, I stumbled into this circle of people who started Access Living. I was in the rehab institute getting therapy at the very moment Access Living was being cooked up. I met Marca Bristo [CEO of Access Living]. We were in the rehab institute literally months apart. Our injuries were months apart. We've known each other since late 1977. So I got involved in Access Living right away. I was on the founding board and started actually working at Access Living in 1984. I went from being on the board to staff, and I've worked there ever since, although now I'm only working eight hours a week.

Disability Is How People with Impairments Live in the World

There are various definitions of disability. For me, when I'm kind of being crude about it, I'd say that disability is how people with impairments live in the world. So impairments are the medical conditions. It's the diagnoses. And disability is a social condition. It's about the surroundings. I always emphasize that "in—the—world" implies something different than just "in the world." It's the idea that there's a relationship between the milieu that you live in and your own personal experiences. It's not just everyday life or everyday experiences, but it's also the little world that you live in. For instance, how disabled people live in Chicago is different from how disabled people live in rural Iowa. So to know disability, you need a context.

When I use the term *person or people with impairment*, I'm really talking about the medical condition. I'm talking about the person who's blind or has a spinal cord injury or whatever.

When I use the term *person or people with disabilities*, I'm referring to an individual or individuals with impairments and how they live in the world.

When I use the phrase *disabled persons*, I'm referring to the social group. I'm not referring to individuals. I'm referring to the social group of disabled persons, and I'm also referring to that social group as an oppressed social group.

And then there are all these problems. For instance, could you have an impairment and not be disabled? Big headache! For instance, what about ninety-five-year-old people, who have all these impairments? They don't hear well, they don't see well, they don't walk well. Are they disabled? The social model asks, *How do society and the surroundings treat old people?* You could say, "Well, they are treated as normal. Old people are supposed to have those impairments."

One of the defining characteristics of disability is abnormality. So where does that begin and end? When impairments move from the abnormal body or the abnormal mind to the all normal? Well, if you get to be ninety-five and you don't walk, it's already assumed that you're not gonna walk well. So it just seems to me that it isn't cut and dry where impairment ends and disability starts. When you use the social model, it makes things more complicated. That's not to say it's wrong! But it's important to remember that it's just a model.

We've Become Invisible

As a social group, we've been excluded for at least a couple of hundred years. Then, over time, what ends up happening is that the social group becomes invisible or it simply disappears. That's why I think the situation of disability and disabled persons is more about disappearance than about appearance. You hear this even in narratives about discrimination when people say, "They look at me but they really don't see me. They just see the wheelchair."

As a social group, we have been excluded to such a degree that we've become invisible. There's this very odd invisibility based on people being excluded, because they're not as valid. You get jobs based on whether employers think you're valuable. It's not just an uneducated feeling or uneducated idea in the head of the individual employer. If you have a social group that's been excluded for a very long time, excluded from work primarily, but also socially and culturally, then it would make sense for the mass of people to assume that the people in that group are inferior. This exclusion has been going on for hundreds of years. We as a group have never worked. Individuals have. I mean, I work. There are individuals with disabilities who have worked. But disabled people never worked. As a group, the unemployment rate in the US is more than 70 percent.

So to me it all flows out of what I would call structural exclusion based on value. That our value is less! Not that we don't have value. But we have less value. In the US, we used to have the term *invalid*. Then there was a big fight to get rid of that word. But in some ways that word is more honest. Because it points to value—less value, less valid. And I think if a social group has been historically less valued, that's where the backward attitude comes from. The attitude comes out of this exclusion. And it's not an exclusion based on steps and not letting you into a building. I'm talking about being socially, economically, culturally, politically excluded. If people are excluded in these areas for hundreds of years, others are gonna come up with some conclusions about that group! Those conclusions are legitimate. They're wrong, but there's a material basis for why other people would think like that.

You hear people say, "In my culture, people with disabilities are considered less." My reaction to that is "Why do you say 'In my culture'? I can prove to you that in every culture disabled people are treated less!" So that would imply that it's not about particular cultures, not about particularities, but dominant cultures. In general, disabled people are just thought more or less poorly of everywhere! They—are—thought—of—as—less! My view is, we are less. We're valued less based on the way that capitalism values people. People with disabilities, like all oppressed groups, have less of what Marx called "exchange value." I'd even go further and say disabled persons are the most devalued.

It's not the way that individuals value other individuals. But we have less exchange value as a group. Not necessarily as individuals. If disabled people go to Harvard, they have a very good exchange rate. Their value is very high. But I talk about the group. As a group, we have less value.

I Just Thought That I Was Being Overlooked

I have a lot of ideas about discrimination, although I don't have a lot of personal experiences with it.

You will hear this from people: "It took me a long time before I realized that I was being discriminated against. Now when I look back on it, I can see that it was a behavior that I experienced over and over again. But I didn't really put two and two together. I didn't fully understand that it was discrimination. I just thought that I was being overlooked."

My Options Are Wider

I think it's really good that you're interested in the intersection of race and disability. Because that's an entanglement. You're trying to access degrees of discrimination or nuances of discrimination, and how race fits into that. I think it's really relevant.

But it's more than race and disability. I mean, I'm white. But I'm also class privileged—more or less. So the way I live in the world and how poor people with disabilities live in the world with various barriers is very different. To me, these barriers are like nuisances. I've always been able to get a job. I have a graduate degree from the University of Chicago. In some ways, and in ironic ways, because of the exclusion and discrimination that people with disabilities face in general, for the few of us who get through those barriers or handicaps or challenges there are some advantages in terms of the ways that discrimination works. Some places actually want to hire disabled persons. And there are so few of us with degrees from fancy universities. The pool is so much smaller. I never really looked for jobs. I've always been hired. And I really think that it has something to do with these ironic effects of discrimination that made it easier for me. I stood out and it benefited me.

So the disability experience is complicated. It's complicated by what I would call the deep structures of race, class, and gender. But there is also the intersection of the various kinds of impairments. So the issue of discrimination becomes even more complicated by this hierarchy of impairment, or hierarchy of disability. My idea is that people with mental illnesses are far more discriminated against than us with "just" physical impairments or disabilities. And then there are the people with severe cognitive problems. In the US we use the term *developmentally disabled*. It seems less pejorative than *mental retardation*, which was used in the old days. These are the people who are the most screwed.

Therefore, the barriers that I'm up against as a white, middle-class, spinal cord–injured man aren't the same as those of a poor African American woman with a mental illness. That's not to say that I don't experience barriers that limit my options. But my options are wider because of my class—my very middle class. So even though there are limitations on me from being a wheelchair user, I still have a lot of choices. The barriers are more irritations for me.

And then again, the intersection is not just about class, gender, race, and disability. Within class or class privilege, there's cultural capital. And that also plays a huge role. When discrimination is operational, when does it really handicap someone, and when does it just become a nuisance or irritation? Cultural capital is such a huge advantage. If you don't know anybody, you're really swimming upstream. In general. And then you add on race and gender and disability.

When you're looking at discrimination and intersectionality, it's very hard to parse out whether persons are being discriminated against because they're black or because they're disabled or because they're poor. They're probably getting discriminated against on the basis of all of the above. You'd never really know.

AN ASPECT OF HUMAN VARIATION

HEATHER GABEL

Heather was a teaching assistant in my class on disability in world cultures at the University of Illinois at Chicago. When we met again half a year later, it was summer and campus felt quiet and a bit deserted. We spoke, and big words, warm smiles, and occasional bursts of laughter filled the empty classroom.

Impairment and Disablement

I do identify as a person with a disability. I have two chronic illnesses. I have type 1 diabetes, although generally when I share that information, I don't include the type. That's strategic. I also have Hashimoto's, which is a thyroid condition, and for me it produces nodules. They're like little tumors in my thyroid, and I have a history of having to get those biopsied. So I spend a lot of time in the doctor's office, and I think, for me, that's why I identify as disabled. Not only because it's included under the ADA protection, which is a valuable resource and a good reason to identify. I feel like I do because my experience points me that way. The ways that my conditions and my chronic illnesses have played out have made it so that I have to have accommodations and I have to make life adjustments. And because I've been making those life adjustments, I choose to identify as a person with a disability. I also think that the disability community is a very powerful one. Who doesn't wanna be a part of that? I definitely do.

I see disability as an aspect of human variation more than anything. What I don't wanna do is to say that I see disability as a limitation. As something that weighs people down. Because I don't think that. On its own, disability doesn't do that. But it does seem like a limitation in the context of society. So I would explain disability as a form of human variation that is observed as occurring within the body, or around the body, or on the body in some way. A human variation that is observed and/or perceived. And perhaps experienced that way.

Disability is also a social phenomenon. There is a distinction between the impairment and the disablement. Because the impairment is like the experience of the variations within the body or on the body, and the disablement is the part that comes from the outside . . . from the barriers set up in the environment that limit you. When I'm talking about disability, I separate impairment and disablement. But there's overlap. And it's messy. Especially when you talk about an individual's experience. Because on a personal level, I sometimes feel my diabetes is a limitation. Sometimes my diabetes—and not the barriers in my environment—is the reason why I can't go to work that day. It's so complex.

At eleven I was diagnosed at the same time with diabetes and Hashimoto's. I had a very rough journey to diagnosis. Because I was an eleven-year-old girl and the main symptoms of diabetes are weight loss, my doctor thought it was anorexia or bulimia or some other kind of eating disorder. He didn't check me for diabetes. He didn't look further. So I was undiagnosed for three months and kept losing weight. I had just started middle school, and it was a very turbulent time for my parents and me. Another symptom of having high blood sugar is sort of erratic behavior. I would throw temper tantrums like you would expect from a toddler. I had all these stuffed animals on my bed, and I remember just throwing them at the door. Just enraged at nothing. My body was so out of whack. One time, I went to the doctor, I was five foot two and weighed sixty-eight pounds, so I was scary, scary thin. Emaciated. Really very uncomfortable. My doctor was out of town for an appointment, and I saw his physician assistant. Immediately, the physician assistant said, "Oh, you probably have diabetes."

So the next week I was in the hospital and starting to recover. I think that whole experience for my parents was very, very traumatic. Before my diagnosis, I recall my parents saying good night to me in a serious way. Because we just didn't know what was happening. Like, *I don't know if you're gonna wake up tomorrow. I need to have this time with you.*

So the diagnosis was a relief. But also scary. Because diabetes requires constant management, and the doctors put that in my hands when I was only eleven years old. My parents helped. But I administered my own insulin. And insulin is like a lethal drug if not taken in the correct doses. With all that said, I think most of what I felt from my parents was worry. It's kind of a hard subject for my parents to talk about. They still struggle with it. The tantrum part of it sort of continued for three years. Because I was going through puberty and had these wild variations in my blood sugar. I was unruly, and I was mean. There was tension in the house all the time. I felt like the problem. Growing up was like that.

When I left for college, everything changed. And that was really good for me. I needed that. Because I felt like I was wrapped in a blanket of worry all the time. In college I got to take responsibility for the first time. And not be in a state of rebellion. Before, I actively pushed away my parents' worry, but in so doing, I didn't manage very well. And I didn't wanna have diabetes at all. It sucks. It sucked then. It's not fun now, but I see the silver linings. I definitely didn't then.

I Can Let Myself Go to Sleep Right Now and That Would Be It

The first two years when I was still in middle school, the stigma around diabetes influenced my self-esteem very badly. It showed through my wardrobe. I went goth in my last year of middle school. I only wore black and picked friends who only wore black because that's all I felt. I just felt very dark. I wrote horrible poetry that probably really scared my parents. I was never suicidal, but I was deeply, deeply sad. A lot of that was because I was aware of my own mortality. At that age kids usually aren't. I was like twelve or thirteen.

I had five seizures in middle school. So on top of sort of being mentally aware of that, there were five times when I woke up with a crying parent above me. [*Clapping both her cheeks.*]

The experience of low blood sugar is haunting in a way. And it happens all the time. Now that I'm pregnant, it probably happens five times a day. I'm dropping low all the time. When I was a kid it happened a lot too because I just couldn't find any kind of regularity. My blood sugar was up, and it was down, and it was up, and it was down. When I am low, which is where seizures happen for me, I feel like, *This could be it. Like I could go right now if I didn't* . . . I would lie in bed and think about that when I was a teenager. I would wake up knowing my blood sugar was low and I would think that it was a possibility: *I can let myself go to sleep right now and that would be it.* So I had a lot of up-close experiences with a sense of my mortality at a young age. In middle school it was really hard.

There is one experience . . . It irks me still. I went in to see a doctor when I was in college. She was a general practitioner, and it was the first time I saw her. She was looking through my chart and she said, "Oh, diabetes. Are you over that whole why-me phase yet?"

And it just made me cringe inside, because what a horrible thing to say. What if I wasn't . . . What if I was still there? And she just asked this incredibly condescending question. I would definitely characterize middle school as a period of seeking answers for why this was happening to me.

I'm Gonna Own Diabetes

In high school I was bubbly again. I think when I got the insulin pump I started to feel kind of cool because it was this external device. People could see it and maybe there was some satisfaction there. Some validation. That it was obvious that I needed something on my body to help me regulate . . . I haven't thought about it like that before . . .

I went into high school thinking that I was gonna turn around everything that had happened in middle school. My first day of high school, I felt that way. It was like a new beginning. I was kind of like, *I'm gonna own diabetes.*

I would talk about it in an informative way. Because I wanted people to know. I wanted to tell everybody about it so that people understood. It almost became a platform for me at that point. So in high school I was hyperembracing diabetes. Because I just needed to regain the control over what it meant that I had diabetes.

College was great. I met my husband-to-be right before we started college. Jessie was a life force of change. He didn't really have any thoughts about diabetes when we first met. So I got to sort of craft the way that I talked about diabetes. And with him I was just like, "I have this thing. It makes me a little bit different, and I like it. . . . What's weird about you?" [*Laughs.*] It was kind of like that. And he was really receptive.

Diabetes Is This Disease That's Deserved

The attitudes. The media plays into this. Diabetes is touted as a disease where people don't care about themselves. People get diabetes because they don't care about their bodies. They don't exercise. They don't eat well. Because of these stereotypes, there's a lot of judgment. A lot of expectations that I'm struggling because I deserve it.

I feel I experience these attitudes all the time. They show up in little comments. Usually. Or even expressions sometimes. On prom night, I remember we went out with a big group. I remember the stares. Oh, the stares when I ordered a mac and cheese. It was just like . . . I don't know. That was one time when I felt that I was being ostracized for my food choice. Even though four other people at the table got the same thing. Like, "Shouldn't you be making better choices?" "You already have this because you made bad choices. Shouldn't you . . . take care of yourself?"

Wow, I haven't thought about that experience for a long time. I order mac and cheese all the time. [*Laughs.*] It's my favorite. [*Laughs incredulously.*]

Some of the attitudes were also about energy level. If I was tired. If I didn't wanna go rollerblading. This happened in my neighborhood. If I didn't wanna go, it would be like, "Don't you need to?" or "Isn't that something that would be good for you?" Whereas I'm assuming if another kid decided that he didn't wanna go rollerblading, that's not a question he would be asked.

One of the big comments from people is "Oh . . . my grandma had diabetes. She died of diabetes." Often it's followed by "She didn't take care of herself at all. She never ate well." I think people are trying to connect with you, but it's really an awful thing to say. [*Laughs.*]

And then as a teenager when I would hear that, I would be like, *Uh. I don't eat well . . . I don't exercise very much.* Then I would kill myself because I wasn't doing those things. *Everyone is giving me evidence that this is something that will likely happen to me because I'm not caring.*

I internalized a lot of the stigma when I was younger. I honestly didn't think I would live past thirty-five. [*Laughs.*]

But then I started attempting to dispel myths about diabetes in a very uncharged way. I worked in a fast-food restaurant my first two years of college, and the comments happened a bunch in there when I was working as a cashier. I have the word *diabetic* tattooed on my arm. When I was handing out money and stretching out my arm, people would say, "You're diabetic? And you work here?"

And I'd be like, "Yeah, actually diabetes is a condition that's more like a spectrum, and most people with diabetes can eat just whatever they want as long as they take insulin."

And then they'd be like, "Oh. OK . . ."

And I'd be like, "Yeah. You learned something today!"

And I felt empowered by that. I felt like, at that point, I didn't internalize it anymore. I was seeing it like this: *You have that attitude because of whatever you've experienced and interacted with in terms of media and your family. That's all about you. You're not commenting on me when you're saying that. You're just demonstrating an idea that you have.* So in college I was able to start separating and stop internalizing.

The attitudes and preconceived ideas is a real constant. It's too much . . . Sometimes it feels like it's too much to do anything about. In general, I'm very optimistic about social change. But every now and again . . . Wow! . . . It feels like the dark ages. I can't believe how insensitive people are. And how wrong people are about what diabetes is.

People still think that diabetes is this disease that's deserved. That we don't eat well. That we don't care about our bodies. That we don't exercise. You see this in media representations. If you ever see a media story about diabetes, pay attention to the B-roll. Just see what's playing behind. Somebody's speaking about diabetes and you see a midsection of bigger people carrying McDonald's cups. It's like every time, even if it's a positive diabetes story. So we have this image at a social level, that diabetes equals don't-care and at-fault and to-blame.

Right now, because I'm pregnant, I do [feel guilty when I eat "unhealthy" food]. But no . . . Like, if you'd asked me about six months ago, I would have said no. I don't take it in when people look at me. I just know very deeply now that when someone sends me a look, it's saying more about that person than it's saying about me.

Let It Be Not About Me

Part of [knowing that] is just growing up. I also do think that diabetes required me to pay attention to what's happening to me . . . I need to be able to feel my blood sugar in order to be safe. That same sort of self-surveillance applied to my emotional state as I matured. So I would watch myself have . . . I would watch that internalization happen, and I would think, *The only person who's hurting is me. I need to do something about that.*

I think it started as a sort of self-protection mechanism in high school. It was like denying and pushing away. After that, I continued to mature as a person and I met Jessie. He had a lot of impact on the way that I processed and self-reflected and self-monitored my emotional state. I then began to actively do what I felt would be best for me. And what's best for me, what gives me the least negativity and the least bad feelings, is to just let it be not about me. I think doing that made me very aware of the social as a separate entity. I didn't see that before.

3 | NO ONE SEES ME

A party. I was there at the dinner table eating my appetizer. People next to me were talking to people next to them, not to me. I made some comments. I tried to get their attention. They didn't hear. They didn't see. Me as a person. I was invisible to them. And there was no one and nowhere to go to that night.

PEOPLE WITH DISABILITIES EXPERIENCE invisibility all the time. Every day. Everywhere. Not being invited. Not being regarded. Being left out. Not being seen as individuals.

Charlotte McClain-Nhlapo is a global disability adviser at the World Bank and uses a wheelchair. In a TEDx talk, she explained how one day she was waiting for a friend.* She was sitting in her chair on the pavement, and she had a can of Coke in her hand. She quickly saw from the corner of her eye this little old lady coming over. And this lady was just about to drop a coin into Charlotte's can when Charlotte gently stopped her: "Oh no. No. No. No. Not my Diet Coke." The reality was that the lady hadn't seen Charlotte. She hadn't seen Charlotte as a person. She hadn't seen Charlotte as a productive citizen. The only thing she had seen was a person in a wheelchair. She had seen her as an object of pity. Giving most likely made the old lady feel good. But I do not think that she considered how it made Charlotte feel to receive.

---

* Charlotte McClain-Nhlapo, "Why It Is Time to Make Inclusive Development Inclusive," TEDx Talks video, July 6, 2016, https://youtu.be/cQg-jnOfHPQ, 11:17.

Throughout history, people with disabilities have lived their lives apart from the rest of society. They have been isolated, hidden, stigmatized, mistreated, and marginalized. As a social group, they have been excluded to such a degree that they have become invisible and anonymous to the majority. People with disabilities say that still today others look straight through them. In this chapter, Susan Nussbaum explains how people do not even notice her until they bump into her wheelchair: "It's a kind of invisibility where you're overseen or you're seen as someone or something that you're not."

Invisibility and social isolation are often the results when friends retreat. Alissa Chung tells us in this chapter about her daughters being infantilized by other children and how friendships went in the direction of inspiration porn. Parents also experience exclusion themselves because of the disability of their child. Many times, parents withdraw from their friends' pity or incomprehension. Alissa Chung describes this: "I think there are a lot of people who either are uncomfortable and don't know what to say . . . or are afraid." The reality is that the birth of a healthy child usually expands the parents' social network; the birth of a child with a disability often constricts that network.*

Inaccessibility has stopped people with disabilities from living their lives out in their communities. Even though progress has been made and communities have become more accessible and diverse, most people still do not regularly interact with persons with disabilities. This is the case in schools, at workplaces, at the local grocery, nail salon, or movie theater. Systemically, people with disabilities have been excluded, and still are. Societies all around the world have made people with disability invisible and anonymous. It is no different in Chicago.

As Ralph Ellison wrote in 1947 of the struggle with social exclusion based on race, "I am invisible, understand, simply because people refuse to see me."†

---

* Andrew Solomon, *Far from the Tree: Parents, Children, and the Search for Identity* (New York: Scribner, 2012), 363.

† Ralph Ellison, *Invisible Man* (orig. publ. 1947; New York: Modern Library, 1994), 3.

YOU'RE LITERALLY NOT SEEN

SUSAN NUSSBAUM

I read the heartbreakingly raw and funny novel Good Kings Bad Kings* *about teenagers living in an institution for young people with disabilities. The story gave insights into a world that is utterly foreign for most people, so I was grateful that the author wanted to talk to me. We met in Susan's apartment in Chicago's Lakeview area and had a long conversation about structural barriers and discrimination against people with disabilities.*

Their Best Was a Lot

I'm spinal cord injured. I was hit by a car when I was a young woman. I'm a wheelchair user.

I was a student when I had my accident. I couldn't continue my studies in acting school.

In my family, none of us knew anything about disability or ever really bothered to check into it. At the time there was no disability rights movement. And even more than today, much more so . . . disabled people were invisible. There really wasn't very much, except for the horrible movies that they did with disabled characters. But my family—I have this great family. They rallied round and did their best. And their best was a lot.

---

* Susan Nussbaum, *Good Kings Bad Kings* (Chapel Hill, NC: Algonquin Books, 2013).

It's as If You Don't Exist

You're literally not seen. It's as if you don't exist in the streets. It's very different in that sense from the kind of paternalism and sexism that women experience. As a young woman, when I was walking down the street there was self-consciousness and a lot of male attention that I had to negotiate. That most women still have to negotiate because they're dealing with this objectification. And there's a certain danger to it at times. Mostly it's just [*sighs*] same old . . . same old stuff.

If you acquire a disability, that objectification is instantly replaced by a sort of invisibility. No one sees you. No one even notices you. They don't see you until they bump into you . . . sometimes. Or they see you but in some really odd, specified way—like they feel they must smile really hard at you. Or they have to ask you how you're doing or if you need help. Which is very invasive and very inappropriate and very, you know, ugh [*sighs*] . . . very paternal. It's a kind of invisibility where you're overseen or you're seen as someone or something that you're not. It steals your own sense of ease on the street.

Today, I have a power chair and I don't need help out there. But people in the street say so many things that still piss me off: "Do you need help?" "Are you all right?" When I haven't done or said a thing that would make people think, that could make anyone think, that I'm in some kind of peril.

I Wanted to Be with Those Folks

A year after my accident I discovered the very incipient disability rights movement in Chicago. It finally found its way here. The moment that I heard about it, I went to check out the place. And there were all these disabled people working there of varying disabilities. I felt instantly at ease and peaceful for the first time [*smiles*] over a year since I'd been injured.

That was where I wanted to go. I wanted to be with those folks. I didn't wanna explain. I didn't wanna think. So when I joined the movement, something inside turned around completely and I felt sort of rejuvenated or back in touch with myself . . .

I discovered that disabled people have this wonderful sense of humor that springs directly from their experience of being marginalized. I think that was the best part. Being able for the first time to really laugh at how outrageous people's responses are in the world out there. To find that community. To understand that the disability wasn't my problem. To understand my tentative feelings about living again. It's not like I was suicidal, but my feelings about putting myself out there, even sometimes going outdoors, were tentative. My shame about what had happened to me. I felt so awkward. When I found that community, all that was sort of shook up. Everything needed to be reconsidered.

Being in the disability community refocused my understanding of what the problem was. The problem was the culture and the institutional thinking on how disabled people fit in. How we fit in is to be dehumanized. To be medicalized. To be devoid of sexuality. To be paternalized in the sense that we are unable to provide for ourselves. Even though the reasons we are unable to do so are the many barriers around us.

In the disability community I got something else that brought me energy, enthusiasm, and anger. I got a political orientation that I felt familiar with. I saw the barriers that had a systemic impact on all sorts of people—including, now, me. I had been very active in the women's movement before the accident and now I had to rethink my relationship with various identities.

You Don't Belong Here!

There are different kinds of barriers. And different kinds of exclusion. There are microaggressions and macroaggressions. I see the systemic stuff as the most oppressive because it's hard to change. It's hard to fully understand. It's so complicated. But it's all the systems that one comes in contact with in one's life. All the systems that have control over various parts of you: employment, health care, education, and so much more. Every aspect of life is somewhat systematized.

All of that was very problematic for me after my accident. I couldn't go back to school. It made no sense. Nothing was accessible. But also at the time, I certainly couldn't be an actress. I mean, I was a wheelchair user! What could I possibly do in a theater? And that mentality was something I internalized. I was angry about it. I was certainly angry about the piece that was structural. I think the only way that one can internalize that is to feel . . . hmm . , . to feel the physical impact as an emotional impact. You know, it's just one message after another that says, *You don't belong here!*

I think social oppression of disabled persons is very real. I imagine I am less desirable as a partner to some people and not others. I've had many part-ners in the course of my life. I think my disability has had an impact on my life . . . for sure. And I think, like everything, one becomes comfortable with that stuff over time. I sometimes wonder, would I have married if I had not been hit by a car? If my disability has had an impact on my ability to attract another person? I don't know. But I can say that I'm very prickly in general. And I may have chosen not to make that kind of commitment in any alternate universe. You know? It's hard to say. Although I did adopt a daughter.

I used to be an organizer for young women . . . high school–age girls in Chicago with disabilities. They were pretty much denied information, not just by the schools but by their families, any information about sexuality or their bodies or things they needed to think about or plan for. In fact, the opposite was the case. The girls were told . . . most of the time that they would not marry; that they wouldn't have a boyfriend. Because I think in the parent's eyes, the teenage child was still an infant in a way. Or it was a thinking that there was something wrong with a disabled person acting on her sexual urges . . . just naturally wanting to explore. So there was no need for the girls to know how their bodies work and to know how to protect themselves during sex or how to get help for various things. Or for the girls to know if they would be able to bear children. And if they were, how they would know if that would be problematic for them.

It's still a new frontier out there . . . for disabled people. We're in the world now. The world—especially when you're a kid—can be a very harsh place for a person with a disability. Lack of information is lack of freedom as well. And the idea that one can be sexual is not always clear. You don't see it much in movies. But oh God, things like gender identity and all that goes with that . . . These are things you learn, that any person learns generally once they're out in the world.

I Just Want Something Else Now!

I think like any kind of oppression, it shapes the way you're seen. It does that for anyone experiencing oppression. You're gonna have to recognize that. You're gonna have to hope and work toward a time when it will ease up. [*Sighs.*] But it kills me when I hear that people feel they might be unwanted or undesirable because of their disability.

I have many stories of feeling invisible. I have many stories of isolation. I think you reinvent yourself all the time as a person in the real world. Certainly, when you're acquiring a disability later, it asks for a reorganization of one's priorities, to say the very least. I feel intensely all the things that disabled people usually come up against. I have felt that.

But I guess I'm tired of focusing mostly on that—the sad and disempowered and vulnerable-to-the-opinions-and-wishes-of-others kind of mentality. I just want something else now!

Disability is difficult in the sense that one has these various conditions that one has to deal with. And all the barriers in the surroundings. But I would say that disability is also really rich. Maybe in some ways more meaningful than certain other life experiences. Because it sensitizes you to something new. Something really hard. And something wonderful.

I FEEL THE DISCRIMINATION LIKE THE DEATH BY A THOUSAND PAPER CUTS

ALISSA CHUNG

I met Alissa in her home in Evanston. She's a clinical and developmental psychologist, and she had a busy day ahead of her. She spent the morning with me in her small office and spoke about her daughters. Alissa told me about her place in the world as a mother of children with special needs.

I've Tried to Be Better About Just Letting Her Be

I have thirteen-year-old twin daughters. Both of whom I guess could be described as being on the autism spectrum. Certainly, one of my twins fits that category a little bit better than the other. The other one, I don't think any one of us really know what she has. She's severely apractic. She has apraxia of speech, so she's largely nonverbal. But it also affects her ability to motor plan anything. It's really hard to know, actually, underneath what other limitations she may or may not have. She's sort of like a prisoner of her own brain. At the same time, she's incredibly physically capable if it's her idea. She's an enigma.

She can communicate her basic wants and needs. What's hard is that we don't really know what she's thinking and feeling a lot of the time. I know basic feelings. I know when she's sad and when she's angry. But I don't know what she's making of the world. I don't know if she knows that there's been a presidential election that we all cared about. I've always said to my husband that I think there's a 50 percent chance that at some point she's gonna pull out her iPad or some sort of device and just start writing. And it'll be like, "Look guys, I know everything. Everyone talks to me like I'm an idiot. I'm not an idiot! I know everything." [*Laughs.*] And a 50 percent chance that this will never happen. I really have no way of knowing, which is kind of strange as a parent. I have a third daughter who's ten and she's typical in every way. And with her, I know absolutely everything [*sighs*] she experiences, feels, goes through. All those things, I know about.

So my enigma-twin . . . she's behaviorally difficult. She might scream in a restaurant or in the movie theater. There're a lot of places that I just don't go with her. And that's what's isolating. It's like living on an island. When my husband's here, we can all go places. But I've been realizing how few places that I can really take her by myself now that she's my size. I don't know what she's gonna do, and I can't just pick her up and take her out, like when she was four. It's still hard to go out in public sometimes. I have these moments where everything falls apart and the whole world's staring at me.

I acutely remember one time where my other twin daughter was ice skating. She'd be in these shows. It was hard for her. She was actually a pretty good skater, but doing all the choreography with her motor-planning problems was really difficult. But she wanted to do it. I will never forget being backstage that particular time. My daughter was having a great time on the ice. She was running around in her costume, and she had her makeup on. She was maybe seven or eight. She was running around on the ice, and she was flapping, which she does when she's excited. And these girls who weren't even skaters, they were just backstage. These girls started running around imitating her and laughing at her. I was so angry. So angry. I said to them, "You know, first of all, don't do that. And second, if you're gonna do something that's that stupid, don't do it while her mother is standing next to you." They kind of did the "I didn't . . ." "I wasn't . . ."

Those experiences are painful. I don't think my daughter knew it was happening. I hope she didn't know. But it makes you aware every time she's flapping in public. Who's thinking what? And what are they thinking? She usually does it when she's happy. But I become so self-conscious about it on her behalf and then it makes me feel bad because it's just an expression of her joy. I don't wanna tell her not to be joyful. I've tried to be better about just letting her be. And just letting her . . . be . . . her. But it's hard. It's hard in the political climate where you've got our president who imitated a person with a disability in the same fashion as those girls did with my daughter. And not even in a backstage area. What does that mean?

Nobody Thinks About Our Kids

I cannot tell you how many times my child wasn't invited to be part of a music assembly at school. Because the teachers couldn't think of any ways for my child to participate. And it's just not that hard! But they don't do it. It feels crappy. It's hard to go to these assemblies and watch these things as a parent. You hear other parents saying, "Oh, look at my angel up there onstage." And my kid's just sitting doing nothing. Because she can't participate . . . in this way . . . in this thing. Couldn't they just have thought of anything that would give meaning that my child could do? Were there no ways she could contribute in the arts? She's just expected to show up. And if she can't do what everyone else is doing, she's told not to be a nuisance. And I feel that says a lot about where we are in our society today.

School breaks are frustrating. My ten-year-old, I could sign her up for programs all summer long. She doesn't even need it. She could play with kids on the block. I could find a million things for her to do. They don't have anything like that for a really vulnerable kid. So I feel the discrimination like the death by a thousand paper cuts. Nobody thinks about our kids. They just don't think about them. They don't think about, *Wow, how would that program work for them?* They're just not even thought about at all. There's nothing. But I don't think it even occurs to people. That there's nothing. It's the invisibility problem.

They Weren't Friendships Anymore

Friends. That's hard. Our one daughter was included in general education when she was little. She had a couple of girls in school that loved her. Loved her. She was never alone. They were friends. She couldn't do the things that they were doing. She was never at their level. But it was genuine. It was easy, and they would hold hands.

The other girls kind of infantilized her a little bit unnecessarily. Like they were putting her on their lap to go down the slide. I was always like, "Come on. She can go down the slide on her own." [*Laughs.*]

But I think that they just loved her. She's a very pretty girl. So that worked through the early primary grades. But starting in about third or fourth grade, the kids still loved her, but they would talk to her like she was a baby. And I don't think they were trying to discriminate. I really don't. I think they cared about her genuinely. She didn't have a language like they had, and they would talk to her like [*very squeaky high-pitched voice*], "Do you remember my name?" [*Laughs.*] And my daughter remembers everything that anyone ever told her and that's ever happened to her . . . forever. So it's like, *Yes, she remembers your name!*

They meant well. But the relationships seemed to us like they weren't friendships anymore. To me, it felt like it was going in the direction that I would call inspiration porn. It's like, *Oh well, how about we make her play on this team? Everyone can stand at the side while she kicks the ball into an empty goal. And we can all feel really good about ourselves.* I don't mean to say that those things aren't well intended. But they don't feel good to me. You know, the first time I heard about them, I thought, *Well, that's nice.* And now they feel like going down the slide on somebody's lap. Well intended but off the mark.

I don't think my twins feel lonely. They have each other. They have that. And they're very close to my parents. They love spending time with their grandparents. Their world is inhabited by adults who adore them. I wish they craved more peer interaction. I'm kind of hoping that as they get older it will become more natural for them.

They Were Uncomfortable

I guess the girls were toddlers. I'd meet these other women. We all had twins within a short period. When it was clear that my kids weren't talking, the interest dropped pretty quickly. I think they honestly felt, *What would my kids have to gain from spending time with your kids?* I think they were uncomfortable.

I think there are a lot of people who either are uncomfortable and don't know what to say . . . or are afraid. And then I think some of them genuinely just feel that there are only so many hours in the day: *I'd rather have my kid hang out with people who can be on her level.*

It was hard early on. It was hard seeing that my kids weren't doing things that other peoples' kids were. It was hard when people would suggest activities that they knew I simply couldn't do: "Oh, let's take our kids to the Children's Museum together." I couldn't do those things. And some people wanted to accommodate that, and some people just didn't. So you learn. You learn—I guess the way that anybody learns when they get through something hard—which friends are there for you and which friends are there only as long as you're convenient.

I was ready to be done with those friends. They also were keenly insensitive in some of the things that they would say. I remember one of them saying to me that she was signing her children up for French when they were like three years or so "because they're like sponges for language at this age. And this is the time to pick it up quickly." And she knew that my kids were struggling to learn *any* language. So it was like a weird conversation to have. And it's not that I don't celebrate my friends' children's accomplishments. I absolutely do. But this woman would just find ways of saying things. Like when her twins were three, she'd say, "I'm concerned that only one of them is interested in reading." And you know, it's absurd. Neither of them should be interested in reading at that age. But I thought, *Why're we having this conversation? I'm happy to hear about your children, what they love and what they do. But why are you expressing your worry about your children's development to me when you know that your children are actually way ahead of the curve developmentally? What's that about?*

I don't want people to walk on eggshells around me. But with my friends who are real friends and who've been my friends all these years, we're just normal to each other. We talk about their kids and whatever struggles may be going on. And I talk about my kids. They're not afraid to talk about their children, and they're not uncomfortable hearing about mine.

My Kids Can't Stand Up for Themselves

Yes. [*Sighs.*] I'm worried about attitudinal barriers in society. Because we're already invisible in this very progressive community in Evanston. Last year, they had a Martin Luther King Day assembly at school for my typically developed child, and I went to that. There were all these messages about peace and inclusion. And then I saw the kids who were in the program that my older daughter used to be in. They were sitting and watching in the back. They were not participating. They weren't invited. [*Laughs.*] Nobody thought of anything they could do to be part of a civil rights assembly. That blows my mind. And I should note that they're 95 percent children of color, in addition to being kids with disabilities. And they were sitting there all day until they misbehaved . . . quote/unquote. Or they started talking, and then they left because they were being disruptive. And I thought, *How's anybody OK with this?* I was walking out, and I was so angry.

And this is in our supposedly bubbly community. So yeah, I'm afraid. It's not been long since the presidential election, and there's been all these things going on with people receiving acts of hate. My kids can't stand up for themselves. So I worry about that and the immediate safety. I worry about the messages that are being sent. I worry that 50 percent of our electorate really didn't have a problem with a candidate mocking someone with a disability. Or was willing to overlook it. That it wasn't a deal breaker for them.

Then I also worry in a more tangible sense about a bunch of things. Health care. No mass plan for people with disabilities. I worry about the fact that we have this whole group of people with disabilities and we have no plan for them. No jobs. Has anybody even thought about the fact that it's a problem? And it's everybody's problem, not just my problem. I have to support my kids, but the day will come when I'm not here anymore. And someone's gonna have to support all these kids.

The thing is, they have skills. They're capable of things. I know that. At least my one daughter has some amazing skills. Her photography would make you cry—it's so beautiful. She's really bright. But she couldn't run her own business. And there are a lot of things that would make it hard for her to hold a job. So what's gonna happen next. That scares me. It's not just their immediate safety. It's this long-term picture. We have so many people with disabilities. But we really haven't thought about how to include them in a way where they can take care of themselves or be supported in some doings. They're invisible, and we just haven't thought about how to value them.

I FELT LIKE DEAF PEOPLE WERE INVISIBLE

RACHEL ARFA

Rachel is an attorney with Equip for Equality.* I had been at the offices of Equip for Equality many times, but the interview was my first meeting with Rachel. We sat in a bare conference room, although I didn't notice it because of the warmth in Rachel's kind smiles and her powerful laughter.

My Whole Life Was in the Hearing World

I was born with a hearing loss. It was a profound fluctuating hearing loss, which meant that every time my hearing went down it didn't come back up again. My parents didn't know that I was deaf at first. I was at my babysitter's house with another boy my age. We would be running down the street and the babysitter would say stop. She noticed that the boy stopped but that I always kept running. She said to my parents, "You may want to have her hearing checked out." So my parents took me to a doctor who told them that I had a hearing loss, which over time would drop to a profound hearing loss.

---

* Equip for Equality is a nationally recognized, private, not-for-profit organization with a mission to advance the human and civil rights of children and adults with disabilities in Illinois. It serves as a legal advocate for people with disabilities and as an independent watchdog. Equip for Equality also strives to level the playing field for people with disabilities and to break down barriers holding them back.

74

My parents were introduced to the world of deafness when I was eighteen months old. I was the first deaf person that they had ever met.

The doctor who did the hearing test told my parents, "She's not gonna be able to walk normally. She's not gonna be able to talk normally. Or to have a normal life." This was devastating for my parents.

My hearing dropped and became unmeasurable. I did not even have enough hearing for hearing aids. I became profoundly deaf. Then the cochlear implant technology started to come out. I did not like the idea of having surgery. But still, I was fifteen years old, and I went to an audiologist with my family. The audiologist gave me the most powerful hearing aids at the time to try on. I put on these hearing aids, and for the first half an hour I could hear again. And then all of a sudden, the hearing aids stopped working. But that half hour was enough to remind me how important it was to hear.

We came back to the audiologist's office, and he faced me directly. No doctor had ever faced me directly before. Most doctors only talked to my parents. I always hated that because I wanted to be my own person. He said to me, "Rachel, do you think that you can survive in a world without sound?" I burst into tears because my whole life was in the hearing world. I knew the meaning of having sound to be able to function in the hearing world. So I ended up getting my first cochlear implant. It was life changing because all of a sudden I could hear the sounds . . . I could hear my own voice.

They Still Rejected Me for Reasons That I Had No Control Over

In school I was never in a class with other deaf students. I would tell the teachers that I needed to be able to read their lips. I would tell them that they needed to face me instead of talking to the blackboard. I know I missed a lot, but I also know that I ended up turning out just fine . . .

I had an experience in seventh grade. I became friends with a group of girls. We went on a class trip, and after the class trip my whole group of friends stopped talking to me. I never knew why. I was very traumatized. It was very hurtful. One of the moms talked to my mom and told her, "It takes too much effort to communicate with Rachel. Why should they bother?" This group of girls would make fun of anybody else who would try to become my friend. So it was one of those moments that really changed the way I thought about the world and about people. They just stopped talking to me. They didn't give a shit.

In seventh grade you want to be friends with the other girls. In seventh grade you want to be like everybody else. I would go shopping, and I would think, *Are these girls gonna like this outfit?* That's the time where you really want to just fit in. It was a shock to me that no matter what I did, even if I bought the right sweater, I still wouldn't fit in with them. They still rejected me for reasons that I had no control over. My self-esteem dropped. It really shook my confidence. It made me very afraid to trust people for a long time, because this is what happens to people who I have trust in. That was the first time I really had a sense of being different. It was the most blatant incident. But these are the experiences that shape you. They shaped me. I took that to become a better person. It had an impact on how I interact with people.

Seeing Somebody Like Me in the Media

I felt that I was not reflected in the media or in TV shows. I felt like deaf people were invisible. I don't think I realized the effects of not seeing somebody like me in the media. But I remember there was a Miss America who was deaf. Her name was Heather Whitestone. She talked just like me. She had hearing aids. I thought it was so exciting that there was somebody deaf who communicated the same way I did. The other incident was the Gallaudet University, which is a university for the education of the deaf and hard of hearing. A lot of students were upset because the university had picked a hearing person to become the next president. It was inspiring to see deaf people advocating for their voice and to see that the protests ended up with the appointment of the first deaf university president. It was talked about a lot in the deaf community. We didn't have the Internet, but we read about deaf people fighting for equal rights in newspaper articles. Those two things stood out to me to be very powerful.

He Just Closed the Courthouse Doors

I went to the University of Michigan for college, and after college I moved to Washington, DC. I worked for Senator Patrick Leahy at the Senate Judiciary Committee for four years. After that, I decided to go to law school and went to the University of Wisconsin–Madison. My first job after law school was at a legal aid society. I became an attorney in consumer protection and in housing and eviction cases. I would go to court and help stop people from becoming homeless. I had to figure out the court system, and I found out that I could use sign language interpreters. Then a new judge started, and he said that I couldn't use sign language interpreters anymore. He said that I was using them to communicate with my clients! I was shocked . . . I had gone to law school. I had passed the bar exam. I had a job and I had clients. And because I was deaf, I needed communication access in the courtroom. And he just closed the courthouse doors in front of me. It was very stressful.

My executive director of the legal aid society became one of my biggest advocates. He told me that he wanted to sue the courthouse. I was nervous about filing a lawsuit because that takes years, and it doesn't always turn out well. And I just wanted to practice law. I just wanted to go to work and do my job. But a pro bono attorney working on my case reached out to the chief judge, and we negotiated a solution. We agreed that I could use the real-time captioning used by court reporters instead of sign language interpreters. The first time after my accommodations were approved, I was very nervous. I had to worry about representing my client, but I also had to think about whether the judge would approve my accommodations.

It was scary for me to think about not being able to work as an attorney. But I learned not to underestimate who my allies in the room may be. My executive director had never met a deaf person before he hired me, and he turned out to be my best advocate, my best ally.

Perceptions of People with Disabilities

I often think about people with disabilities in elected office. What if I wanted to run for office? What does that mean for sign language interpreters and making sure that communication is accessible? I think that we are not there yet. But if we had more people with disabilities in elected offices that would change the perceptions of people with disabilities. If people choose to have someone with a disability representing them, they realize that a person with a disability is their voice in elected office. I think that would be a big thing. I really believe that political engagement is the way to make changes to people's attitudes toward disability.

About two years ago, I was part of the Deaf and Hard of Hearing Bar Association. We organized and got sworn in to the Supreme Court bar. It turned out that Chief Justice Roberts knew sign language. On the day, he signed, "Your motion to be accepted into the bar is granted." That was very exciting, and it made news in national and international newspapers. And it made me realize how many people don't know what people with disabilities can accomplish. I didn't think that this moment would be so important. But it turned out to be a great reminder for me that there is still a lot more work to do to challenge people's expectations about what people with disabilities are capable of accomplishing.

We Could All Be Better Communicators

My number one message to anybody who wants to learn about disability is, try to have an open mind.

Number two is to challenge your own biases about people with disabilities. We all have biases, and as we become more informed about people with disabilities, it's important to recognize our own biases. There are people who say that deaf people can't be doctors, that deaf people can't be nurses. But we have seen that deaf people become doctors and nurses, and even lawyers.

Number three is not being afraid of talking to someone with a disability. Being willing and open to communicate in a way that you may not normally communicate. When I communicate, I read lips. I am watching, and I am also looking at the facial expressions and the body language. I believe that if more people would look at each other when they talk, they would understand each other much better. I think we could all be better communicators.

4 | EMBRACING DISABILITY

AS A SOCIAL GROUP, people with disabilities are often seen as a burden. To their relatives. To their local communities. To society in general. They are told that something is wrong with them. That they are broken. That they should be fixed to become genuine members of society. They are not accepted as the persons they are with the disabilities they have. They must try to fit in. They must keep quiet. They must make an effort to pass as normal. The intolerance continues to be immense, and to protect themselves, people with disabilities often stay invisible.

Not being accepted as a person with a disability puts a heavy burden on the individual. It is no simple task to embrace or disclose your disability when you constantly get the message that having a disability means that you are a broken person. Preconceived ideas and stigma create an environment where many individuals see no other way than trying to hide their disability. This is particularly true in the area of mental health.

Still, in spite of stigma and attitudinal barriers, many individuals do embrace their disabilities. They go against expectations of family and larger society. They come to understand and manage their disability as a matter of identity and not of illness. In this chapter, Matt Perry explains that he "had a period of coming out, almost like a young gay man would come out to his friends." In chapter 5, Curtis Harris describes his experience: "I tried to be . . . so-called normal. I learned about five to ten years ago—there are no normal people. You are who you are. You accept disability. You reject normalism!"

So people with disability increasingly acquire their identity from a peer group, which is what Andrew Solomon describes as a horizontal identity, in contrast to the vertical identity that most children share with their parents.* Claiming disability as an identity often involves the replacement of a false consciousness of self-pity and helplessness with an awareness of dignity, anger, and empowerment. The raised consciousness is a real appreciation of the self and, as explained by James Charlton, not the manufactured images and projected values and interests of the dominant culture.†

Zachary Richter writes about the turning point in his self-knowledge, "I have always been disabled. But for quite some time, disability was not an identity; rather it was a series of symptoms or gaps between me and other people. [. . .] They now unite me in solidarity with a wider community through my new self-identification as autistic."‡

Today more people with disabilities do what they like to do instead of what people think they should do. They are empowered by not having to pretend. In this chapter, Pam Berman explains, "That's also when I truly became free in my life, I feel. 'Cause I don't hide that I'm blind anymore."

People embracing their disability talk about the power of peer support and solidarity with other people with disabilities. They discuss family and friends who now see them as they are, not ignoring disability but rather recognizing it. Timotheus Gordon explains in this chapter how people like himself are proud that disability is part of their identity: "I know people now who see me. They see my autism as part of my personality. They don't see my autism as a joke or a burden."

Also, people who acquire a disability report that it can potentially be a transforming experience and a transformation for the good. Rene Luna explains in this chapter how he went back to school and college after a traffic accident: "I didn't like school when I was younger. But in college, I found new skills, talents, abilities that probably were there but just never brought out."

---

* Andrew Solomon, *Far from the Tree: Parents, Children, and the Search for Identity* (New York: Scribner, 2012), 2.

† James I. Charlton, *Nothing About Us Without Us: Disability Oppression and Empowerment* (Berkeley: University of California Press, 2000), 16.

‡ Zachary A. Richter, "Contours of Ableism and Transforming a Disabled Life," in *Barriers and Belonging: Personal Narratives of Disability*, ed. Michelle Jarmin, Leila Monaghan, and Alison Quaggin Harkin (Philadelphia: Temple University Press, 2017), 48.

I KNOW PEOPLE NOW WHO SEE ME

TIMOTHEUS GORDON

*A couple of months after I interviewed Timotheus, I saw him at a university sum-
mer picnic. He had just been admitted into the PhD program at the University
of Illinois at Chicago. I wasn't sure if he preferred to eat by himself, but I asked
if I could join him anyway. He had explained his experience of embracing his
disability so vividly to me that I felt like I really knew him.*

Like I Came from Another Planet

I was born and raised in one of the African American neighborhoods of South
Chicago close to the University of Chicago. At the time, the neighborhood
wasn't that bad. It was a little rough with crime activity and poverty. But it
wasn't as bad as people made it seem.

As a child with autism, I would rub my hands and flap my arms. Some
people said I had a speech impediment. Basically, in a nutshell, my family
did whatever they could to fix me. They wanted me to be like anybody else:
"Speak properly." "Don't flap your arms." "Don't talk to yourself." They
worked real hard to try to make me pass. I wasn't allowed to be myself.

My community treated me like a broken person. I wasn't allowed to speak
in our church. The pastor always prevented me from speaking.

My mother didn't want me to become involved in street life. Being a child
with autism, I didn't really socialize. People were nervous what I would do.
Let's say that I would walk in the street and somebody would put a gun to my
head and ask for money, pull out a knife, or try to beat me up. My response
should be to give the money right away. But because I was nonverbal and

because I didn't know how to approach such a situation, I would probably have hit the person. And that would have had consequences afterward. So I was made busy in sports and park district activities. My mother protected me. She kind of saved me from getting into bad things in my neighborhood.

Academically, I loved school. I got to sit in class. I got to read books—not just books but encyclopedias and science books. I enjoyed the activities in school. I excelled.

Socially, I didn't. I was bullied because of the way I spoke. I got teased for my obsession with Pokémon. I got mocked because I was smart. They imitated my voice. My voice was a squeaky voice that was easy to imitate. They imitated how I spoke and what I talked about. I didn't understand some of the jokes. They were cruel anyways. I didn't have friends to tell me how to approach other people and how to joke. I didn't get the jokes. I got bullied for that also. I don't think I made any friends. I got a lot of attention, but no friends.

I felt like an alien. Alone. Like, I'm flesh, bone, and tissue. I'm made out of bone and blood like everybody else. But I felt like I came from another planet. I even feel that sometimes now. I guess my brain is wired differently. Even though I know I'm on this earth, I feel like I'm from another planet. I feel like a foreigner, a visitor from another land or another country.

People were scared of me initially because of my screaming when something bothered me. That was when I couldn't communicate. But later on, I don't know why. I got confused. I didn't know why they were afraid of me. Was it because of my size, my looks, or the way I talked? Was it because of the way that I viewed things? Or because they couldn't figure me out? Even today some people get scared. I guess they haven't dealt with an autistic adult before who's not Rain Man.

In school I didn't understand why I couldn't make any friends. And in high school I didn't understand why it was harder for me to try to date. I thought that if I was a nice person, then everybody would love me. That wasn't the case. I learned over the years that I had to be perfect socially in order to attract any attention. I learned that the hard way by trying to pass as typical or normal.

Growing up African American lower middle class, I had to work hard just to fit in. I had no place to be autistic. In other social classes, you have.

And you don't get bullied for it or pressured to be somebody else. But I don't blame my family. My family didn't know any better. I blame my community. My community is talkative and playful. I wasn't as playful. I was excluded for that, and I was excluded because people didn't understand me. Disability, and especially mental disability and autism, is frowned upon in my community. It's seen as something that should be fixed, something that's demonic or something that's been made up. It took a long time for people to get a glimpse of who I really am. For people to see that I'm not a broken person.

Football Taught Me How to Be Stronger

It was freshman year in high school that I started playing football. I had very little self-esteem before. From football I learned to be tough and brave. I learned that I could work and fight through situations that seemed troublesome. I could succeed. Literally, football taught me how to be stronger.

I guess the toughness came from how to deal with losing a game without throwing a severe tantrum. Without hurting someone. I learned to use other ways of fighting through the pain. That could take the form of volunteer work, academics, or doing something positive. Before, I had some nasty anger issues because of the bullying and because of being excluded in my community.

My football experience translated into navigating social relationships, whether it was friendships or romantic relationships later on in life. I used my newly felt toughness to navigate college and the adult world. Even to this day, whenever things aren't going the way I want them to, I fight through it. Even if something seems impossible, I do whatever it takes to get the job done, and I feel good about myself afterward. I continue to do what's right and what feels good.

It's funny that I said tough. Because it's also my community's model when things get hard. Get stronger. Persevere. Even as a child, if I cried, I was told to man up. That mentality may have backfired a little. But it was how I was able to move on from the nightmares of my childhood. It made me more respected.

I'm Autistic and I'm Proud

In college I didn't experience discrimination. That's the great thing about large universities. There are so many people that you can fit in to pretty much any group. There are more opportunities. That's when I became more confident. I also met people who were more open minded and friendly and shared some of my interests. That's when I got more social guidance in partying and hanging out with people and stuff that other people do. It was the first time in my life that people didn't see me as a weird person but saw me as me. I even joined a fraternity. I guess the stereotype is that autistic people cannot fit in socially in a fraternity. But I did!

In graduate school—that was really when I fully embraced that I'm autistic and that I'm proud. I realized who I really am. I realized that I didn't have to be like everybody else. I could just be myself. That's when I felt better. I learned to keep on moving. I've been hurt by the bullying so much. I've been misunderstood so much. I kind of got over it. If someone made fun of me, it was his own problem. I know people now who see me. They see my autism as part of my personality. They don't see my autism as a joke or as a burden. Also my family—they see now that I'm not broken. They see that I can do things.

I put my energy to what worked. I learned what a true friend and a true partner look like. I learned from close friends after college what to look for in a person, like important values. I learned sometimes with help. Other times I learned the hard way—through trial and error.

[The hurt from those years] doesn't cause me to question myself. It doesn't stop me from having friends. It doesn't stop me from having girlfriends from time to time. I dated a few times. In fact, I can say that autism is my character by now. I can also say that autism is my superpower.

I'm thinking more now that I don't have to prove something. That I can just be myself and do things because I like them and not just try to excel every time to shove it in people's faces. I tried for so long to prove myself in sports, in academics, and in social life. I would try to be normal, to fit in. But once I got into things I liked to do instead of what I should be doing, I felt much better.

I still love sports. And that's a good thing to like in American culture. I talk about football a lot. I love it. And it doesn't matter whether you are autistic. If you like football, you like football. We can talk football all day.

I had to accept myself. And I get asked a lot, Who am I? To be honest, before, I would describe things that I do: I do this and I do that. I hated adjectives. But then I realized that I'm autistic. I realized the things that I like. I care about people. I built up my self-confidence. I became more confident in telling people what I like and what I liked to do.

Sometimes when I apply for a job, I get through the application process and get to the interview. They always ask me to tell more about myself. When I get this question, I don't know how to approach it. I also don't know how to describe my response to social situations in a work setting. I don't know how I'm supposed to answer these questions when I have only had two full-time positions and a few part-time jobs since I was eighteen years old. In these jobs I have just worked, worked, and worked. So how am I supposed to respond to questions on how I would react to a social situation? I cannot tell. I feel that because my social skills aren't the same as my peers', I cannot get a job. Even though my résumé is amazing.

I don't struggle with low self-esteem anymore. I may struggle with not being employed. And why I am not employed. I may struggle with the fact that my peers are married and now have children. I cannot even keep a relationship longer than a year. But I realize it may not be for me. Or there may be other things that I need to do before I get to that point. I try not to worry about the haves and have-nots, like I did before.

A PART OF THE WORLD
THAT WE DON'T TALK ABOUT

MATT PERRY

Matt is an advocate for social justice. As a person with a mental illness, he has often experienced people telling him he would not succeed. I met with Matt several times. He showed me his cousin's brewhouse in Evanston. Our conversations went on for hours as we discussed our shared love for details, words, and the importance of individual narratives.

The Child That Never Smiled

I grew up in an upper-class family in a very affluent suburb on the North Side of Chicago. My father's a private investor. I'm the oldest of three kids. I never grew up with a concept of what depression was. I think everyone in my household had some self-deception on the matter. Part of the problem was that I always seemed like a pretty competent kid who was normal enough. So I don't think my parents suspected or thought that something was seriously wrong. Also, upper-class families have too much space for their own good. My parents have a big piece of property and a big house, so I was much farther away from the individual members of my family than you would be in a middle-class or lower-class home. There was much less contact. So I think a lot of emotional connections were lost in my upbringing, and I was able to go under the radar.

My second-grade teacher gave me the nickname "the child that never smiled." I was just kind of always sad. I think some people did notice. But nobody ever took me aside. I was a quiet, lonely child, but I didn't feel like a total outsider. I did have very depressive symptoms at a young age. I would sometimes go to bed at night hoping not to wake up. I didn't think of that as suicidal at the time. But that's what it was.

I Thought It Was a Character Flaw

It was during college. I went to Santa Clara University—a school in Northern California. By the wintertime I was just deeply, deeply sad to the point where I couldn't deny it. After so many online tests where you fill out the boxes of symptoms and so many tests coming back saying that you're chronically depressed, I ultimately accepted that I had depression. I had a lot of anxiety and a lot of dread. I wasn't sleeping very well. I think, privately, I cried a lot. My weight dropped. I didn't have any appetite. I didn't care for myself. But I was also making friends in college. I made some really good friends. And I still keep in touch with them today—some very interesting people.

I think I had a lot of moralistic views of mental health at that time. I wasn't ready to admit to any deep problem either in biochemical makeup or problems of living. I thought it was a character flaw. That I just needed to work through that . . . And that ended up being very ingrained in me.

My sophomore year, I moved out of the dormitories and moved in with my older cousin, who was two classes ahead of me. I moved in with his friends. As outgoing seniors, they would drink and party a lot. I got caught up in that. The alcohol and the partying mixed with my depression, both became more severe, and that was when my academics really started to drop off. I started as a physics student. I was an A-student and did very well. Then I became a B-student my sophomore year. And then I started getting a couple of Ds.

My parents became more and more stern in their approach. I would be calling them . . . We did weekly phone calls on Sunday afternoons. We would chat and they knew about my depression. There was something very cheerful and complacent about their tone on these phone calls. It would never get deep into my state of affairs. But when I was really depressed, I would be really desperate on these phone calls. I even cried a couple of times. I think my parents had decided that just being hard on me was the way to do it . . . I remember one time I was near the point of bawling. I was so despondent and I think they had just gotten sick of it. I think that . . . I don't know . . . I would say, "I love you. I love you." And they just were kind of like, "Yep. Yep. Yeah" [*sighs deeply*], not saying it back. I remember that hurt me a lot.

I continued to ignore depression. I thought that I just needed to do things better: eat healthy, exercise more, be more social, and try to be happy . . . the tough-it-up mentality was very strong in me. So I got into long-distance running. I started spending a lot of time at the library. I read a lot of literature and got into classical music and watched a lot of films that were totally unrelated to anything that I had in school. I found art to be a very powerful diversion. It seemed to add some meaning to my life. But my social environment became kind of frustrated with me.

There was this cycle of just ignoring myself and exhausting myself and drinking heavily. My first week back to college for my senior year, I ended up in the emergency room. The doctor told me, "You're an alcoholic. And also you have anxiety."

He gave me some Librium, which I subsisted on. After that, I just ran with the label of alcoholism. Now I don't identify as an alcoholic. I drink casually just fine. But from that point on, I was in a state of deep, profound madness. When I look back at it now, every part of how I saw the world was completely different. My life was always frantic. There would be times where I couldn't get two [*sighs*] coherent words across. I'd always . . . I don't know. I don't even know . . . I'd go to the library to try to do schoolwork. But I had no cognitive abilities whatsoever. I could read the same page over and over and over. And nothing would register. But I would stay and do it anyway and just waste all my time and get nothing done. My schoolwork went to absolute shit. I barely stayed afloat. I'd get some Cs in class—enough to stay just barely on course for graduation. I wasn't out sick. I didn't seek counseling. I still kept working out a lot. It helped marginally. But there was always something off. My dreams were always very anxiety ridden. I had horrible, horrible nightmares. My social skills began to fall apart. I became more awkward. More anxious. I wouldn't know how to talk to other people. [*Fingers tap, tap, tap.*] I feel at times I might have had hallucinations. It's hard to say . . . It's hard to say. I might have heard some things that weren't there. I would write a lot.

I remember reading my journals from that time. It would just be rambling and rambling and rambling. And that was how I spent the rest of my senior year. In my last quarter there, I got a 0.0. I failed every single class. That was . . . that was that year. I ended up leaving college without a degree.

The Burned Hand Teaches Best

In June of 2012 I was back in my parents' house without a college degree. I came home having bottomed out academically. And that was when we finally said, "OK. Something's . . ." [*Laughs.*] It's like the level of self-deception and denial was so amazingly high and so deep that I really had to bottom out completely before anybody ever said, "But what the hell's going on with you?"

So me and my parents had to face reality and figure out what was going on. Everybody had been very complacent. I had certainly been in a lot of self-denial. My parents had also had a high amount of self-deception going on.

So my parents sent me to counselors and psychotherapists who talked to me a bit and told me that I had issues with severe depression and anxiety. I was still in a state of not really wanting to accept it. Like, I didn't wanna be on drugs. I still thought that I could work my way out of it. And that's how it went for a while.

I couldn't find something to relate to. People had always spoken very dismissively of taking psychiatric drugs or of people with depression. I mean the phrase quote/unquote "depressed loser" was pretty common in my social network. People would say things like, "Oh, you know, they're just trying to get attention." "They're just weak." The key was, you know: *You have to grow up!*

People would say that about suicide a lot: "Suicide is cowardly. People are just trying to get attention." I don't know how that logic works out. I don't know how wiping yourself off the face of the earth gets you any attention. It just gets you off the earth. [*Laughs.*] There's nothing that comes with it.

Do you know *Lord of the Rings* by Tolkien? There's a line in *The Lord of the Rings* that says, "The burned hand teaches best." [*Laughs.*]

And after a certain while, I had just gone through so much failure and humiliation that the point of denial and self-deception was ridiculous. So around January the following year I started seeing a psychiatrist, and I agreed to get on meds because my mental health was just terrible. I was constantly fatigued. I felt like I was hearing things at night . . . I don't know why I suddenly started to accept it. I think that because things were going so miserably I thought, *Why not? Let's get on the meds and see what we can do.*

And the meds were fine. At first it was really hard to be on it . . . But it gradually got a little better . . .

I ended up enrolling in DePaul University full-time. I transferred all my credits from Santa Clara and decided to go for a psychology degree.

Keep Your Chin Up

I had a period of coming out, almost like a young gay man would come out to his friends. I made a point of saying, "This is what's happening to me. This is who I am." And it was very intimate and very serious. A lot of my friends in those conversations were kind of like, "OK, cool. Whatever . . . I get that." Some of them were uncomfortable, and they didn't wanna talk about it or they just said, "Keep your chin up. Stay positive." [*Laughs.*] Some would just change the topic immediately. But after that the conversations never went too deep. And I think part of it is that they didn't understand how intense depression was for me.

I Ended Up Being an Outsider

I did a lot on my end to push the image of madness or depression or mental illness aside, and for that reason, I think a lot of people didn't suspect it. Maybe they didn't have a concept of it. But there would be glimpses where my illness would come out. And it would be very despairing and very despondent and that's when people would get scared or nervous. And that's when something would change in the way they would see me. I think their reactions even led me to continue on that path of trying to fake it. Just trying to fake it.

But there were times when I was clearly just a very mentally ill person. There's a kind of depression that's so thick that you can see it. You can see that the person is weak and so covered in something, very despondent. It's his physicality. It's how he carries himself. And that was the kind of person that I was. So people noticed. But nobody talked about it. And if I tried to talk about it, they changed the conversation very quickly or they'd get frustrated with me.

I think there was a good amount of people in my social circles that quite clearly lost respect for me. You know, I got called some pretty nasty things. I was called the freak; I was called pathetic . . . straight to my face. People are pretty nasty to people who are weak or dirty. They'll openly roll their eyes and say, "Here he comes again. What the hell's wrong with him?"

People were frowning their eyebrows, giving me the mean looks. Frustrated gestures when I would speak. You know, just coldly kind of turn away and give me the cold shoulder. Quickly darting away when I approached the room. It made me angry and frustrated. [*Laughs.*]

People stopped talking with me. They stopped socializing with me. I imagine that I was a very difficult person to deal with at that time. I probably wouldn't have wanted to be around me. But there was also no real semblance of a deeper reaching out and saying, "So, what's going on? Are you OK?"

I ended up being an outsider. I had some friends who stayed close. I had some other friends that just never looked at me in the same way and haven't talked to me since.

I remember going out with old high school friends in Chicago. It was after I'd come home from college and I was like twenty-two or twenty-three. At that time I wasn't drinking. I also hadn't finished my college degree. I would be at a bar and have a standard conversation with somebody, and the obvious question would come up: "Why is it that you're not drinking?"

My response would be—if I was being honest—"Well, I have a major depressive disorder and mental health challenges."

At that point their eyes would maybe bulge up like they were getting nervous or frightened. Or they would literally shake in their stance or take a nervous sip of their drink or just simply walk away.

There was pretty much never a point where I could say anything about mental health challenges and expect the conversation to go [*laughs*] in that direction for more than five seconds. I mean, nobody wanted to talk about it. Nobody wanted to associate with it. So I became very . . . I just . . . I don't know. The social life was hard during that time of recovery, because it was always one question away and I had no choice but to identify and disclose it and just face up to those—I guess—little gestures of disrespect. After disclosing, people assumed a sense of superiority. It was like the things I said from then on didn't really have a ton of significance and that they didn't wanna talk to me any further. Certainly they didn't wanna talk about mental health and stuff like that. The issue was that when I got into quieter spaces where I knew that people weren't deliberately getting together to entertain themselves, the response was no different. I mean, the same standards would apply; it would be too depressing to talk about.

It was everywhere I went. People were always deferring the conversation to another place where it was quote/unquote "appropriate" to talk about mental health, and that place was nowhere. There would be no place where people would talk to me unless I wanted to pay for a counselor or a psychiatrist.

They Didn't Have the Words to Talk About It

I tried to explain my situation—certainly when I was in recovery . . . I remember a conversation like on a Saturday: "I'm feeling miserable. I can't go out."

"What do you mean?" I tried to explain depression, and then it was just like, "Well that's life. Just get over it."

"No, this is actually something deeper." I wouldn't necessarily have the words. And they wouldn't necessarily be sympathetic or understanding to it.

Again, the mentality was *Get over yourself. Toughen up.* And that just goes nowhere.

I don't know. I think just enough people having the same experiences should let it be trusted. But you gotta get those people to talk, and that's very hard. We need these individual stories.

I know my parents felt the stigma. Their inability to talk about my illness and the fact that they didn't have the words to talk about it really crushed them. They would try to go about the relationship with me like it was normal. And normal means that you don't talk about mental health! They wanted to be loving. They wanted to be caring. They wanted badly for me to be better. But they didn't know how to talk about the things that I was giving them . . . the pain. I remember one session with my psychiatrist where my parents came along. To see them sit next to me and look at my psychiatrist as we sat to talk about depression. The look on their faces was like a combination of being both dumb and very concerned and very eager. They were so desperate. It was causing them so much pain. So the attentiveness to what the psychiatrist was saying about what they could do was just so . . . It was very heartwarming to me but also very sad at the same time. Because it was clear they wanted the answers. They wanted for things to be different so badly, but they didn't have the tools.

It goes back to what you were saying earlier. Mental illness is in every household, and yet not every household knows how to deal with it. Simultaneously, it's something that you're very familiar with, and yet it's totally foreign to you at the same time. I don't get it.

All These Little Lessons That Discouraged Disclosure

I think I had an awakening when I started to look at my life and look at all the little things about mental health that were taught to me. How people treated mental health. How mental health was treated at the university. How it was treated in the media. There were just all these little lessons that discouraged disclosure and discouraged you from taking mental health seriously or talking about it. And it was just so consistent throughout that it stopped looking like it was a mere coincidence. In fact, the discouragement was really systematic, like it was part of our social world. Like some time ago people decided that if you're going to be a fully accepted member of society, you have to be sane . . . whatever that means. And that people who aren't sane constitute this quiet, invisible second class. A part of the world that we don't talk about!

So I became very passionate about looking at mental health through the lens of social systems, similar to how gender studies look at women's issues or African American studies look at black issues. What I realized when I started to get into these areas and look up to them as models was that mental health wasn't part of the conversation. I would try to look up things about stigma and mental health that would be like a parallel to feminist studies or African American literature. But there was close to nothing. Everything I found was talking from a psychiatric or psychological point of view. When it came to persons experiencing discrimination or what I would call quote/unquote "sanism" as a real social phenomenon, it was virtually off the radar.

Today, I'm very passionate about trying to take after previous movements and do a similar thing for mental health. The main reason is that I feel my problems were really related to our system or values around mental health. How we treat it and teach it. If those values were more enlightened, that would have been the difference between me being a miserable college flunk-out to being someone who is pretty well adjusted and could comfortably talk about mental health and not have to take this multiyear backtrack on my life.

If it hadn't been for stigma, I'm sure that my response would have been totally different. There wouldn't have been this tendency toward shame and repression. There wouldn't have been the constant hiding and self-medicating and trying to live up to some ideal that was inauthentic . . . that was just some phony version of being normal or successful but wasn't about being myself. Yeah, I think absolutely everything would have been different.

A LIBERATION
TO BECOME TRULY BLIND

PAM BERMAN

We met at a quiet café on the periphery of Andersonville on the North Side of Chicago. I saw Pam walking past the café, and I went outside. She was upset because her guide dog is normally good about finding the door. We had lunch and talked for hours about disability. We discovered a mutual interest in books and discussed scenes from our favorite novels.

She Didn't Want Me to Be Blind

I have an eye disease called retinitis pigmentosa. A lot of people call it RP. It's very popular—very hip. [*Laughs.*] Some people even say it's progressive, which I think sounds fun. It's a degenerative eye disease. I like to think of it as a young person's macular degeneration. But I don't get hung up on what people's eye disease is. Because we're all in the same place.

It was diagnosed when I was seven years old. I have three older brothers. Once, we went out as a family on my brother's boat. When we were getting off the boat in the evening on Lake Michigan, they gave me all the towels to carry. And I walked off the other side of the pier. Into the water. So night blindness is the first thing that happens.

When I was young—ten or twelve—I remember going to the eye doctor with my parents, as we did annually. We were coming home one time, and I heard my parents go, "Oh, *Got zol ophiten.*" In Yiddish that means, "God forbid."

And I was a kid, sitting in the back of the car, my eyes dilated. "What? What happened?"

There was a man that was walking down the street, blind. And he had walked into the bushes. What this left in my head was, *It's really bad to be blind. It's really bad 'cause you could walk into the bushes. And worse than that, people are watching you and not doing anything to help. They're just feeling sorry for you.*

I didn't ever want people to feel sorry for me. I had this eye disease where I was losing my eyesight. I couldn't change that. So why not wear it proudly? *I can be the person who doesn't walk into the bushes. I can be the person who does all these amazing things.*

And humor has always been a big part of who I am. I would laugh it off. So being the blind person in college that falls up the stairs to the dance floor because she can't see, that's just not funny. That's not cool. But the girl who's partying the night away and had too many drinks and falls up the stairs, that's understandable. That's considered funny. It was better in my opinion to be drunk, to be perceived as being drunk and hip than being blind.

My parents didn't think that it was cool to have a disability. Their way of dealing with me being visually impaired was to not discuss it. If you don't talk about it, then it's not a problem and you don't have to worry about it.

My parents were firm believers in tough love. I remember my dad giving me a hard time for walking into things: "What's wrong with you?" "Why don't you pay attention to where you're walking?" They would think that I was very clumsy. But I was just slow. At least I thought I was.

My parents were also really classy—and my mother especially was a very classy lady. I just adored my mother. But they wanted everything to be perfect. I think being Jewish had something to do with it. Not wanting to draw attention. Wanting to come across as the chosen people. Because there was that in my family.

There were many things that my mom could have done differently. When she was in her eighties, I was visiting her and she had me sign some important financial papers. I hate signing my name! My mom got so angry with me. She was like, "I can't believe you can't even sign on the line. You're deliberately trying to upset me!" I think at that time I probably even had the dog.

I really think my blindness was something she struggled with. She didn't want me to be blind. But she ended up accepting my blindness just before she passed away.

My parents are both gone now. I think that they did what they felt was the right thing. It wasn't what I would do. But they didn't know where to go for help.

It Was Not Cool to Have a Disability in Grammar School

I went all through grammar school in regular Chicago Public Schools. My grammar school was a small school. I grew up in West Rogers Park on the North Side. It was primarily Jewish at the time. The teachers were all fine to me in grammar school.

I had help in math. You know, they write the numbers on the board, and I had trouble seeing it. I could understand the concepts but I couldn't completely get it because I was a visual learner. So in grammar school, I did have a tutor, and I would be taken out of class periodically. But then again, I preferred people to think that I was just slow, kind of dumb—rather than to think that I was visually impaired and that I needed assistance. I wanted to be cool. It was not cool to have a disability in grammar school.

Knowing That Because of Me, People Were Educated

My major discriminatory experiences have been after I got my guide dog in 2007. I think the first week that I was home with my dog, I went into a Dunkin' Donuts. The woman told me that I had to get out because of my dog. It was upsetting, but it was also a nice experience because there were a couple of people who worked there—young kids—and they were telling the lady, "Oh no. No, you can't do that."

Shortly after that, I went into a restaurant in Chinatown. The guy behind the counter told me that they could not serve me in the restaurant. I could get food to go, but I couldn't sit down in the restaurant. The reason being that they had other patrons that were not comfortable with my dog.

I think when it happened in the beginning I didn't know what to make of it. I was appalled. I couldn't believe it. That that kind of stuff would happen. So that's the bad part. The good part is that after the Chinatown experience, I reached out to the woman who had raised my dog. I said, "I can't believe what happened. I'm home a month with my dog, and this thing happens."

She said, "Pam, you have to do something. You have to report it."

She said it with such strength. It wasn't like a question, like is it OK or not? But *you have to do something.*

And I did. I filed a complaint with the Commission on Human Relations. And I won. And not only did I win, which is very rewarding, but the whole Chinatown area had an educational session with the chamber of commerce. Different agencies in the city all went, telling them about guide dogs for the blind. It was a really nice feeling knowing that because of me, people were educated. It's important.

I have tried it other times. And when it's happening, my chest starts beating. It—it's a very unsettling feeling, somebody yelling at you, telling you to leave the restaurant. And even though the police tell you that you can go in, think about it. Look at my dog. He's my eyes. But he's much more than that. He's my buddy. He's my pal. He's my child. He's my partner. So how do you take care of your child and your partner? You don't throw them into a situation where there's some moron that's screaming and yelling and hope that it's not gonna happen again. So you go to another place. And that's what I do. Mostly.

It's very exciting to win a case. Not just to win. You get monetary compensation. I donated some of it to my guide dog school. I bought bones for all my guide dogs in the group that I work with. All the women that I met with one night when I was thrown out, I took them and their families out to another restaurant for dinner. That's exciting, to celebrate the right thing.

It thrills me that the restaurant owner had to do disability training for all his staff. He had to put a policy in place so that everybody understood about guide dogs. So that part makes me feel good. But when it's happening right there, I get real shaky.

It's Been a Liberation

Oh, I can be very hard on myself. I can be really, really hard on myself. When I was younger, I had no interaction with the blind community at all. I was not involved. Now I have a lot of blind friends. And I learn so much from them.

I've mostly felt the discrimination after I've become truly totally blind. It's hard to say exactly when I became blind. But it's within the past five to ten years. And that's also when I truly became free in my life, I feel. 'Cause I don't hide that I'm blind anymore. I don't hide that I can't see.

Before, if I were to meet you, I would never ever—never before have recommended meeting you outside my house. I would only say that we'd meet in my house. Because it was comfortable.

I think for me disability meant, *You are weak! You are less than!* That's what my parents showed me. I didn't want to be weak. I didn't want to be less than.

So it's been a liberation for me to become truly blind. I can't pretend anymore. I can't! I used to get on a bus, and I would hold on for the longest time. And then I would slowly move, so I could slide my leg around to feel if there was a seat. I would do things like that. To others, I looked like *Oh, I don't want to sit.* In reality, I just didn't know if there was a seat.

DISABILITY AS A TRANSFORMING EXPERIENCE

RENE DAVID LUNA

Rene was young in the 1970s. When we met, I sensed how his wisdom and warmth came from a place of experience and insight. We talked for a long time. His energy and engagement was that of a young person.

I Was Limited

I grew up in Indiana, close to Chicago in a small steel town. I had an automobile accident at twenty-one. I had been working in the steel mills for two years. My injury was a result of the accident. This was back in the 1970s. I was in the hospital and rehab for about ten months. Trying to survive. Doctors believed that I should go into a nursing home. I had a spinal cord injury. But my family didn't think that was a place to go. I'm of a Latino background, and I think in our culture we feel we're responsible for one another. We wouldn't send anybody to a nursing home.

People in my family saw me as someone needing care and help. But they never discouraged me from going on to pursue my interests. Before the accident I was a pretty rebellious kid, rebellious in terms of drinking too much and smoking too much and having a good time. I wasn't interested in school. I cut school a lot, and I didn't have a high school diploma at the time of my accident. So after the accident I got my GED. It's a test you can take in lieu of a high school diploma. I wasn't going back to work in the mills.

Before the accident I had lived with my grandmother in East Chicago, Indiana. When I finally came home after the accident, I went to live with my mother and her new husband in Chicago. They had to buy a new house. My mother was very maternalistic toward me, but I got an opportunity to grow. After my GED I went to college and got my BA at DePaul. I was the only student in a wheelchair at that time in 1979.

I was limited in college. The only building that I went to was the academic center, where the classes were. The student center across the street, where people go to the cafeteria to sit down and chat and socialize, had three steps down to get in. And only rarely did I ever go into that building, maybe two or three times in the four and a half years that I was at DePaul. That was exclusion there. Environmental exclusion.

I didn't have any interest in having girlfriends. At the time I had the accident I had a girlfriend. We'd been on and off. But after my accident she lived in Indiana and I lived in Chicago. So I told her to stay home, that we should separate. There was a song: "If You Love Somebody Set Them Free." So that's what I did. I concentrated on reading and writing and books.

In college I made some good friends. I didn't have a large number of friends, but a core group of three or four women. Relating with guys was a little bit different. We talked sports, a lot. But going out and getting drunk with them and having a good time, I didn't do that as much. Hanging out with the guys in Indiana? I couldn't really do that. We were separated too. I was kind of estranged from them. So losing that social contact was important to me. I did feel somewhat alienated in college. I don't think anybody pitied me, which was a good thing, but I also didn't allow myself to be pitied. I went through depressions. I still have a lot of issues in that regard. My car accident involved some friends that were also in the car. One of them died, and I was driving. So there were also moral issues, guilt issues.

I struggled through. After I graduated, my professors helped me to get into Rutgers University in New Jersey. I had tried Berkeley, but I wasn't accepted. Berkeley was the area where disability rights had emerged—the mecca. I did go there to the campus to see what it was like. It was somehow like utopia. All the sidewalks were accessible. The buildings were accessible. The people and students with disabilities were all pretty united. There was bonding there. Even in the community, in shopping areas, bookstores were accessible. People were friendly and accepting. Even the hotel, they had set up a personal assistant to help me. They had a van to pick me up at the airport. It was the utopia. Wow. It was like it should be.

When I went to Rutgers, I had to get a power wheelchair so that I was able to run around the campus. There was a lot of accessibility. I lived in the dorm. The others that stayed in the dorm were all pretty friendly. I went to classes. It was a very rigorous program of political theory. Talk about reading a lot; it was a lot of writing and reading. I had a hard time adjusting because I had never lived independently. So I ended up getting pressure sores and had to come back home . . . back to Chicago. [*Sighs.*] I left Rutgers, and that was very disappointing.

I'm Kind of Demasculinized

After the accident, I was focusing on academics. Maybe it was an escape. An escape from myself. While I learned a lot about myself, I also disengaged, particularly with the sexuality, the social relations.

Sometimes I have internalized what people have said to me. But how do you distinguish? Sometimes I had depressions. Why did I have this accident? Why did my friend die? I would think back to who I was before. The mind plays tricks with you. Sometimes you feel sorry for yourself. Mostly you don't. But when it does happen, it hurts.

I think there's one area that we probably don't talk about enough. It's the sexuality point of view. I'm older now, but I do feel that when I go to bars . . . I even felt this when I was younger. You know, people don't look at me the same. Women don't look at me in terms of somebody they might settle down with or want to go to bed with. I'm kind of demasculinized in some way. That's a problem on a very personal level. I cannot say that anybody blatantly is saying, "You're less than." But I feel it. Just because I'm just not seen as human in a lot of ways. As a sexual being.

Pity Is a Four-Letter Word

After I left Rutgers I couldn't find a program of political theory that I was interested in here in Chicago. At that time the Chicago Transit Authority started to run a door-to-door paratransit service. They didn't have accessible transportation. This is another interesting thing. At DePaul I was the only person with a disability. So I didn't develop a disability consciousness. I wasn't uniting with other disabled folks. The irony is that with this door-to-door service, this segregated service, I came across other disabled people, and I never really had before that. Some of them talked to me a lot about how CTA was discriminating. I said, "You're right, why don't we have access to mainline transportation?"

So I became involved with Chicago ADAPT.* We began blocking buses and doing protests at CTA meetings. My activism emerged. Unfortunately, that came at the expense of my academic interests. It was about 1985. I learned about Access Living around the same time as I participated in ADAPT. They hired me as a public speaker. I would go around to high schools and talk about disability. But I didn't talk about it in a negative way. My ideas about disability were more politicized. I wasn't talking about myself from a self-esteem point of view. I didn't talk about disability as a "you don't want to end up like me" kind of story, which some people do. Because when I say that you don't want to end up like me, then unknowingly people put down disability. So I tried to be careful about that. I understood disability in a broader way than just my own experience.

I kind of felt in between worlds sometimes. My name Rene can be considered male or female. But in the Latino culture it's almost always a guy's name. And in American culture some people don't understand this. So I felt these cultural differences. In the Latino culture I felt at home because I had certain levels of binding with the culture, language, traditions—you know? But there was more of a pity attitude in the Latino culture than in the American culture. It's hard. But I understand that it's a process of education and that it's ignorance. I understand that the medical model is more engrained in Latino culture; it's embedded there. Some of the language in our culture has been very negative: *invalido*, which means "invalid"; *incapacitado*, which means "handicapped" or "incapacitated." It's changing now.

My identity issues came later. I didn't grow up with a disability, so I didn't feel excluded at a young age. I was always rebellious and never able to focus. But after the accident, my schooling obviously shaped me too. You know, I

---

* ADAPT is a national grassroots community that organizes disability rights activists to engage in nonviolent direct action, including civil disobedience, to assure the civil and human rights of people with disabilities to live in freedom.

hadn't graduated from high school. I didn't like school when I was younger. But in college I found new skills, talents, abilities that probably were there but just never brought out. So in some ways I see disability potentially as a transforming experience for those of us who acquire disability. A transforming for the good.

When we look at disability as a tragedy . . . I would say my family looked at my disability as a tragedy. I don't know how we cannot look at somebody having an accident not being a tragic experience. But it doesn't mean that you should look down at the person as tragic. *Pity* is a four-letter word. There was a group in Chicago that fought pity: Piss on Pity. I was never accepting of pity. That's not to say that I haven't felt bad or haven't had bad experiences.

Race, Disability, and Class Marginalize People

There's definitely more disability awareness today. And yet the issues of race, disability, and class marginalize people in ways that we still don't even recognize. The mainstream disability community—and here I really mean the white middle class—they've grown up as part of liberal traditions and liberal conscience. They don't accept discrimination against anybody. But they don't understand the class discrimination. The way people of color . . . the way poor people are marginalized and excluded. I think that's a problem. It's multiple discrimination. And nondisabled people still don't see disabled people as equals.

The Americans with Disabilities Act has opened some doors. People know not to discriminate. They still find ways of getting around it. But there're also more people with disabilities that have come out, so to speak . . . Still, society isn't prepared for these issues. Even with an aging society, people forget that disability happens to everybody. It's a natural thing. It can happen today to anybody. You can have an automobile accident like I did. You can get hit by a car. You can get shot [*laughs*], at least here in Chicago. You can get some type of illness. And you get older.

We still struggle to be part of the political process. To have a voice. To be considered as equals—beyond just fighting for services, for budgets—as having a political view that's valid, that's important.

But it's hard to be respected—to be regarded.

5 | ALONE AT SCHOOL

CHILDREN WITH DISABILITIES EXPERIENCE being sidelined from the game all the time. It happens in school. It happens after school. They get bullied and called names. They're excluded from social life. They're not invited. They're talked at. They eat alone in the lunchroom. In this chapter, Curtis Harris describes it this way: "The other students treated me like crap. They treated me like a piece of meat. Jumping on me. Saying that I was retarded."

Today many children with disabilities are mainstreamed in school. It is a legal right to receive free and appropriate public education, regardless of disability. An integrated educational system benefits many children with different disabilities and other horizontal identities; it likewise helps those who share a classroom with them. So building a compassionate school system benefits not only those who are newly tolerated but also those who are newly tolerating.*

These are positive developments compared to earlier times when children with disabilities were sent away from their homes to special institutions and boarding schools. However, mainstreaming and integration do not equal inclusion. Children with disabilities might be part of the typical academic program with varying degrees of academic achievement. But the mainstreaming does not necessarily mean that they are included in the social lives of the other children. In this chapter, Andre explains how as a child she did not have

---

* Andrew Solomon, *Far from the Tree: Parents, Children, and the Search for Identity* (New York: Scribner, 2012), 687.

words to describe her blindness, but how she began realizing that she was different: "It began to click why the kids in kindergarten and in first grade were laughing at me."

As adults, many people with disabilities are still marked by experiences of exclusion and bullying during their school years. In this chapter, Erick Allen discusses low self-esteem: "It lingered with me for a long time. Oh yeah. A long time."

Children with disabilities need their parents to be strong advocates. And parents of children with disabilities may not follow the typical trajectory where children leave home to go to college or in other ways become independent. Jennifer Wheeler explains in this chapter how she and her husband will never be empty nesters because she will always be parenting her oldest son: "I will always be close with him in that way. So it has a silver lining."

YOU'RE STILL A PERSON WITH A DISABILITY AT THE END OF THE DAY

CURTIS HARRIS

I was embarrassed when I first met Curtis. The night before, he had called me to confirm our appointment. Because of his accent, I did not understand what he said on the phone. I thought he was a sales representative. I was having dinner with my family, so I had rudely cut him off. When we met, his face revealed no reaction to my apology. But he also did not seem to mind talking to me.

He Was Devastated and Had Tears in His Eyes

I was born in 1977. I was diagnosed with autism when I was four and didn't talk until I was six. Back then, I was just labeled autistic. Today, I use the labels of Asperger's, developmental disability, learning disability, ADHD, and depression anxiety disorder.

I grew up with my family in Chicago. My dad had a lot to do. He took me to psychiatrists and psychologists for evaluations. He was devastated and had tears in his eyes. He didn't know what to expect. He got the news that I wasn't gonna talk, read, and write. That I was to be taken care of for the rest of my life. He was told to put me in institutions. They said that I should be in a state-operated developmental center for life. But my dad didn't like the conditions of the institutions, so I stayed at home. And the Chicago Public Schools opened the autism program for me. I was the first student to be enrolled in the autism program in 1984. I was six, and my mom had just died four months earlier.

I lived with my father and my sister until she went off to college. I mostly grew up on the West Side of Chicago—the Austin neighborhood.

They Treated Me Like a Piece of Meat

In the beginning, it was fun going to school. We were doing beanbag games. But I didn't do much academic work. I didn't get enough academic education. I was in the special program.

For a year, I was in a mainstream social studies class. But I was taken out because I got obsessed with the fire alarm. I had thoughts of pulling the fire alarm. At another school, I had pulled it. I couldn't help it. Most of my school time, I was in a severe learning disability program. In eighth grade my dad took me out, and I was put in a regular mainstream class.

The other students treated me like crap. They treated me like a piece of meat. Jumping on me. Saying that I was retarded. They called me "fat," "retarded." I got attacked by students. Toward the end of eighth grade, my dad kept me home several days. I didn't like school.

I got in trouble. Kids told me to do things. To pull the fire alarm. To dance.

After I graduated from eighth grade, I didn't know where I was going. Because there was no program for me. So my dad got some lawyers and fought with the Chicago Public Schools. They created a new high school program called the Inclusion Program for students with severe learning disabilities, autism, severe developmental disabilities. I did go to mainstream classes the first year. I did fairly OK.

The high school students were cruel. They made fun of me. I was naive. They said that I was slow and retarded.

It was bad. It never changed. Because those students were in gangs. Students with disabilities and students without disabilities had gang ties.

I felt bad about myself. Depressed. Being in that environment.

During my first two years in high school and in my junior and senior year, I only once got picked to play in a basketball game. Because of my autism. Because of my personality. I was just dejected. In spite of the fact that I played football and was elected the homecoming king. Still excluded. I know that being a homecoming king don't change you. It's just a popularity contest. You're still a person with a disability at the end of the day.

Low self-esteem. Rejected. Dejected. I felt torn. Hurt.

But I had no self-esteem to tell the coach or to stand up to the other students. I didn't really have friends. Not really. But I had a sweetheart. She wasn't my girlfriend. But she left my sophomore year because she aged out. At that time, when you turned twenty-one, you had to leave the Chicago Public Schools.

I did have some football teammates standing up for me. Most of them did. But there also was bullying from some of them. Including this big guy who was the biggest and tallest athlete in the school. He set me up for trouble. He attacked me. He also had a poor attitude.

So I attacked. I hit students. Because they hit me. Before I went to this school, I was soft. I was a soft a person. I did not stand up for myself. I did not stand up for others. But when I got in that school, they taught me how to defend myself. They taught me how to stand up for myself. To fight back.

Classmates [taught me]. In the severe learning disability program.

So I started fighting to defend myself. I felt better. But I also don't like violence. Because my dad didn't teach violence. So my dad said, "We're gonna do something about this." He talked to the teachers. But by junior year in high school, damage was done. I was going to college unprepared.

They Made Me Dance for Them

I lived in a gang-infested neighborhood. There was a group of gang members. I saw them out the window, and I went to them with my basketball. I was after the gangs. I was bored at home with nothing to do. I had no social outlet. I'd just started college and I didn't have any assignments due yet.

So I went to the gang members and I told them about their gang lifestyles. That they were at risk of going to jail or dying. They took my basketball. They lied, saying that it wasn't my ball. They made me dance for them. They made fun of me. I was called retarded. They beat me up. And one of them took a glass bottle and hit me in the head. So I went home by myself, bleeding. Told my dad what happened. He said, "What's wrong with you? Why on God's earth did you leave home and go to them?"

Instead of him criticizing those boys, he—he [*stutters*] fussed with me. He was seriously pissed off with me. Someone told him to file a police report, but

I didn't know the names at the time. In the emergency room, I talked to the police. I had eight stiches put in my head. My uncles wanted to retaliate. My dad told them, "You don't need to do that."

[I kept seeing them] for three more years after they beat me up. They kept saying, "Retarded people can't work" and "Retarded people can't go to school and drive." Now all of them have been killed by other gang members.

I moved out of that Austin neighborhood in 2010. I got hit in the head in 1996, and I left over thirteen years later.

To This Day, He'll Say That I Got Distracted

I went to college. But I wasn't the same person after I got beaten up. I did pass classes. But fifteen months after those boys hit me in the head, I left. I had to take a break from school. It'll be twenty years next Saturday that they hit me. It was right after I started college. So the rest of that year was just rough.

Toward the end of my college career, I was advised to leave school. I was told to stop telling people that I had anxiety attacks. And panic attacks. Then I was advised to leave school for a break. For one semester.

My dad was devastated. 'Cause he had worked so hard for me to go to school. Worked overtime to pay for tuition. To this day, he'll say that I got distracted by being part of a black journalism organization.

My dad don't talk about [my not finishing college]. He don't bring it out.

There Are No Normal People

I tried to be . . . so-called normal. I learned about five to ten years ago that there are no normal people. You are who you are. You accept disability. You reject normalism!

When I came to Access Living, I realized, *Hey, I don't have to be normal.* Disability is part of my personality. I don't need to be fixed or cured. There is no cure for autism. There is no cure for mental illness.

Stand up for your rights. Stand up for yourself. Fight for yourself and others. It gives me a sense of pride. Self-esteem. Self-attitude.

It helps me in a lot of ways. Like my sister . . . She tells me that I don't need to work. I get a check. But I tell her that I wanna work. For myself. I wanna earn more money than what I get now through social security. She's saying that I've got people taking care of me for the rest of my life. I'm OK. But . . . that's not what I want.

I'm not working now. I would like to work. In retail. Like stocking merchandise. Or working in grocery stores stocking food, toiletries, cat food, cleaning restrooms and pushcarts. My sister tells me that I'm overqualified because I'm almost forty. I'm competing with teenagers and college students for those jobs.

I still live with my dad.

YOU STUPID NIGGER CHINK. CAN I CATCH WHAT YOU HAVE?

ANDRE

It was a hot and heavy August day in Chicago. I was sitting with Andre in her apartment in Lincoln Park; the windows were open, and outside jet fighters and other special airplanes were practicing for the Chicago Air and Water Show. The roars of their engines interrupted our conversation as they flew right above us. We still talked for hours. There were long pauses of silence.

You Don't Know What a Baby Sees

I grew up in Chinatown. I enjoyed living with family and neighbors in very close proximity to each other. My aunts were in the building to the left. Down the street there was another lady. We called her auntie even though she really wasn't related. It was just kind of one big family. Cousins. Close friends around.

My mom and I really didn't get along very well. We had a lot of differences. She had problems dealing with my blindness. I was born premature—at seven months. Everything was OK, but she knew that something was a little bit different about me. She couldn't explain what it was. My mom said they had lots of colorful things over my crib. I didn't look at them, and they didn't soothe me. I just didn't pay attention. She knew something was different. The others tried to hush her up. "Oh, this is your third child. You should know that babies don't see very well until they're six months old. You don't know what a baby sees. You don't know what babies are thinking."

My mom felt guilt. Like it was her fault. Which it was not! I think she blamed herself for my premature birth. She was really, really protective. But then my father would give me to his sister, who lived next door. And even though I had a home, I would spend a lot of time there. Because I was just like one of the kids there. My aunt had five kids, so I was like kid number six. She would say things to me: "Do this. Do that." My father would do the same, and my mother would always say, "You know she's blind. You know she can't see."

"It doesn't make a difference. She's got to learn to do things. We're not gonna be here all her life. She gotta learn to do things."

I remember dropping a ball, and he made me find it. My mother thought it was the meanest thing he could have ever done. It was in the yard. It wasn't in the street or anything. It was in the backyard. "I'll find the ball."

Being proud—my father was full of that stuff. I remember once he brought me a bike. I wanted a bike so bad. I wanted a big girl's bike. I didn't want a tricycle anymore. He said, "OK, well, if you want a bike right now, I think auntie has a bike that she would let you have." He painted it. He put the reflectors on it. He put a horn on it and a bell. It was all pink. I got on the bike. I had a good time on day one. I rode up and down the sidewalk on day two.

I knew how far to go on the bike by the way the sun felt, by the way I saw the sun. If the sun was a little to the right, I'd gone too far. In the morning, the sun would shine in a certain way.

Maybe about a week or two after I got the bike, there was something . . . I think my dad had adjusted the wheels a little differently. So I went over and tilted to the one side. The bike just tumbled with me on it and fell on top of me. We fell into the street.

My mother said, "Oh, I told you. I knew this would happen. Why didn't you . . . ?"

Wow. Everybody was just . . . Of course, I was more scared than anything, so I was screaming. My dad picked me up. He took me into the house and washed off my wounds. I was pretty scraped up, but nothing broke or anything like that. Then he said, "Are you ready to go back outside?"

And once I'd calmed down and stopped sobbing and all that: "Are you ready to go back outside?"

And I was like, "Yeah."

He picked me up. Took me back outside. Did not let me walk because there was a gauntlet of people. Some were yelling at him in Chinese. I don't know what they were saying. But I was told it wasn't very kind. "Hey, you don't want her. I'll take her." "What're you doing?" "Stupid man, what are you trying to do? Hurt that baby." "I'll take her. If you don't want her, I'll take her."

Some of the women were cursing at him. And he still held me. We walked. I was on top of the world. I was in daddy's arms, you know. He put me back on the bike. And my mother came running and started screaming. "*Nooo! Nooo!* Don't let her ride that thing no more. I was going to throw it away."

And he just looked at her. My aunt came running and said, "Come on. Come on. Let's go sit down. We'll talk about this."

And my father said, "Leave me alone. I know what I'm doing. Maybe you could take my wife and she can help you with dinner."

And that was basically telling her, you know, to get lost. My father put me back on the bike and the one word he said to me was "Ride."

I was four or five by then. I'll never forget that.

I had no reason to fear. When my father said something, he wanted you to pay attention. He wanted to be listened to. You obey. There wasn't any other way. It was definitely his way. I guess he went back and got my aunt and my mom. He said to them, "See. Look out the window."

And there I was, riding past the house on my pink bike.

You Will Be Educated

My father would always say, "You're going to school. Even if we have to teach you what you need to know, you will be educated."

There was a state school for the blind. My father was taken there, and I guess his mother went along for the ride. My grandmother didn't like that the school was too far away from home. That was her first complaint. Her second complaint was "How would she know who you are?"

There was a white house parent at the school, and she would say, "Oh, you leave them here, and they will become our children. This child will become my child. I will treat her just like my own child."

My grandmother took offense at that. "Because how would she know who her real parents are, if this other woman was raising your child?"

So I went to a Catholic school. It was down south. It was all white, an Irish Catholic school. I was somebody of color. I don't think they quite knew what to do with me. [Laughs.] The school had a special program. I stayed in the resource room where all the blind kids were for a few months. And then I started having classes with the regular first-grade class. You know, I was mainstreamed. After a couple of months, I was full-time in second grade. It was vastly different. You couldn't get up and walk around. You had to sit in your seat. You had to work. You couldn't cry. You didn't get cool things to eat. The teachers didn't bring in little snacks like they did in the resource room. Rules were very, very rigid. You did your homework. You stayed in your seat. It was nothing like the resource room.

For the teachers, it didn't matter that I was blind. I had to sit in my seat and do my work. That's the way it was. They treated everybody that way. Back then, they had real big classes, like sixty kids.

When I was seven I did not have words to describe my blindness and I did not comprehend what blindness meant. Then it began to click when I was a little older—maybe about seven and a half or eight years old—that I was different than the other kids. It began to click why the kids in kindergarten and in first grade were laughing at me when we would play games. I would not quite end up in my own square. I would end up in somebody else's square and sit on somebody. And it caused a major uproar and made lots of laughter in the classroom. I began to understand why that was happening . . .

My grandmother taught me how to get to school. My mother was not for that. But my mother was hospitalized for depression. She was schizophrenic and stuff. So my grandmother had me a lot of the time. She was along the same lines as my dad. You know, "We're not gonna be here all the rest of your life. Now that you've learned how to use a cane, you're gonna use it."

And she would stay far behind. The first few days, she'd walk with me, and then she would stay farther and farther behind. And then one day, she wasn't there at all. It was nice. I liked the independence.

I Was Caught in the Middle

There was a camp that I wanted to go to with some of the other kids from school. "You can't go because you're not white."

It was my color, the color of my skin. The other parents told me that the camp wouldn't allow black kids. At the time, I was like, "Me? Black? I'm Chinese."

Then I became aware that my mom was black and my dad was Chinese. That I was biracial. It was different from then on. Just very different.

The white kids would play together—even in the resource room. All the white kids would get together. "Oh, can Johnny come over?" And I noticed that the others, Johnny and Susie and Jamie, would always get invited to each other's houses. But I never got the invite. This was probably when I was nine or ten.

I did manage to go to the Lions summer camp. But, oh, I got called names [*laughs*] by the kids. "Nigger." "Nigger chink." "Commie." I think somebody called me a whore once. But I didn't quite get that one until I was a little bit older.

I didn't understand why. Or what was going on. For some reason, it made me angry. But I didn't understand my anger, you know? They would be polite. But then all of a sudden, if I would get mad at one of them, then they would say, "You stupid nigger bitch." "You stupid nigger chink." "All you people are f-ing communists. You're all communists." "All you wanna do is bomb the United States."

I was about ten then. They were just starting to talk about the Vietnam War and stuff like that. I was born in 1955. This was in the 1960s.

I formed a few friends. Yes, there were people that stayed away from me. I'm too dark to be white and too light to be black. I was caught in the middle of the Black Power struggle. I hung out with a few people who were really close. Some of us still keep in contact today. I'm not saying that I wasn't discriminated against. But I learned by then that some people are not in your life for a reason.

I would hear comments like "Why don't you go back to China?" and "Why you gotta be here?" Some of the blindness issues would also come up, like "How come you do that? How come you walk with a stick?"

But I also learned that there were people who accepted me for my stick and for my Chinese father.

In high school, as long as I didn't bring up my background, I was OK. Some girls would say, "Don't mention your mom."

"Why?"

"Because they don't like people like your mom."

At that point, I didn't like my mom either. But it wasn't because she was black. It was basically because she had issues, and I didn't realize. It took a toll on her life, losing my dad. My dad died when I was seven. My dad was the one that learned Braille. We did things together. He came to the school stuff. They came together to the conferences, but my dad was always more involved. He took the nuns from school to Chinatown. He kind of introduced them to Chinese culture. So it was nice. Over time, I began to notice things with my mother. Like my mother staying in bed for long periods. Just her being very unhappy.

After my father died, we stayed in Chinatown until I was eleven or twelve. And then we moved down to the South Side of Chicago to a black neighborhood. That was interesting. Before that, I never thought of myself as different because I was blind. I was just part of the people that I was with. And I had a good time. But then there were stares and stuff like that. Probably more so from the grown-ups.

I hated it because it wasn't what I was used to. I wanted to go back home, to where my aunts and uncles were. I was lonely. It was a lot different from what I was used to. I felt different because I was blind. 'Cause some of the people asked me, "Can I catch what you have?" "Can my kids catch what you have?"

And I was like, "Me? No, I don't have anything."

I was sort of naive. I didn't get the reference line, you know? As far as I was concerned, I didn't have a disease.

I Caught Hell

Things got to be different around fourth and fifth grade. My body started developing a little early. I started growing breasts.

I remember I got a major whipping. It was a month before my tenth birthday, and I got my period. I was wearing this cute little pink playsuit. My sisters would make comments: "Oh, you're getting a big girl's shape."

But they wouldn't tell me what that meant. I remember going on a picnic somewhere with all these boys. And I came home with blood on my playsuit. Boy, I caught hell. "What did you do?" "Who did it to you?"

And I was like, "Who did what to me?"

"You have blood in your playsuit."

"I don't know. I don't know how it got there."

And I didn't know. It was just like I opened my legs and they happened to see the stain. My mom told me that she didn't expect to have this conversation with me for a long time. And I was like, "Why did everybody . . . Why did Grandma get so mad? Why did she ask me who did it to me? Who did what to me?"

My mom said, "Oh, she thought that one of the boys raped you."

And I was like, "What? What's that?"

The Only One You Can Change Is You

My mother. It was kind of hard to socialize because my mother sat on top of me. If a boy was sitting here, then my mother would be sitting between us. I managed to get out from under her. I felt bad because she was lonely. But I couldn't . . .

It got better in college. Because college is different. I started liking school. Liking challenges. Liking . . . almost loving learning.

In college, I still experienced people talking at me. "Does she want this or that?" "Does she need me to read for her?"

I would have friends or professors saying, "Well, ask her. Don't ask me. She's a person." "Don't talk at her. Talk to her."

I would always say, "Yes, I'm a person. Talk to me! There's nothing wrong with my hearing. My eyes don't work too well."

I wanted to be a lot like my sisters. I wanted the husband, the house, the backyard, the swimming pool. It just didn't work with this man! He's the father of my daughter. It was too much craziness. Too much drama. Not knowing when he was gonna come home. Not knowing if he was gonna come home at all. I just couldn't do that and raise a child.

It was not easy.

Someone taught me—I don't know if it was my dad or my grandmother— you can't change people. The only one you can change is you and how you're affected by people.

DON'T LET ANYBODY SIT ALONE AT LUNCH!

JENNIFER WHEELER

Jennifer lives in Plainfield, Illinois. She's an attorney specializing in family law, and she has three sons. We talked on the phone one morning after she had been to court. We were both in our homes in a quiet corner.

All Three of My Boys

My oldest son, Tripp, is almost fifteen years old. When he was two, he wasn't verbal, not speaking, not making any kinds of sounds. So he was developmentally behind the benchmarks where he should have been. He was extremely focused on spinning items. He persevered with some very atypical behaviors. He had difficulty recovering from emotional stressors. He had meltdowns often. He couldn't cope or reregulate. So we received the autism diagnosis and started with an active and intensive course of treatment that involved primarily therapy. Lots and lots of therapy. Speech therapy, occupational therapy, developmental therapy, and social therapy. That has made all the difference in the world. Right now he's verbal. He has a blended school program. He has some strictly special education classes, but he's also mainstreamed into the general population for the other parts of his classes. He's about fifty-fifty in terms of special education classrooms versus mainstream classrooms. But I expect that next year when he goes to high school that might change. He might have more vocational training and focus on independent living skills. I don't expect that

119

he will live a fully independent life. I expect that he will need assisted living of some sort—just in terms of being functional and not being taking advantage of by members of society. That's my oldest.

By the way, all three of my boys—although the primary diagnosis has always been autism—all three of them also have a diagnosis of anxiety disorder, as well as ADD. Those overlapping diagnoses have proved extremely significant in terms of having an impact on what they can do and how they cope with things. So it's the overlapping diagnoses as much as the autism diagnoses that provide them with some challenges every day.

My second-oldest son, Wheeler, is twelve. He also has autism. He's very, very high functioning. He's extremely intelligent [*laughs*], like off-the-charts intelligent. He's completely introverted. However, not with our own family, where he feels comfortable. But he's not interested in developing or maintaining social relationships at all. So while being extremely intelligent, he's really less concerned about the world around him. He has a great big kind heart, but he really doesn't value relationships with others as much as a typical-developing person might. He likes to put his nose into his books and read all day. He will do great, great things, probably scientific or mathematic. But then again, I do have tremendous concerns about his ability to keep and maintain and benefit from social relationships such as having a spouse. I think that's gonna be a problem. His ADD is extremely significant in terms of his functioning every day. He'll be facedown in a book, and the rest of the world goes by. He's not really checked in. Honestly, the practical tasks that are required—the ability to multitask, like driving and things like that—I don't know . . . He can probably cure cancer someday, but I don't know if he's going to be in a position to drive a car. He's mainstreamed for all of his classes and receives very little support in school.

And finally, Tate is my youngest. He just turned eleven. Of all my three sons, he's the most functioning. He's the most typical with his peers. He has some significant ADHD concerns. He's got hyperactivity. He's very busy, busy. He also has some sensitivity to social situations. Other people's interpersonal interaction is challenging because he's highly sensitive, highly emotional, and highly reactive. So Tate is very checked in to a point where a lot of it has a hyperimpact on him. But socially, he can hold it through. However, it's always a tricky game whether he'll succeed in that. But he does OK. It will just always be a work in progress.

He Still Eats Lunch by Himself in the Lunchroom Every Day

Across the board, I feel like my children, for the most part—knock on wood—are well accepted and understood by their peers. Even if they aren't accepted as equals, I do feel that they are accepted with kindness. Because it's not a secret that they're different. The peers have always grown up with them and at least in the classroom, they are very understanding and very cognizant. They are mindful and aware of the fact that something sets my children apart. Even if the peers don't go out of their way to be particularly helpful or to make my child their project or their buddy, at a minimum they are certainly kind, understanding, and patient. I'm one of the lucky ones, I truly understand that. There have been very few incidents of unkindness and nothing that I know of—I should say—but there hasn't really been anything that rises to the level of true bullying, in my opinion. So I feel very fortunate. I just want to fall to my knees because I'm so grateful that my children so far have been treated with such kindness. But we have a long way to go . . .

I know I've said the word kindness about seventy-two times. But kindness is my goal for my children and for the world and people in general. To be more kind to one another.

There are lots and lots of different examples of how certain kids in class will ask to work with Tripp for group projects or partner projects. And it's usually the girls. Girls are usually mothering to him. So it really feels like his peers have taken some kind of responsibility for him—at least until now. However . . . However, when it comes to the social, things are different. The kids are into the opposite sex now, dating and texting, going to the basketball game on Friday night. They don't necessarily include Tripp in the social pursuits. While they're able to and interested in engaging with him in the classroom academically, in the social pursuits they haven't really thought to include him. I think they also understand that he's not interested in the things that they are interested in socially. So I don't feel that it's coming from any place of maliciousness. I feel those kids are just thinking that Tripp really wouldn't want that.

And I will say . . . he still eats lunch by himself in the lunchroom every day. And that's heartbreaking for a mother. Just heartbreaking.

It Is Isolating

I've experienced isolation because of it. Mostly it was when they were younger. When they were younger, we almost couldn't go anywhere. We couldn't go out to eat. I was a single mom as well, with sole custody of my children. I was a single mom from the time that Tate—my eleven-year-old—was three weeks old. When he was three weeks old, my other guy was one year old, and my other guy was three years old. That was when I became a single mom. I was doing it on my own for a good four years, and that's when all the diagnoses came in. So it was a pretty miserable, lonely period of my life. And that's when I felt excluded and isolated.

I kind of solved the problems of exclusion or isolation by seeking out like-minded individuals and parents, people who understood exactly what I was going through. People who understood exactly what my children had. And we all kind of supported each other. So the fact that I exposed myself to a fraction of people who understood me was very helpful in preventing feelings of isolation and exclusion.

But I couldn't go anywhere. They were babies. They were melting down. They had no language. I couldn't carry them. This was before iPads and devices that could have helped me. So I couldn't go out to eat with them. I couldn't go to the movies with them. We just couldn't make it through anything. So there was a lot of self-isolation because I was like, *Forget this. I'm not going anywhere. I'm not leaving my house with my children . . . ever.*

I had no family near here to help me. And to cope with going through a divorce and having all of this on my plate and all these diagnoses, I started to run marathons. I joined the gym just so that I could have the free childcare. Because I had no break and no help. [*Laughs.*] So I figured, once a day, I'll go to the gym and drop my children off for forty-five minutes and have some time to myself. First, I just went and took a shower without babies in it. And then I turned it into exercising.

I remember one incident at the gym. The children were young, and I couldn't get them out of the facility. They were screaming and melting. This older lady went by and she just gave me the dirtiest possible look. Literally, I was holding one child up by his ankle trying to keep him from falling to the floor. The other children were screaming. I was clearly frustrated and clearly on my own. And she gave me a dirty look. I'll never forget it. I thought to myself, *Why aren't you offering to help me? Why are you being nasty? Clearly, I'm not doing this for fun.* I don't think you can call that discrimination. But that was one of the first times where I was like, *Man, there's a difference between me and them.*

Another similar experience was when I tried to go to my church back then. People would give me dirty looks because I didn't keep the children quiet at church. The children were kind of wiggling and wandering and making noise. It was just like, *If I can't be accepted here . . . If I can't be offered kindness or help or just a smile here, well then, where can I?* I stopped going to that church.

So it's not that people have isolated us. But it is isolating . . . But boy, the hardest thing for me has been watching my children not being included in social things anymore. First it was birthday parties. You know, when all the kids are little the whole class is invited. All the boys and girls play together. The older they get, they stop having these birthday parties and you also stop having boys and girls together. You just invite three or four of your closest friends for your birthday. And at that point probably close to fifth grade my sons stopped being invited to things like that—anybody's special occasion and anybody's celebration. And that has been hard for me to watch. Because I know that they would still enjoy going. I know they would enjoy being part of that, being included in that. They would love to be invited to a birthday party.

It's been a constant decision on my part to be proactive. I was a teacher. Then I became a stay-at-home mom, and I felt that this was gonna be hard. I'm already fighting with insurance companies. I'm already fighting with the school.

My children's diagnoses had an impact on everything. It had an impact on my divorce. It had an impact on health care coverage and services and options and school placement. So I just thought, *I'm gonna have to get better at doing this if I'm gonna be the mom that they need me to be for them. Because I'm on my own, and I better figure this out.*

So that's when I went to law school and became a special needs attorney. I think that probably has prevented some potential opportunity of discrimination against my kids. [*Laughs.*] The fact is that people know that this is my life. It's my profession. It's my personal life, and it's my professional life. So just don't be that way! Just don't do it!

I Worry That Somebody's Gonna Take Advantage of Them

The future worries me. I feel like, for as great as my children are, I worry that somebody's gonna take advantage of them. Somebody who is socially unaware or just socially uncaring. They're gonna see the vulnerability in my children as an opportunity for evil, to be honest with you. And that can be in physically disturbing ways, it can be in a criminal way, it can be in a financial way, where they want to take advantage of my children.

I worry all the time. I worry . . . all . . . the . . . time. I worry because there's a whole other element of people out there who don't care. They don't care about the elderly, they don't care about special needs groups, they don't care about people who are different. And honestly, it terrifies me. And I think it's always been there. And it will probably always be there, but it just makes me panic that my work will never be done. My job will never be done with my own children. I'll never ever be able to relax and step back and let them be on autopilot the way that they should be able to be, if they were typically developing. Not because of what my children have or haven't learned to do, but because of other people taking advantage of them. That's an exhausting prospect. And once again, thank goodness that I'm now married to a man that understands that my work won't be done. His work's done as soon as his kids are gone for college. They're following the script. They do this, they do that, they graduate, and then they go off. That's not an option for me. And that's a great divide too.

So you know, that's an absolute game changer between them and us. Where normal parents are empty nesters and moving on and celebrating their new-found independence, I'm just like, *Well, that'll never be me.*

I'll always be parenting my oldest son, Tripp. The same way that I was parenting him when he was younger. That's a pleasure too. That's a very, very happy thought for me. I will always be close with him in that way. So it has a silver lining. But you know, that's not our job. Our job is to make our children independent. So no matter what happens, I wonder, did I fail because I couldn't . . . I couldn't accomplish that? I couldn't help him that way.

Be Aware of That Kid, the Kid Who's on the Fringe

[I would like to ask their peers] to continue always being kind, and that can be just as easy as saying hello. But also to be hyperaware of the loneliness factor or the isolation factor. I would say, "Just sit with him in the lunchroom." "Just ask him to play at recess." "Just ask him—even if you know that he's gonna say no. Just keep asking him if he wants to play." Because the happiness that my kid would feel just from the fact that you asked is really underestimated.

So if I could ask children to do one thing right now, it would be, be aware of that kid, the kid who's on the fringe. And even if you don't feel like you can bring him in—and even if you don't feel that he wants to come in—at least always reach out to that kid somehow.

And don't let anybody sit alone at lunch!

Because the other thing that's bad, that's socially isolating for them, is from the outside looking in. It's not only the fact that they're sitting by themselves, feeling lonely. But the whole rest of the school is watching. The whole rest of the lunchroom is seeing that this child is sitting alone, and they are saying to themselves that there must be a reason that that kid is alone: *He must not be likable. He must not be fun. He must not be friendly. So I better not engage with him either.*

YOU KNOW ABSOLUTELY NOTHING ABOUT ME

ERICK ALLEN

The phone was beeping. Erick apologized but checked the messages. His daughter was texting him on her way home from school. She was by herself. We spoke about being street-smart and feeling safe, as a kid and as an adult. Erick talked about coping with discrimination. About how it is "the others" having a problem and not him.

It Was Easy for Them

I grew up in Chicago. Born and raised in South Shore, just south of Hyde Park. I'm African American. My father was a policeman. He's been retired now probably longer than he actually worked. [*Laughs.*] But he was a policeman for thirty years. My mother who raised me was actually my stepmother. My birth mother passed just one month before my fourth birthday. I have a brother almost two years older than me, and a sister eleven months younger. My mom passed, and my father remarried a couple of years later.

My stepmom, my mom is Irish, South Side Irish. This was interesting [*laughs*] growing up in Chicago. But you know, it was all I knew. It was family. A few years later, I had a younger sister. She is seven years younger than I am. So there were four of us in terms of siblings.

My disability . . . My family didn't know. It was my stepmother who took the bull by the horn and made the observation. It was right before kindergarten. I wasn't formally diagnosed before. But my mom sent me to doctors, and they diagnosed that I had a nerve disorder in my eyes, optic nerve atrophy.

I went to kindergarten in special ed with all the support that they could muster. Which wasn't much.

I was in public school through fifth grade. Then I transferred to a Catholic school with my brothers and sisters and finished there. Academically, I was fine. I was an above-average student. That changed in high school. As I got older, my perception of the disability and how I thought I was being treated deteriorated. I think people made more of a big deal out of it than I thought they should. I guess, as my world started to expand, it was always the first thing people would notice. They would ask how I was reading, how I was seeing, what materials I had to use, if I had a magnifier, or why I needed this or that. I probably didn't respond very well. I don't know if it was shame. Or if it was just me not understanding why it was such an issue. And what difference it would make.

I think I hid [my anger] behind humor for a long time. But looking back now through the lens of over thirty years, I was definitely very angry and very upset. In high school, I don't think that I handled it really well from a maturity standpoint. I didn't focus on what I should have focused on in terms of the work. I focused more on trying to manage the relationships with the other students. There was teasing, name-calling, kind of labeling. Like blind man's bluff—just anything related to blind, or bad.

I don't know what was so funny. I could never figure out what was funny. It was every class. It was constant. I don't know if it was a comic relief that they needed. It was easy for them.

It affected my academics. Trying to manage the social piece, I didn't pay attention to the academics as much. I was really inconsistent. I was up and down for four years.

I was angry and frustrated about the whole thing. I was all by myself in high school. There was nowhere to get help and advice.

I Would Rather Not Do Things Than Ask for Help

My self-esteem was pretty low. I think outwardly I tried to expect things. I tried to portray a certain ability. But I think inwardly it was hard to muster any kind of sustained confidence. High school was hard.

It lingered with me for a long time. Oh yeah. A long time. You know, I moved on to Loyola University. Going through all that, maturity was an issue. I wasn't a very mature student. I didn't have the skill, the academic skill to really be successful in the classroom. That affected my grades early on at Loyola. Again, I was inconsistent.

Finally, my parents stopped paying for school. [*Laughs.*] I think that kind of pushed me to say, *Oh, now I got to start paying tuition.* So that helped, to be honest with you. That helped. It became more of a *How do I accommodate this? What tools can I get to be successful in the class and on campus at Loyola?*

It became less of an issue socially. I was out more on my own. I kind of got a sense of how I could fit in and be more independent. I could get around. You know, there was public transportation. I could work; I was functional. I kind of built a pool of friends with whom it wasn't an issue. That helped. I spent much more time on academics. As I got older, the teasing went away. It became less of a barrier, less of an issue.

It was an academic struggle in college. But I found freedom. Social freedom. I could come and go as I pleased. I was quote/unquote "independent."

I don't make friends easily [*laughs*], to be honest. I'm not really . . . Well, most of my friends are a few really close friends from high school that I'm still close with thirty-five years later. New friends—I can probably count on one hand the people that I actually call friends. I feel . . . I don't know if it's self-esteem or just not wanting to go through the effort of explaining, "This is who I am. Will you or will you not accept this?" It's easier to just sort of hold back. Although I've come to the understanding or the belief that my vision is probably not as big an issue as I've made it out to be over the years, it's still an issue. I think it's affected even my close relationships or friends that I've had for years, you know.

Going out and doing things, my travel and how I get to things have to be accounted for. Sometimes that becomes an issue: "I can't get to this place. Can I get a ride?" And my . . . I was always reluctant to have to be that needy person. I would just not go. I would just not ask. It was a deep desire to be able to do it on my own. To show that I could do this. I didn't need anyone's help. I remember having huge arguments with my brothers and sisters as they got older and started driving. For the most part, they were very supporting. But they were in their teens and twenties. I would say, "I'm not a package. If you don't feel like . . . Let me know. It's OK. I'll find a way." [*Laughs.*] "I don't need you to make me feel that you're doing me a favor."

I would rather not do things than ask for help. Or make it really hard on myself just to get it done without the help. There were times when asking for help might have been easier. I didn't attach it to self-esteem. But it probably was a self-esteem issue.

I Didn't Feel Recognized, Welcomed, Accounted For

Loyola had its issues with race. The Catholic Church had its issues. There were maybe 25 African Americans in my graduating class out of 170 graduating. We were a small group. We used to joke that we would take three lunchroom tables in the entire cafeteria of 2,300 kids.

There were definitely issues. I was a victim of a race-based attack on campus during my senior year. It reminded me of what city I lived in and what school I went to. [*Laughs.*] It was me and a couple of friends. We got assaulted by a bunch of white kids.

Loyola didn't do a good job in managing race relations or making different cultures feel welcome on campus. I didn't feel recognized, welcomed, accounted for. I got comments from some of the students.

It still helped me somehow. I gained a sense of the world. If you want to live in the real world—in Chicago that's so diverse—as a male minority, you have to learn how to cope. You have to learn how to succeed in spite of what they may think of you.

It's Their Issue

I started to learn—and I really try to tell this to my daughter and my son—"It's not your issue." You know? "It's their issue!" When I'm looking back, I really would start to understand that.

To be honest, sometimes it's been hard to really stay the course with that mind-set. But it really is . . . If you have an issue with my disability, that's your issue. Because I'll figure out an answer. Or if you have an issue with my race, that's truly your issue. Because neither one has anything to do with what I'm capable of.

I remember when I was in my twenties and I would go around in the city with public transportation, my mother would say to me, "Just be careful now."

And I would say, "Mom, trust me. I'm not the one that people are looking to take advantage of. It's the exact opposite. They think that I'm out to get them."

You see people move away. You see people cross the street. *You know nothing about me.* [*Laughs.*] *You know absolutely nothing about me.*

I don't think it ever made me mad. I feel bad. I feel sorry for them. I really do. *This is your only reaction and it's the only encounter you've ever had with me. You have no idea who I am.*

If I'd have to say one thing has had more impact than any other, I'd say my disability. 'Cause it's . . . I like to believe that we've come to a point where I can overcome my race. If that's the right wording . . . With performance, with credentials. But I do believe there's still very much ignorance and impatience against folks with disabilities. And intolerance. If I'd had to pick one, I'd pick my disability.

While I've tried not to make my visual impairment an issue, I've realized over the years that it's profound. How you take in information is primarily visual. I remember sitting in on an eye exam for my son with an eye chart in the room. My wife was reading. I remember saying, "What line are you reading from?"

"It's the bottom."

And I was like, "People can actually see that?" [*Laughs.*] I thought that it was a "made in Taiwan" thing. Oh my God. It gave me a sense of what I don't see. It's profound. So there have probably been social interactions over the years, social clues that I have missed. Communications that have taken place, maybe directed at me.

My kids are in special ed, and being a mentor is really what I try to be for them. To say, "Hey, it's OK to be upset, but what are you going to do about it?" My kids have the same kind of disorder and visual impairment as me. What I'm hoping, just from a self-esteem standpoint, is that they don't let it get to a point that it really has a negative impact on them. [*Sighs.*] We'll see. I tell them all the time that I was in sixth grade myself. I get it. I also didn't want to stick out. But I'd rather get an A versus not using my glasses.

6 | TO BE LOVED

LIKE MANY OTHERS IN society, people with disabilities struggle with confidence, or the lack thereof. They are suspicious when others show interest. It is often easier to shut people out than let them in. In this chapter, Candace Coleman describes this: "I mean, how do you accept yourself fully, who you are, and let someone else see that?" In her book, Susan Nussbaum gives voice to a young woman with a disability:

> His family is large, and they are religious. I mean, they are Religious. Apparently, Ricky is the only non–Pentecostal Jehovian Catholic Witness among them. I'm just worried they'll think I'm an "invalid," or poor childbearing material, or the worst imaginable choice for their son, brother, et cetera. I am trying to compartmentalize and enjoying some success.
>
> And even though Ricky and I don't know what might happen in the future, for now we're good.*

Exclusion and isolation because of disability during childhood and young years often cause additional blows to the self-esteem of people with disabilities. Sharon confides in this chapter, "I probably wouldn't have married the men that I did. I've been married twice . . . and divorced. I had the idea that I didn't have a choice. I'd have to take whatever I could get." Also in this chapter,

---

* Susan Nussbaum, *Good Kings Bad Kings* (Chapel Hill, NC: Algonquin Books, 2013), 270.

Rahnee Patrick describes how in high school she had "enormous crushes, but in terms of dating, I was not involved in that. I think it was because . . . I felt for a very long time I was a monster."

More fundamentally, persons with disabilities often experience being seen as asexual creatures, incapable of being lovers and partners. In chapter 4, Rene Luna explains, "Women don't look at me in terms of somebody they might settle down with or want to go to bed with. I'm kind of demasculinized in some way. [. . .] I'm just not seen as human in a lot of ways. As a sexual being."

For many, it is controversial to imagine people with disabilities having sex. History shows how persons with disabilities have been denied expressions of sexuality. Young people with disabilities are often not taught about sexuality and healthy sexual practices.

The reality is that many persons with disabilities still today experience not being seen as full human beings. People in their surroundings focus exclusively on their impairments. In this chapter, J explains his frustrations: "Some women, because of my disability, they might not see me. They always see something that's missing. What about what I do have?"

SHUTTING PEOPLE OUT IS WHAT I'VE DONE

CANDACE COLEMAN

Candace was the first person I interviewed for this book. I was nervous when we met in a small meeting room at Access Living, where Candace works as a youth community organizer. She had so many stories to tell that I soon forgot my own worries about being a good interviewer. When I left the room a couple of hours later, I was deeply moved. Candace is a very empowered yet vulnerable woman.

They Never Allowed Me to Think About My Disability First

I grew up on the South Side of Chicago in Englewood, which is right now deemed as one of the most dangerous places in the city. But not when I was growing up. I lived on a very community-centered street. I grew up under my grandparents. I have a very young family. My mother was seventeen when she had me. So my grandmother kinda took over with me. I'm my mother's oldest child, and I grew up in a house with both my grandparents and my mom. My aunt and my uncle stayed in the basement. I have two sisters who are five and six years under me.

I had an interesting upbringing because I was always in the hospital. I have cerebral palsy, but I also have severe asthma. So believe it or not, the asthma kept me in the hospital more than cerebral palsy did. Every time the wind or the weather changed, every time any allergy triggered me or a bee stung me, I was in the hospital. From maybe three days to two weeks. That kept me in and out of school a lot. I grew up more identifying with medical stuff than school stuff because I was always around doctors and nurses.

My family is very family centered. We take care of one another. We do a lot of things together. They never allowed me to think about my disability first. Like, "You can do whatever you wanna do. You just have to deal with some things." They never let anyone say that I couldn't do something. So I grew up not knowing that I had a disability. It wasn't until I had to deal with outside people, who would look at me strangely or point at me.

I always believed that there's a bigger purpose of my life. The part of the story that I didn't tell you about is that my mother hid her pregnancy. No one knew that I was coming. My mother wasn't even getting prenatal care. I was born premature. I was supposed to come on Valentine's Day and I was born on Thanksgiving. Because of prematurity and because my mother was bleeding while giving birth to me, there was a lack of oxygen. I think I was born to fight. There was just a lot of stuff that could have taken me out. From the time that I entered the world. From the time that I began existing.

So my grandmother didn't know about me before the day that I was born. My mother was wailing in pain in a pool of blood on her bed while they were trying to get the Thanksgiving dinner ready. My mother was very small. In all her pregnancies, no one could ever see that she was pregnant. So while they put her on the stretcher and rolled her down the hallway in the hospital, I popped out. Just knowing that part of my story, I think, spiritually, that I'm a person who's a fighter.

A lot of times growing up, when you have a disability people walk over you. They talk about you. It's like my head is here, and the person—the system I have to deal with, whether it's the doctor or the school—is standing over here. And then there's my mother standing in front of me, and they're all talking about me, over me. And no one is really asking me what I want to do. That's the experience that I had many times. The experience of realizing that . . . The feeling that I don't matter. [*Laughs.*] It felt like everybody was always making decisions about me for me. And no one was asking, "And Candace, what do you wanna do?"

Even when my family was supportive, there were still things that they thought I couldn't accomplish. Like getting married or being in a relationship. Even now, oh my God, I'm still battling with the idea that I can live by myself.

I've never lived by myself, but it's something that I wanna try. And I believe I can do it with the right help. And my mom is like, "NO!"

Always the Butt of People's Jokes

When I went into the school system, I was discriminated against a lot. The first school I went to was a special school for kids with disabilities. But it was for kids with learning disabilities, and they actually ended up kicking me out because I was teaching my classmates how to read and write. The doctors had told my mother that I should start in a special school. When people know that you have a physical disability, they automatically assume that it's your mind as well.

I wasn't walking. I didn't start walking until I was three, and when I started walking, they kept serial casting me. They put casts on my legs from below my knee to the tips of my toes, so I wasn't able to physically move around a lot growing up. I guess they put me in the special school to accommodate that.

Later, in first grade, I went to a school in the suburbs where they had more resources. I was able to flourish in that. It was a school in Calumet City. They really embraced my learning style, and I was able to actually be in the gifted program in that school. I got socialization and everything that I needed. It wasn't until I moved back to the city that they treated me like, "Oh no. She should be in special ed." So I struggled a lot in elementary and middle school.

I remember one incident in middle school. I went to a college prep school in Englewood. They tried to ingrain in you pretty early on that you're going to college. And I remember one incident in sixth grade when a teacher did not want me to go on a college tour because he did not want to accommodate me. My mother had to fight, like, "She's going on this trip; y'all need to do everything you can for her to go."

That was my first experience having to advocate for myself. I remember my mom being really frustrated, and I just couldn't understand. "I want to see colleges too. Why can't I be on this trip?" I think they felt like I was more of a liability. Like I was a fragile person. Like if they would do something wrong, I would break or something.

I've always known that I wanted to go to college. But there were a lot of times where I could have died. And hospitals have always told me something that I can't do. They said that I couldn't walk. I walked. They said that I wouldn't live past a certain age. I lived past that age. They said that I wouldn't be able to do physically the things that other students did. I surpassed all those expectations. So we were going on this college tour, and I thought it was important. Because I was like, "I don't care what you all think; I'm going to school. I need to go on this trip to see what it's like. I want to go on this trip."

So they had to make arrangements. It was like a series of meetings, just for me to get to go on this trip. My family contributed; they funded me. The community pulled money together so I could go on this college tour. I went, and I had a very good experience. But even in that experience, I saw how much school wasn't accessible on a college level. It restricted the stuff that I could see. This was another moment of *Aha, you're still a person with a disability.*

When I got to high school, kids were mean. [*Laughs.*] You have to do team projects and different things like that, and it was always "No, I don't wanna work with her." Because people automatically assume that when you have physical disabilities, you must also have a type of disability where you're not able to think. That created a silo of people not really wanting to engage with me on an academic level—and also on a social level. I was always the butt of people's jokes, so the bullying played another key factor in me developing as a young person with a disability.

I wanted everything that anyone else wanted. I wanted to have friends. I wanted to be in a relationship, have fun after school, and socialize with peers. I was not able to access that.

It was even worse in college. Again, students thought that just because I had a physical disability I was not smart. It was a continuous cycle. I always had to prove myself. I always had to prove that I was smart. I grew up in an education system that really believed in developing teams. But in college, students didn't want to be on my team. They would flip out if they got assigned to me.

I used to hear comments in the lunchroom. I don't know why people thought I couldn't hear them. But I would hear comments like "She's stupid. I don't wanna be in a group with her." That really hurt my self-esteem. It was like, *You don't even know me.* Like, *What is this?* So that's like a twofold thing—either a teacher not challenging you enough because they don't think you can do it or a student not believing you can do it. So that was a double whammy for me.

I thought college was supposed to be different. [*Laughs.*] I didn't think it was this big social thing, where people would come up with all these stigmas and live them out in the culture of the school. So I didn't even wanna engage. I disengaged myself socially. I did *not* wanna go. I barely wanted to walk around campus. I really wanted to just hide. The thing that brought me out socially was my friends. They would literally drag me to different events. Because I didn't wanna go. [*Laughs.*]

In high school and college, I wish I would have known about self-advocacy and self-identity. I wish I had seen people with disabilities living a full life. If people were exposed to know that they can do whatever they want to do, including with a disability, then stigma wouldn't be so hard. Then the bullying wouldn't have penetrated my whole life. So having a community and seeing yourself in art, in pop culture . . . You know? Seeing yourself as something that's valuable. That would have been valuable.

Believing That I Can Actually Do Something

One of the major things that I deal with even as an adult is believing that I can actually do something. Being a student with a disability, there were times where teachers only gave me a grade because they were excited that I was in class, instead of actually grading me on my skill set—so that I could know where I was good or where I needed to learn more things. In college there was one class where my teacher gave me grades just because I was present.

Knowing if I've done well has always been a challenge for me, even now that I'm an adult. I'm like that. "Are you just telling me that? Are you just glad that I completed it? Or did I actually do a good enough job?" So, having that stigma in the grading skill . . . People are like, "Oh my God, Candace came to school. You're such an inspiration." That was another form of, I guess, pity or discrimination or inspiration, or all three. That still impacts me now. I'm still like, *I don't really know if I did that right.* Sometimes I struggle with knowing what my best work can be. Because a lot of people think, *If you just do the work, it's great.* That's an ongoing struggle for me professionally.

I Don't Do Relationships

I just turned thirty, and I am in shock. Because when you grow up hearing "You're not gonna walk that far. You're not gonna live that long," when you hear that, the only thing you think about is surviving, or making it. So now, I'm in this place. Oh my God, I'm thirty. I made it. What do I do with my life now? I'm possibly thinking about a family. I'm possibly thinking about shifting my career, or maybe even buying a house. All these things were never even brought to my attention growing up. Because, again, the limitations of people telling me all the stuff that I couldn't do. "All you can do is to live!"

So now that I'm living, what the heck do I do? What do I do with this time? How do I engage? One of the things that I'm struggling with is actually dating. I mean, how do you accept yourself fully, who you are, and let someone else see that? So I am growing in that socially. I avoided dating from high school though college. Everybody else had boyfriends when they were young. I went to prom with my best friend.

It's superbly hard because people think at a different age you're supposed to be a different level. But I'm still a baby in this particular area of my life. I honestly don't know what to do. [*Laughs.*]

In college I didn't think that people would look twice at me, and if they did, it was literally out of a joke. Like, "How can I sleep with her? She's different, you know." That just totally made me a recluse in terms of being vulnerable. Again, I don't know why people think I can't hear them. [*Laughs.*] People just think I can't hear what they say. I remember one guy having an exchange with a person who said he was interested in me: "You should try it out. Just do it because she's different. It might be different." It was just like it was a challenge or a bet or something. So I heard this, and I was like, *OK, just go back to your corner and stay in your room again.*

I don't do relationships because of this trust thing. "Like, are you . . ." Now I'm gonna cry. "Like are you . . ." [*cries*] "Like are you . . . Like are you . . . interested?" [*Cries.*] Just . . . "Are you really interested in me as a person?" And shutting people out is what I've done [*cries*]. So that is what I've done. Shutting people out is what I've done. [*Weeps softly.*]

It's just this automatic response. Get to know a person. You help them, and then you let them go. So I don't hold on to people. I don't hold on to people. I have a serious sense of abandonments. Because when you're in the hospital, it's the doctor doing what he gotta do to you. And then he leaves. Usually it's a painful process. So it's the pain of a person fixing you walking away. Or your family has to leave because they gotta go to work. They can't be in the hospital with you all the time. I was homeschooled [*sobs*] in middle school as well. My teacher came to my house. So I was only able to develop friendships for a very short amount of time.

People would leave. That's how it was. So, now it's like, I'm starting to trust people. I think that they're gonna be there for a long haul. But I really, literally, can engage somebody for maybe the max of six weeks and . . . then I'm waiting for you to leave. [*Laughs.*] So when people stick around, I'm shocked. I'm really shocked. "Are you still here?" [*Laughs.*] And then I notice that I overcompensate. So if I wanna hang out and someone can't: "Oh, I'll pay for you to come with me." Or "I'll help you do this." I'll go above and beyond socially to make sure everybody's happy. Yet I'm the one who's usually not.

Where Do I Fit?

The world keeps saying that I'm disabled. And I keep saying that I'm not. But in every systemic thing that I've tried to accomplish, they keep saying that. "You're disabled. You're disabled. You're disabled." And then the Department of Human Services rejects services and says, "You're not disabled enough!"

Where do I fit? For a long time, I tried to fit myself in a box as a black girl, as a poor person, as a girl with a disability. And I never fit in anywhere. So now I guess I'm saying, "I carve my own ways. I mark my own footsteps."

I developed my disability pride within Access Living—in my job. Oh man, I'm not the only one with a disability. It boosted my confidence. To be OK with who I was. To not have to feel ashamed. Before, every time somebody would point at me, every time a kid would point at me, every time an adult would point at me, every time somebody would talk over me, around me, behind me, I would hear them. That just made me shrink. I would not look people in the face. I would never, never . . . I would never go into a place by myself. I used to be that person that always had to have somebody with me. Now I go to movies by myself. I drive wherever I wanna go. I have no problems. If there's a problem, it's your problem. [*Laughs.*]

How does disability make you feel when you're not even part of society? Before, I always felt that I was alien. [*Laughs.*] And that's how people treated me. Like I was foreign. Like I didn't belong. Like I couldn't contribute. So I think having a community, and the confidence . . . I think seeing other people living a life and being happy just by being themselves and making their own choices. If I had had that growing up, I would be the president right now. [*Laughs.*]

White people can get resources and services and not even know that they have a disability because they have the support that they need to accommodate the stuff that they lack. In my community, we don't even want to identify disability. It's so negative. So you don't get the support that you need. There is less recognition in the black community. It's a race thing. I think it's literally a black thing. Because we deal with all these traumas. I mean, people getting shot. We deal with stuff that's so tricky. You have a kid who just saw a cousin or brother getting shot, and then you expect him to go to school and be OK.

It's also about class. Dual intersectionality. Accommodations on the South Side . . . there are none. I can't take my wheelchair home. It stays here at work. Because I don't have an accessible place to stay. But even if I had an accessible place to stay on the South Side, stores are not accessible. There is no community structure to welcome people with disabilities. So it's dual discrimination. Not only are you not getting what you need because of your race, but you're also not getting what you need because of your disability within your race. Because they don't know, don't care, don't wanna know.

If you are not set free from the limits that the world is putting on you, you're imprisoned three ways: mentally, physically, emotionally. And when you don't get the accommodations that you need, that layer of racial discrimination adds on. So it's like a three-layer whammy.

NOBODY WANTS ME

MAN CALLED J

J walked toward me with this cool walk and a big smile on his face. Then he started talking. He couldn't stop telling stories. After two hours we stopped the interview, but I talked to him again on Skype a couple of weeks later. He had moved out West to stay with his sister for a while.

I Call It Swag

I'm a man of color with a disability. Description of my disability? I call it swag. For those who are not familiar with the term, *swag* means basically your own style, your own walk, your own looks . . . the way you talk. A lot of people like the way I talk and express myself. Especially as a young adult, I started to develop that style naturally. And then my walk is, like, just my walk.

If you want to get technical and medical, like the medical model of disability, I have mild cerebral palsy. I'm blessed and humbled because this disability in particular has a lot of degrees to it and a lot of variations. I'm blessed that it only affected my mobility. I was able to walk when I was almost five years old. I'm thirty-one years old now. Blessed to have made it this far.

Right now I'm suffering from certain chronic physical issues like prearthritis in my hands and feet. My joints are hurting. I'm suffering from that and severe fatigue.

I heard people say, "Oh, you know, he's just sick."

You grow up with this thinking that there's something wrong with you because you're different. There is something wrong with you because you have a disability. But the truth is that disability is part of life. Disability can

141

happen from birth. In the middle of your life. When you're a child. When you're an adult.

I would tell my family, "You need to stop saying that I'm sick. You need to stop saying that I have a disease." I've broken down and told my mother, "Look, I have a condition. I have a disability. And it's a part of me."

She knows that, but because of the time she grew up in . . . Back then, it was like polio, cripple, and all these other things. They didn't know any better. But we're not in the '60s no more. I keep telling her that this is a part of me. My older sisters still use words like *handicapped*, they still use words like *retarded*, like *mentally retarded*. Those are things that are not positive and not empowering to the person . . . to me. You're supposed to put the person first. You're supposed to say, "A person with a disability."

Basically, my disability is just an important part of me. But it's not all of me. You know the typical thing they say, "Oh, I'll look past . . . I'll look past that."

"No, I don't want you to look past that. I just want you to take me with it. I want you to embrace it with me. I don't want you to make any assumptions about me because of my physical disability. Because I'm still a good person."

I Could Pass for Different People for Different Reasons

My family is political refugees from the Pinochet military regime in Chile in the early '70s. My parents were Allende supporters back in their younger days. I'm a product of that. Me and my sisters. I'm the youngest. We're all a product of that. Our parents were politically persecuted and had to flee. So two years after the coup in Chile, they had to leave Santiago.

I was born in 1984 in Michigan, and when I was one year old we moved to the Chicago area in Illinois. I lived here till I was nine. I was able to get surgery and get real good treatment through the medical services. We do have one of the best rehab services for certain disabilities in Chicago. We still do. I was blessed with that.

My mother taught me to be a little gentleman. I was young, and I was surrounded by people, older cousins, my elders, my play uncles. We had a lot of extended family growing up. So we called each other cousins. My blood cousins were my cousins, of course. But we also had play cousins. We developed a relationship so even to this day we call each other cousins. It was those of us who grew up in Chicago. We were all political refugees from the Pinochet regime. We all met here in Chicago in the '80s.

I had a pretty average childhood. I really wasn't aware of my disability. I knew I had a disability, but I was just a happy kid. At least up until I was nine. At that time my parents wanted to go back to Chile. They'd spent about seventeen years in the States, between California and Illinois, with a stop in Michigan and maybe a couple of stops in Venezuela in South America. Venezuela was one of the only countries at the time that didn't have a dictatorship affecting its people.

Growing up I didn't have identity issues until we moved to Chile. The whole family went back. On New Year's Eve of 1993, we all decided to move back. Our parents wanted us to get to know where they came from. And that's when all the identity issues started. That's when the disability kicked in. Because even though I was in special ed up until the third grade in the US, I never really experienced discrimination. It wasn't until I was about nine years old when I came to Chile.

One time in Santiago, I remember some people giving me money. I was just walking in the street and all of a sudden someone gave me money. I didn't know how to say thank you. They gave me like twenty dollars because they felt sorry for me. They felt sorry for me because I had a disability. They didn't know how to say it. They didn't say it. But they were saying it by giving me money. They just gave me money like I was a charity.

My family was very loving and supportive all the time. They would always tell me to be myself. They taught me to be a man, to have manners and to be generous. Then, as I grew older, the more protective my mother became, the more frustrated I got. My mother wanted me to be happy. I felt like she didn't want me to get hurt by the outside. When I was twelve or thirteen I started going out with my cousins, taking public transportation in Santiago, Chile. That was helpful. But I always had to have somebody with me. I always had to have a chaperone. I understand her concern, but at the same time, I had to grow up eventually.

Throughout high school I excelled when it came to writing. When it came to school stuff, I was doing great and my family was really proud of me. They were always supportive. They showed me love, and I spent some of the best years with my family there. I don't know what I would have done if my family wasn't there to support me because the city itself and the people in Chile were pretty socially conservative. They have this thing where they pity you and they don't even realize that they pity you. In many communities of color, especially black, Caribbean, and Latino, we tend to lean on faith. But we lean on faith sometimes for the wrong reasons. We try to cure or fix disability. I grew up hearing things like "cripple" all the time. I'm part of all those communities. I'm culturally and ethnically mixed myself. I could pass for different people for different reasons.

My sisters loved me. But I felt like I was a burden to them. Like they rejected me. I would want to go out. Or we would go to the store, and then I would be too slow. Again, this is how I used to feel. We have a much better relationship now. But then I felt like I was a burden. We used to always argue. I was just an angry, angry frustrated teenager. Like most teenagers. No, let me take that back. Not like most teenagers. Because there were a lot of things that I wanted to do that I couldn't do. And I was really mad. I was jealous for years. I was jealous of my sisters for years. Because they were out there living their lives, doing what they wanted to do.

One time I remember we were having this family moment on a Sunday, and I was really upset. And I said, "Every time I try to go somewhere with you, if I go dancing or go to a party, you act like you don't see me. I want you to see me for who I am. Why can't you just see me as your brother? Not treat me like . . . I already have one mother. I don't need three mothers."

I just wanted them to see me for me. And to see things from my perspective. To see me. I needed them to see me for me.

They Would Look at Me Like I Was a Piece of Meat or a Mutant

I was a happy child. But as soon as puberty hit, to be honest, that's when things really started getting murky and difficult for me.

Back in those days, especially in Chile, they didn't know how to handle people with disabilities. In school they used to say I was a cripple, make fun of my walk. I'm talking about schoolkids younger than me. They verbally abused me. They pushed me. I went through bullying, and that's a type of violence. Verbal and psychological bullying. They would say that I had a funny walk. They would call me names. They would look at me like I was a piece of meat or a mutant or like I was undesirable. Like I was a freak of nature. I didn't react in the moment. I turned the other cheek. So then, when I reacted, it was worse because I got emotional. I got aggressive, and I was upset.

I didn't have a social life. I had a life with my family. I had a family life. I hung out with my uncles and cousins, and it was all good. But when I was outside that, when I was trying to meet people outside, people my age—I barely hung out with them. So if you ask me about my social life in high school, I didn't have none. I didn't have none. You know, I was just seen as the angry refugee.

I didn't really see disability till I went to prom when I was a freshman in high school. The seniors liked me, so they invited me. I remember this one moment where I really wanted to dance. At the time I hadn't had my last surgery. So I didn't have my swag like I have now. I walked on my toes, and I had a little bit more difficulty moving around. I didn't dance as much. And then this girl was, like, standing there. I stood there and then she looked at me like I was ugly, like ugly as ever, and I just wanted to dance: "You're dancing with me like you don't want to touch me, like I'm going to break or something."

That's when I started to really feel my disability. When I started to go to social events. And people would always pat me on my back and say, "Oh, you're a good friend." "You're my buddy, you're the perfect buddy to hang with. It's nice to talk to you about my relationships. It's nice to talk to you." Like, *You're cute and all and you're handsome, but I would never date you.* They would never say that out loud.

I hated high school. When you talk about dating, when you talk about kicking it with the guys and hanging with the boys, I didn't have none of that. I didn't have none of that outside my family.

I Want to Be More Than a Buddy to Somebody

I'm starting to believe my own sarcasm, and that scares me. And even people who're closest to me don't want me to talk like that. "Don't talk about yourself like that!" I just feel like nobody wants me. I'm telling myself, *Oh well, there's always the robot.*

But again I can't afford it. I'm poor. I can't afford it. I'm drowning in debt as part of my student loan crisis. I just want to live a life with somebody.

I'm really tired. I want to be more than a buddy to somebody. I want to be more than . . . I'm worried. My family . . . My friends don't want to see me like the asshole that I've turned into today.

Some women, because of my disability, they might not see me. They always see something that's missing. What about what I do have? What about my smile? What about my dancing? What about my writing? What about my . . . [*Sighs.*]

TO CONSIDER ME,
EVEN THOUGH I COULDN'T SEE

SHARON

I visited Sharon in the neighborhood of Andersonville on a hot summer day. We could hear cars speeding by on her busy street. Inside Sharon's apartment it felt homely and pleasant. There was a clock ticking.

It's Never Any Fun to Be the Only One of Anything

I grew up on the South Side of Chicago. At that time my neighborhood was all white. It was a Polish neighborhood called Hegewisch about five minutes from Indiana. It used to be very industrial. When the steel mills all closed down there, it really hurt the neighborhood. The kids in that neighborhood didn't necessarily go to college. They got basic jobs. My younger sister still lives there, and it's a more mixed neighborhood now.

I'm sixty-five. My mom always said that I was born at six months, which I truly don't believe. [*Laughs.*] My parents were married in July of 1950, and I was born five and a half months later. To have as little trouble as I have and be that early is just impossible. To have total blindness as a disability and no other neurological problems or developmental issues; I just don't believe I was born at six months. But she went to her grave believing it.

My mom was eighteen when I was born. My dad was twenty-two. They were really young. The doctor said to them that I wouldn't amount to anything and that they should institutionalize me. They said, "No. That isn't going to happen."

147

They were also told that they should have another child right away so that the other kid could take care of me. My sister has never gotten over that. She just turned sixty-four the other day. All her life, she's complained because I was always just such a pain. And frankly, I've been more successful than she ever thought I would be. But she's just a crappy old woman as far as I'm concerned. And if that's what she wants to be, then that's fine.

When I grew up, my parents really didn't want to participate in parents of blind children groups. I think they felt like if they didn't acknowledge my blindness, maybe it would go away. They never felt like they were part of a blind children's community. They just didn't want to associate with it.

I have three siblings. My one sister is seventeen months younger than me. My other sister is seven years younger, and my brother is fifteen years younger. My brother and I are the only ones that went to college. I'm the only one that's got a master's degree.

When it got time for me to go to kindergarten, it was a problem where I was going to school. I ended up going to a school near my aunt's house. Back then you couldn't just choose to go to any school. You had to go where there was some kind of monitoring and where there was a resource room. You had only certain schools that you could attend. So I went to Catholic school. They had to bus me there. That's part of my discrimination thing. That's the way in which education was provided at that time.

In first and second grade, there were two classrooms of blind students. I only remember some of the people in my classroom. We were segregated. We were in a classroom with only blind kids. As we learned to read—because we were taught Braille right away—we were integrated into the regular classroom. The school was far from where I lived. It was in Evergreen Park, which is southwest. I lived southeast in Hegewisch. My dad had to take me to my aunt's house because that's where the bus would come. So a lot of times I stayed there during the week because it was easier than having to leave home by 5:30 in the morning to get to my aunt's house by seven to get the bus. I knew the blind kids on the bus. There's still a woman that I keep in touch with on Facebook.

When I went into fourth grade, my parents moved and the bus wouldn't go to that area. They decided to enroll me into my parish school, and that was pretty much unheard of. My mom was a very feisty woman. She decided that was what she was going to do. She was going to get me enrolled in the parish school. It was only a few blocks from where we lived. I remember going to school the first day. She took me. I was going into fourth grade. It's never any fun to be the only one of anything. And I was for all the years that I was in elementary school there. I had what they called an itinerary teacher who would come around and help me with things that I needed help with. There were sixty kids in our class. We all operated at the lowest common denominator. I don't think we made a lot of progress. We all just got through it. I was the only blind child. I had Braille books. I had to learn how to type when I was in fourth grade because the teachers couldn't read Braille. My dad used to read out my math assignments for me.

The high school where I went was another Catholic school. It was an all-girls' school. It wasn't very kindly called snob hill, because the girls there were all wealthy. Their fathers were doctors and lawyers. My dad was a welder.

I took the bus to high school, and it took me at least an hour and a half each way. I hated high school. I hated it. There were a couple of blind girls there, but I didn't fit in. I couldn't really interact with people because of the distance involved. The long bus rides and then homework. So high school was something that I just endured. It was just something I had to get through. I was excluded from social life. I couldn't stay after school. If I missed the last bus that came to the school, I had to walk four blocks to get to a bus. It was walking along the street and hoping that someone else would come the same way. It wasn't a good time at all.

I had some friends and stuff. But they lived farther away. I didn't see them much. I met some blind kids from the North Side and we would spend time on the phone. I had pen pals that I wrote to. It was a way in which to have socialization and a peer group if you will. But it was pretty isolating.

One thing I remember from high school . . . I used to like to write and I finally got into a creative writing course in my senior year. We had to write a short story. I wrote what I thought was a really good story. It was certainly not politically correct, but it was about a baby. It was written from the perspective of the baby. I think the baby was unwanted or something. And the teacher said to me, "You can't write about things that you don't know."

I said, "I don't know anything. Does that mean that I can't write about visual things because I can't see them?"

Anyway, I was the last person to read my story. It was near the end of class. To me, it was a very emotional story. After that, I was crushed. I used to think about getting into journalism. But after that, I was like, *I can't do that. I'm not doing it.*

Over the years, I have often thought, *You have no idea how something that you say can really tear someone down.* We don't have the right to do that to anybody. No one has the right to ruin someone's dream. I just felt so bad after that. I didn't even want to go back to the class. After that experience I felt like I was nothing. I didn't measure up. And still to this day—fifty years later—I still feel that it was a good story. I had been looking at colleges for journalism. But after that, I just said, "I can't do it." That was a truly devastating experience.

Later, I went to Elmhurst College in Elmhurst, Illinois. College was great. I lived in a dormitory. I could get around campus. It was a small campus. I felt included in things. I had roommates. There were three or four other blind students. But I didn't live with them. We were completely integrated. I did make a point of not just hanging out with the blind people. I didn't feel like I had to do that. I could go to meals. I would go with people. I would go by myself, and somebody I knew would find me and sit with me. I could do more socially than I did in high school. We all had the same issues: roommates, meal complaints, dorm complaints, teacher complaints. I felt equal. These were the best years because I was equal for the first time.

You Have to Be the Best!

My parents always said that I had to work. That was understood. But they didn't know what I was going to do. They expected me to do things. They taught me how to do things. I didn't do as much as some kids, but I did whatever I could do. I spent a lot of time with my aunts. If they hadn't been around, I wouldn't have been the person I am. They taught me a lot. They didn't have any other kids, so they focused on me. It didn't make my mom very happy. But I thought it was very wonderful. My aunt used to say, "Hang these clothes on this line. This is how you hang them up. Clean those stairs. This is how you clean the stairs. This is a bucket." [*Laughs.*] "Cut this meat. This is how you cut it."

My aunts were just wonderful. They really taught me such good values. They were always very positive toward me. Always. They didn't know other people who were blind. When I was young you would see blind people standing in the streets with cups. You know, blind people begging in the streets. And my aunts would say, "You're not going to do that." No, I'm definitely not going to do that. [*Laughs.*]

I wasn't always an outgoing person. I wasn't always very confident. But it happened over the years. I developed confidence and strength. It just happened.

I still do as much as I can by myself. Because I can. If I need help, I'll ask for it. But then I'm sixty-five now, and I figure that if I haven't learned it by now, I'll never figure it out. [*Laughs.*] I've been on my own the last fifteen years. I think that's been the time that I've really come out. Because I didn't have to be brought down by my ex, who was such a downer. I can be myself. I can be happy. I can get involved in the things that I want to do. So these have been the best years of my life. I feel included. But I push myself into things too, you know? I've gotten into a lot of activities. In some ways I've always felt like I have to do the best. Because you're blind, you have to excel. You have to be the best!

That just gets kind of tiresome after a while. But I think that I've done it anyway. I think I still have that mentality.

I Never Dated a Sighted Man

[If it weren't for my experiences of exclusion,] I probably wouldn't have married the men that I did. I've been married twice . . . and divorced. I had the idea that I didn't have a choice. I'd have to take whatever I could get. I think if I'd had different social experiences and had more confidence in myself, I wouldn't even have considered marrying. But things happened. And I have my kids. They have been a real blessing. I have two grown sons who are married, and I have five grandkids.

I always think to myself, *Why did I always get involved with males who weren't very desirable? And how come I never got a man who was sighted who would think enough of me as a person to give me a second look?* You know, to even consider me, even though I couldn't see? You know, to even look at me as a person to go out with, or just spend time with, or whatever? I never dated a sighted man. I don't know what I've done wrong.

I've never been able to figure it out. [*Sighs.*] But I've reconciled myself to being on my own now and having a good quality of life. I'm not worrying about it.

I FELT FOR A VERY LONG TIME I WAS A MONSTER

RAHNEE PATRICK

Rahnee has the most contagious smile. We talked, we laughed, and we shared our worries. "But it's so nice to spend time with you," she said after my last question. I felt the same way about her.

This Ostracism That Occurs to Families When They Have Disabilities

When I was eight I got my first spot of psoriasis on my scalp. Then it started on my neck and just kind of grew from there. I have it all over. My joints started aching when I was ten. That's when I got arthritis. I have what they call psoriatic arthritis. It's arthritis that affects the tendons and small joints. My depression . . . I think I really understood it after reading *Romeo and Juliet*. Romeo described himself as melancholic—having melancholy. Oh, that description is very familiar to me. That was in ninth grade, so I was about fourteen.

I remember when the Chicago Bears were playing at the Super Bowl, and I could vacuum the floor in the house. There were other times when I couldn't. I couldn't move the vacuum cleaner. I would usually clean the house before my dad came home from work, and I remember feeling guilty about not being able to vacuum.

My recognition of arthritis was like waves: in and out—in and out. I think when you're adapting to an experience you expect it to go away like a flu. But then there were times where you'd be adapting to it and accepting it. So it kind of goes in and out. But the psoriasis was always constant. There were always flakes coming off me, red skin. I was feeling dry and uncomfortable . . . feeling asexual, like not feeling pretty or attractive enough. That was kind of a constant thing.

I think my parents really wanted me to work harder. I wasn't a perfect, compliant patient. I wouldn't always do the exercises. They would find pills that I hadn't taken. Looking back on it, I can't find any explanation why I didn't take the pills. I know that I probably felt that they weren't working. I didn't really see any changes. I think it was some kind of a feeling: *Arrrrh, this isn't working.*

With my arthritis, things got harder. And to take care of psoriasis, there's definitely a lot of lotion application, gooey things that you had to put on your skin and your hair, multiple washes. I had to do it all over. And my parents had two children—surprise children—at the same time as I acquired my psoriasis and arthritis. They were kind of crushed by the amount of time and energy they had to use to take care of me and the younger ones. Also I couldn't help as much with raising the kids . . . my siblings.

My parents—I think—really, really just wanted me to get better. They tried very hard. But with the depression, I was slowly just folding in on myself—literally and figuratively. I think I withdrew from them. I definitely stopped speaking at dinner. I would just stop talking. I think my family was at a loss about how to handle me.

My mom looked exhausted. There was this whole social expectation that families did this to themselves. So therefore they must take care of it themselves. It was totally this ostracism that occurs to families when they have disabilities. Now I'm getting kind of macro about it, but I feel socially there's a pattern of that. And I feel my family was playing within those social constraints: "Don't ask for help!" "You're responsible for this."

I feel in much more control of my life now. I have people who come in and help wash me and help me take care of my home. For all the ways that I need support, there are people who are paid by the state to do that. And that's very different from what I had when I was a young person. I didn't know about those things until I went to college and met this other woman who had arthritis. She had a shower chair, and I was like, "Oh. Wow! I can sit in the shower and not sit on the floor of the shower and have the water so far away from me. I can sit and the water will be close to me."

My parents never asked for that kind of help. I think it was a combination of them not knowing what to ask for . . . and embarrassment. Definitely there's a lot of shame around it.

I think maybe because of my melancholy, I mostly remember the sad stories. Like my dad saying, "Well, who wants to share a room with you?" He said that to me when I was in my senior year at high school. I was applying for colleges. He was embarrassed, I guess, about me not being able to wash myself. "Who's gonna want a room with you?" He flat out just said that to me. I was like, "Oh, that's a good question. I don't know."

It didn't work out. I went to community college and stayed at home with my parents.

It's Very Dissonant for Me When People Wanna Hang Out

In school I think I was kind of mean. [*Laughs.*] I think I was kind of a mean girl. I was tough. Women had rights, and I was fighting for them. I was also an organizer. I was definitely a leader: "If you wanna know what's the smart thing to do, you should talk to Rahnee about it." "If you wanna know what's the good thing to do, you should talk to Rahnee." Because I was known as a very moralistic person. I didn't have Jesus in my heart, but I was still very moralistic. [*Laughs.*] I was a fighter. If I learned that somebody had crossed a certain line of injustice, I would get super mad and fight.

For sure, I was different in school. But I think that came from being Asian. My mom is from Thailand, so always at one point or another my family was being made fun of for being Asian. That was one difference. In terms of the disability pieces of difference, they didn't pick on me. I think they felt bad for me. My school classmates were a very cohesive unit. It was a small town in Indiana, so we pretty much aged together. And I think people felt really bad for me. I don't think they dared pick on me.

In college the most connections that I had were the disabled students. I also worked in the computer lab, and I still have a couple of computer friends. Also, my creative writing was really good, so I won a couple of awards for creative writing. All the artistic kids, we kind of hung out, and they included me. I have always been able to get friends through my creative outlet and through my disability. I think people are surprised to hear that I struggle with my self-esteem because people often do like me. But I'm surprised. It's very dissonant for me when people wanna hang out. I'm like, "Are you really sure? Do you know?" [*Laughs.*] "OK, I'll try."

My Monster Self

When I went to high school, I think socially I made choices for myself about not being included. If someone was an object of my desire, I would stalk them [*laughs*]. Everybody knew that I had crushes. I had enormous crushes, but in terms of dating, I was not involved in that. I think it was because . . . I felt for a very long time I was a monster.

The feeling about being a monster, I don't know for sure when I first felt it. I drew a picture of it. It was a very childlike picture, so I must have been very young when I formulated this idea. [*Sighs.*] It must have been because of the psoriasis. I remember one time when a friend of mine . . . He and a friend of his were smoking for the first time. They were like in third grade. Very young—long before you're supposed to smoke. They had been trying out cigarettes and started a fire in the field. The volunteer fire department came, and my friend was crying. I wanted to hug him. But I was so self-conscious about my skin because I was wearing a little girl's tank top. I wanted to hug him, but I held myself back because I felt he would be repelled. He probably wouldn't have, but that was how I felt about my skin. The drawing of my monster self had very sharp teeth, big eyes. It was a monster in a cave, like you couldn't even see it—it was so deep in the cave. And then that monster existed inside a box that would have very large locks. That's a child's picture. Yeah . . . I've been carrying that around for a while.

It was limiting because everything seemed to be unrequited. I always had this feeling: *Oh, it's never . . . Your feelings will never be returned to you. You might like somebody, but then they don't . . .*

I think I was well trained on that—like from a young age, only having crushes. My first sexual experience was after college at a disability advocacy training. I met somebody. He was blind. I figured, *Oh, perfect. He can't see me. So he won't see who I am.* But I forgot that . . . I didn't even think about the fact that when you have any sort of intimacy, the person's gonna touch you. [*Laughs.*] It worked out fine. But, you know, that's how much I protected myself. That's the kind of actions I took. The level of self-loathing was super, super high. So palpable for me.

My Activism Is My Therapy

I started identifying as a person with a disability in college. We had a student group. It was awesome. We had a really good group, and that helped me. One of the members was cut off from the door-to-door transit service. She went on a strike. She stopped eating and only drank juice. She went public with it. So I started looking into protest groups and got involved in ADAPT. I organized protests, and I really, really, really embraced it.

Somebody else has said, "My activism is my therapy!" I really rose up in the range nationally in terms of leadership and doing this type of stuff. But what I think kind of got me to draw back was that it's not paid. I had to pay attention to my paid work. [*Laughs.*]

Hatred Toward People Comes Out More Strongly

Sometimes people act like they can't see me or can't hear me. It's like these microaggressions, and they just kind of stack up. They're not good for someone who has depression. [*Sighs deeply.*] Frankly. I'm testy already. [*Laughs.*] My God! And I have a big mouth. I do have a big mouth. I have no problem about saying stuff. I will react. In today's United States, I'm not quite sure if that's a good thing. But I do react. I'm a little scared now with the current presidency, I'm a little more withdrawn about it. I'm more nervous about it. I think it's a combination of being Asian with curly textured hair . . . there is a nonwhite look to me, plus having a disability. All of that comes together, and then not being Christian too. It all makes me much more anxious right now.

Even though insurance for people in poverty is crappy, it's still there. I worry that it will be taken away completely with Trump. If I lose my job, I'm back on that program, and I'm really freaked out about that. I'm also freaked out about the unleashing of people . . . that they can just say what they wanna say . . . verbally or physically assault me in any sort of social setting. [*Sighs.*] I'm freaked out that hatred toward people comes out more strongly. I'm anxious about that. [*Sighs deeply.*] I'm very nervous about it. Hate speech is not OK! All this hatred was there already, and that's what's most unnerving to me. It's been a surprise to me. I feel stupid for not knowing that.

7 | THERE'S SO MUCH DIGNITY IN WORK

PERSONS WITH DISABILITIES EXPERIENCE being put in boxes all the time. And more seriously, they experience widespread exclusion and discrimination based on their disabilities. More than 70 percent of Americans with disabilities do not have a job. Discrimination is not the only reason for high unemployment, but it is a reason.

So much talent is going to waste. Beyond meeting typical job qualifications, persons with disabilities are often tremendously resourceful in overcoming the barriers of their everyday lives and surroundings. This creativity and innovation is an asset that could benefit the labor market, businesses, organizations, and governments, as well as persons with disabilities themselves.

There is identity and meaning in having a job. And there is dignity, recognition, and daily bread. In this chapter, Susan Aarup describes it: "Just that whole purpose. We don't get that because people don't see us." Most employers see the disability before they see the person. It becomes a constant reminder of a person's disability.

People with disabilities find it difficult to even get a foot in the door to the labor market. They are often seen as not being "qualified." Mary Rosenberg describes in this chapter how she experienced a headmaster of a school telling her, "To be a teacher, you have to have a lot of energy to be able to run around. You have to be able to climb the stairs. So we just don't think you're qualified to be a teacher." Mary remembers thinking how ironic it was that the principal didn't think that she was qualified to teach special education:

"You know what I mean; a person with a disability wasn't qualified to teach children with special needs!"

The reality is that people with disabilities often are not expected to work. Instead of working, many family members, friends, and social workers expect persons with disabilities to get disability benefits and to stay on these benefits. In this chapter, an anonymous woman tells about being recommended to apply for Social Security Disability Insurance (SSDI) by a social worker: "I went to college. I did graduate school. I worked for fifteen years. And this is what they tell me to do!"

Discrimination because of disability is real. Undoubtedly. And it is against the law. The Americans with Disabilities Act prohibits such discrimination in employment situations. Allen West explains in this chapter how he went to all kinds of job interviews: "I remember this one guy that I met, and I hadn't told him that I was blind. So I walked into his office, and he grabbed my shoulders and started spinning me around." Discrimination is very difficult to prove, and few people with disabilities initiate legal proceedings in situations where they have experienced such discrimination applying for jobs.

Discrimination, negative attitudes, stigma, and other barriers to participating in employment often make persons with disabilities feel unfulfilled in their adult lives. Susan Aarup explains, "I'm gonna get my degree, and I still won't be able to get a job, because society cannot get over the fact that I have a disability! And doesn't want to see what I have to offer."

Moreover, people with disabilities continue to be directed to sheltered jobs, which contributes to further exclusion and dependence. It is a waste.

SOCIETY CANNOT GET OVER THE FACT THAT I HAVE A DISABILITY!

SUSAN AARUP

I was used to hearing Susan's voice in the office at Access Living. She was a volunteer and would have lengthy phone conversations about meetings and projects in the disability community. A new world opened when we finally sat down together and I heard her stories. She told me about growing up and never being seen as the person she is. I also had not really seen her.

They Never Really Accepted My Disability as a Part of Me

I grew up in Chicago in the suburbs. In a small town. I'm the youngest of three girls. So there were five of us. I'm the only one who has a disability in my family. That kind of shaped my childhood.

My disability is of a physical nature. It happened at birth. It affects my growth and fine motor skills for daily living activities. I use personal assistants for things like cooking, cleaning, dressing, bathing. And I couldn't do it without them. If I didn't have personal assistants, I would be in a nursing home. They're very liberating for me, even though I would prefer not to have them sometimes. [*Laughs.*] My brain—there's nothing wrong with my brain. There's nothing wrong with my processing. There's no learning disability. It's all physical nature.

I had a very supportive family growing up. They had high expectations. That's always come through. But there were some disappointments because I had a disability. So I had to deal with the fact that my parents wouldn't . . . They couldn't . . . They never really accepted my disability as a part of me. I

159

thought it was just a part of me. But they wanted to make it better. They wanted it to go away. I've been around all my life with a disability. And my parents still live in an inaccessible home. I haven't been at their house for three years. "Oh, we don't need to build the ramp, because it might look bad."

It's frustrating. But I still love my parents.

In a way, it's like my parents missed the boat. There was such denial. But they wouldn't see it like that. So when I was nine, they built a house from the ground up. They put a staircase in the house. I couldn't climb it. I used to sit on the stairs and get up the stairway that way. My mom just wanted the steps.

So one time I asked her, "Why did you build this house when you knew it would be difficult for me?"

And she said, "Your dad and I thought that you'd walk at the age of fifteen."

They kept hoping. It was kind of like, *There's something wrong with you that we need to fix.*

I started accepting my disability at the age of four—realizing that this was how it was gonna be. That I would have to fight and that I would have to explain and that people wouldn't like me. But I was gonna be OK because apparently God liked me. I grew up in a pretty religious house. God is my main focus for everything that I do.

I read a lot. I figured it was their problem, not mine. I had enough problems to deal with. So I didn't want to worry about everybody else's problems. I didn't care what the neighbors thought. Well, I did to a point, just because I didn't want to embarrass myself or my parents. Because if I embarrassed them, that was a bad thing. And I didn't wanna do that. I didn't wanna disappoint them. I had a disability. I had already disappointed them that way. I didn't need to disappoint them any more. So I wouldn't do things. I wouldn't eat certain foods. Even today, I don't eat certain foods out because it's messy. I never eat a taco out. Appearance meant a lot to my parents. So I've kind of internalized that. But by the same token, I'm like, *If you don't like me, that's just too bad. If you're not willing to see what I have to offer, then that's too bad.*

Basically, I disappointed my parents. Nobody wants to see their kid in a wheelchair. It was also this whole guilt thing. Nobody did anything wrong. But my parents think they did. It just came across that way: *Why did God do this to us? Why did God do this thing to us?*

Now it's more like, *What can we do to make Susan's life better?* And they can't do anything. 'Cause I'm an adult. The problems are gonna be there, whether they're here or not. And knowing that they can't do anything about it . . . it eats them up. So they have a lot of guilt. Yet they're happy for me. They're proud of what I'm doing.

My Parents Became My Best Friends

Until eighth grade I was mainstreamed in school. I was born in the late '60s, so I was, like, the first class that they mainstreamed back in the '70s. We had special ed. We had a resource room where there would be an aid if we needed physical help with tests or writing. Or if we needed help with personal care. And we had activities.

I went to my hometown high school. I was the only person who had a disability in the whole school. I had an aid for tests and writing, who would be with me in class. I took regular classes. I didn't take any special ed classes. So the aid was like an accommodation. I was a pioneer for everything because I was the first one. I didn't really like high school. It was very cliquish. I was kind of isolated. I did have a few friends. [*Sighs.*] They were older, usually.

I can remember that I would not be invited to the school dance. Nobody would want me to go. Or I wouldn't be included. My parents became my best friends. My mom and dad were my support. My other two sisters had gone off to college. I can remember my mom when there was a school dance. She would say, "Just go over to show up for a little while. Go to make an appearance. Go to be a part of the community. Just so they know that you're there. That you're part of the class. But then call me when you wanna leave."

The dances would be over like at eleven. And they started at eight o'clock. I'd call my mom by nine. So I'd be at home watching *Miami Vice* instead, or eating chocolate with her, or going to a late movie or something.

I did have friends over. But there weren't that many. I didn't like how it was. And I thought it was unfair. But I lived in such a small town. I just thought that small-town life was stupid. So I wanted to get out of there. I didn't take it in too much. It was more *This is not how it's gonna be all the time. Yes, I might have to deal with this all the time. But not everyone in the world will be like this.*

So I went on to college, and that was a whole different experience. It was more accepting. Just being able to be a part of the community. They had tunnels so I didn't have to go out in the cold.

There's So Much Dignity in Work

I've gotten a lot of noes in my life. I've gotten a couple of yeses too. I've learned to use my disability as an asset instead of a detriment. I don't know exactly why. I guess I just knew that I was better than people said I was. I marked my disability as a diversity tool. It was a way to understand marginalized societies. Because I'd been marginalized.

I used to do prison counseling. To counsel prisoners is like . . . It's like, you would get these huge, huge guys who didn't want to talk to anybody. Because nobody would understand why they would do a drug offense. But they always talked to me. Because they knew I understood. In a different way. Not in the same way. I'm never saying that. Because you can't know for sure what anybody goes through. But sometimes they would say, "Oh. It happens to you too."

Most discrimination occurs in employment. I've applied for job after job. The hardest part is the fighting. The convincing. The discrimination of "Yes, I have this degree. But I may need a personal assistant on the job, or a trackball for the computer, or . . ."

I have applied for two or three hundred jobs. I have three master's degrees. I recently went back to school because I was laid off from the city because of the budget crisis in 2009. People with disabilities are the first fired, last hired. I worked full-time for the city for eleven years. I have not worked full-time since 2009. I've had some part-time jobs.

You know it's there. [*Sighs.*] But I can't prove discrimination. That's one of my biggest issues about going back to school now. OK, I'm gonna go to school. I'm gonna get my degree, and I still won't be able to get a job, because society cannot get over the fact that I have a disability! And doesn't want to see what I have to offer. Because I've got a lot to offer. But you gotta look. You have to be willing to sit down and talk to me. And if you're not willing to talk to a person with a disability about jobs, then you probably don't want people with disabilities having jobs. Discrimination is just a really hard thing to prove. If I'd think about it all the time, it'd drive me crazy. But it makes me frustrated to the point where I want to change the system.

Jobs are really the hardest thing. And they're so important because there's so much dignity in work. I finally got a part-time job just recently at UIC [University of Illinois at Chicago] as part of a research grant. It's five to ten hours a week, but it's something. Just that whole purpose. We don't get that because people don't see us.

My Righteous Anger

People with disabilities are not visible in all aspects of life. They're not visible in churches. It's the whole religious disability thing again: "You gotta be fixed." "You did something wrong." Like it's a major sin or something. But that's not how it goes. I didn't do anything. Except being born. And that wasn't even my choice.

But, you know, you can choose how you respond. Sometimes you can't choose your life circumstances, but you can choose how you respond to them. It's hard to fight all the time. So yes, it's frustrating. But the system is frustrating. That has nothing to do with me as a person. I want to change the system. I want to make it better for everyone, for all the world because the whole world is messed up. So if I can help in my little corner . . . Yeah, I get frustrated. But I know that I just have to keep on going. Because the only other option is dying. And I ain't dying. I told somebody yesterday, a friend of mine, "I can't die until I'm ninety, because the world is too stupid!" I can't imagine being around that long. It seems like so long. But the world is too stupid. So I guess I have to stay around for a while.

I think we're gonna keep teaching society. And there's only one way you can teach society. Don't say, "Oh, you're wrong," "Oh, you're stupid." You lead by example. It's a long haul.

It's powerful—my desire to make a difference. And that's what I think people don't see. Because they don't take the time to look! I call it my righteous anger. My anger has a purpose.

I DON'T BELIEVE IN GIVING UP

ALLEN WEST

I met Allen in a Dunkin' Donuts shop in Irving Park on the Northwest Side of Chicago. It was not a quiet day in the coffee shop, so we walked outside in the clear October morning. Allen works for the Chicago Park District, and he took me to Athletic Field Park, where cars came rushing by on the expressway. We sat on a bench in the sun behind the old field house. We drank our coffees and talked.

Anything She Didn't Want Me to Do I Would Do

I was born blind. Or three weeks after birth, I started losing my sight. I lost the remainder when I was seven years old to congenital glaucoma. I grew up here in Chicago on the South Side of the city. I come from a family of six boys and four girls. I'm number five.

My mother initially had this bad habit when meeting people, telling them, "This is my blind son." Which drove me crazy.

So one day, we had it out [*laughs*]: "Don't do this to me!" People would look at me and tell I was blind anyway. I was like, "Why does it need to be emphasized? Treat me like my siblings." Like, "This is my son Allen. And this is my daughter Regina."

My mother was actually very, very protective. But I was one of these people growing up; if you told me not to do something, I would do it. So anything she didn't want me to do I would do. I was determined to do it, just to show her that I could. One of the issues was getting around the city independently. We had fights about that when I got to eighth grade. We had really, really ugly fights about it. But I was determined to break her. By the time I went to high school, she had no choice because we didn't have school buses. So I had to take the bus independently. It got to the point where my mother wanted to go into the city and she would ask me for directions. My father was very supportive. He was like, "He's gotta grow up. He's gotta be independent. We're not gonna be here forever." That was my dad's attitude.

High School Is When I Began to Feel the Real Racism

In grammar school I had a teacher named Ms. Berta. She was my first teacher. Back then . . . This was in the early '60s. I started school in '63. Back then, if you were an African American, a black person like me, you're supposed to say "Yes ma'am, no ma'am" to anybody white. Once in school, I said "Yes ma'am" to this teacher. And she told me, "In this class, we don't play the race card. It's 'yes.' Like everybody else." I was really cool with that. I liked her a lot. She was extremely supportive.

I went to a regular school. But they had a Braille room, which today they'd call a resource room. That's where you'd have a teacher who knew Braille so when you did your papers in Braille, she'd submit your answers to the regular teachers.

High school is when I began to feel the real racism. And in college, that's when I really, really felt it.

I applied to Loyola University and got accepted. I went on a tour in March of '77 for accepted students. We were told that we would be notified when it was time to be registered for classes. So in June, I started calling. I kept getting transferred or they put me on hold. When I finally spoke to someone, they said, "Well, Allen, we don't have a record on you."

I said, "I have an acceptance letter."

But they didn't even wanna see it. They didn't even want to see the acceptance letter that they sent me. How the hell could they lose my records?

This really, really bugged me. So I met a guy from the Catholic Church and told him about it. And he said, "Oh, really. I had this fight with Loyola before. They're notorious for doing this to black people. We're gonna fix this problem." What ended up happening was that he told me, "You go home and stay by the phone. I'm calling Loyola now, and in two hours you're gonna get a call. You will be going to university this fall."

So I got in there. But housing gave me such a hard time. I wanted to stay on campus. I finally went there and asked to see the director of housing. And they said, "Oh well, he's in a meeting."

It was nine o'clock in the morning. I just said, "Well, I'll sit here and wait for him."

"But you know, he's got meetings until three o'clock this afternoon."

And I said, "Well, then I'll just sit here and wait until three o'clock."

And then, you know, fifteen minutes later, I was seeing the director of housing. [*Laughs.*] That was when I really learned to stand my ground!

Is This What the World Expects Me to Do?

Discrimination happens. Sometimes it's very covert. And sometimes you don't realize it's happening. Sometimes people do things to me based on my race, but I don't even know it. Sometimes people do things to me based on me being blind, and I don't even know it. That happens to all of us. I see myself as a person who doesn't walk through life dwelling on why people don't like me. I treat everybody fairly. I don't care what your race or color is. It doesn't matter to me.

I treat everybody the same. I treat everybody equally. That's important to me as an individual. But you know, as a group, I do see a lot of discrimination against the black, against the blind: almost 75 percent of blind people in the United States are unemployed. I was determined to be among the 25 percent. Throughout college, I always worked in the summer and then went to school full-time throughout the year. I graduated from college in May of 1982 in the middle of the recession, and this was where it really started. I couldn't find a job. Here I have to tell you—when you graduate, you walk across the stage, and you get a standing ovation. All right. It's like, you would not believe it. It's the greatest scene that a blind guy graduates!

In August of 1983, more than a year later, I said, "OK, I need to go apply for SSI [Supplemental Security Income], because I'm absolutely out of money."

And I didn't really wanna do that. But I did. And as I was applying for SSI, this guy said to me, "Mr. West, you graduated in May of last year. Why are you just now applying?"

And I got really pissed off. Because I'm like, *Is this what the world expects me to do?* Expects me to go get an education and then go get a government handout? I said, "I'd be dammed if it gonna be me!"

So I went to all kinds of job interviews. I remember this one guy that I met, and I hadn't told him that I was blind. So I walked into his office, and he grabbed my shoulders and started spinning me around. "We can't do this. You're blind. You cannot do this job. There's no way."

I don't even remember what the job was, but I thought, *You know what? Even if I was able to get an interview and sit down with him, I'd get rejected. Because he's so freaking narrow minded.* So I just left.

When I finally got a job in 1985, I started working in food service. I worked there for fourteen years. I left and started working for a blind association. After that, I started working for the park district. I have been so determined to be employed and not rely on SSI.

I don't believe in giving up. Sometimes it's a fight. But it's a guaranteed failure to accept defeat. If you're cashing the chips, just because someone tells you no, you're a failure right then and there. It points to perceptions in life. What people perceive you can do. If you believe from the outset that you can't, then the world is gonna walk on you. If you don't go out there and try it, if you give up, you actually walk out on yourself.

I used to teach cooking classes for blind kids. And the parents let them come cooking. I'd say to the kids, "OK, I need you guys to go home and practice."

Sometimes the parents would come up to me—"Well, you know he's not gonna use my stove. My knives."

"What? You gotta have confidence in your child!"

Wear Your Perseverance Hat!

After that meeting with SSI in '83, I said, "It will not be me."

I try to encourage other blind people. "Wear your perseverance hat!" "Wear your confidence hat!" "Let's make this happen!"

Some will. And there are many that just won't.

Yeah, I have been called arrogant for not giving up. I get called all kinds of stuff. "You think you're better than other people."

"No, I don't think I'm better than you. Why don't you come and join me in my fight for employment?"

I don't think I'm better than anybody. It's just that when I set my mind on something, no matter how long it takes, I'm gonna keep at it.

A big influence is that I have some guys that I grew up with. We fought in grammar school. We supported each other in grammar school. We're all blind. All of us went on to college after high school. All of us have worked. One of my friends is a very, very successful attorney with the county. One of them does a lot of work with the department of rehab. One of them just retired from the IRS. But we were among those who just decided that we were not going to just accept what the world expected of us. We still get together. In fact, in 2018 we're gonna get together and take a trip for our fiftieth anniversary. We've known each other for fifty years.

Still, the constant rejections do influence you. I would be lying if I said that I didn't have my down times and thoughts about giving up. It gets like that. But guess what? I refuse to accept it. Sometimes I talk to my friends. Sometimes it's all within me. You just learn in life that when you give up, you don't succeed. And really, my idea is also that if you have a dream, then take that dream and make it into an expectation. Because dreams don't come through. It's not dreams that come through; expectations come through. You set expectations for yourself, and you say, *How am I gonna do this?*

And yes, of course, there's a world around us, and discrimination is a part of that world. It will try to beat you back. But you gotta work that into your expectation. You gotta expect this to happen and make plans.

My coping strategy has been not to give up, to fight back. To tell you honestly, my mom may have had a lot to do with that. Because I would always fight with her to prove that I could do things. [*Laughs.*] Where did it really, really start? I'm not sure. If my mother would tell me not to do something, I would go out and do it. I loved cooking, and she didn't want me to do that. I was like nine years old, and I started asking questions about how the stove worked—"I wanna learn how to cook."

I bugged my brothers and sisters to answer all my questions. When I was ten years old, I would get up early in the morning and cook breakfast. My mother was still asleep. One day she woke up when I was still cooking. And she was like, "Allen, you didn't cook that."

"I did."

"I thought I told you not to cook."

I said, "Yeah, but this I why I'm doing it." [*Laughs.*]

After that, I started cooking dinner for all of them.

SOMEBODY'S GONNA TAKE ONE LOOK AT MY WHITE CANE

ANONYMOUS WOMAN

We met at her college in a small town north of Chicago. The hallways were buzzing with students, and she guided me quietly through the crowds. We ended up in a meeting room where we could talk in private.

I Was the Surprise

I was born early with the eye condition ROP [retinopathy of prematurity]. I can see a little bit of light out of one of my eyes. But it has to be very bright, like right in my face. I assume that you have the lights on in this room? But I can't tell.

My parents pretty much treated me like anybody else. I have a brother, and he has the same eye condition as me. But he has a fair amount of usable vision. He's actually my twin. He's technically older by a couple of minutes. I was the surprise. My parents didn't know they were having twins until they did. So it was just my brother and me.

I think my parents decided that two was probably enough. They treated us like quote/unquote "normal" kids. They expected the same of us as they would from any other kids, at least as far as I could tell.

Mostly by Choice I Didn't Go to Dances

By the time I was in school, it was pretty well established that you had the right to go to a public school if you wanted to. And fortunately, that was what my parents chose. School was pretty good. I was in all mainstreamed classes. I was the only one who was totally blind. My brother was a grade behind me, and he needed some services, but not as many as I did.

I don't remember not having friends or not being able to participate. The only class I remember sometimes not being able to participate in was gym. Sometimes, depending on the instructor, they were good about adapting it. But by the time I got to high school, I think they kind of had given up. I just had study hall. One semester they didn't know what to do with me. So they put me in a weight training class with the football team. It was awful. [*Laughs.*] It was bad. I guess most girls would have been excited. But I just thought, *This— is—so—bad.* I was embarrassed. The first day of class, the football coach said, "OK, gentlemen. This is —— and she's gonna be in your class. If she needs any help, you have to help her. And you all better be gentlemen and be polite."

I think he meant well, but I was very embarrassed. I was just . . . you know, I'm not a very strong, physically strong person, and they were all lifting hundreds and hundreds of pounds. I was like, "Yeah. I can't lift the bar on the bench press." [*Laughs.*] Fortunately, it only lasted a semester, and after that they put me back in study hall.

I had friends. We hung out and did things. Mostly by choice I didn't go to dances. I didn't go to the prom. I had no desire to go, in part because of how much it cost. It just seemed kind of silly. I was totally happy not going.

I Don't Think You Should Really Take This Class

My parents always made it very clear that my brother and I were both expected to go to college. And that they would prefer that we picked a college that was far enough away from home that we couldn't come home every weekend. It was time for us to leave the house. So I went to college. It was interesting because this was in the early '90s and the ADA had just recently been passed. So the colleges were all trying to figure out what to do. "What are we supposed to do with these disabled students?" [*Laughs.*]

I had one professor who didn't want me in his class. For some reason I signed up for earth science / geology, which was probably not a good idea in the first place. But I thought I should take geology. The professor was very . . . I think he was concerned because a lot of it was visual. But I got to class. After like two or three weeks of class, we were having a quiz. So we did the quiz, and he said, "OK, the last question on the quiz. I'm holding up a hunk of some mineral; what color is this?"

I raised my hand and I said, "Can I have a different question?"

He said, "No. No, you can't have a different question. What color is this?"

I had no idea.

So I went and talked to him after class. He said, "I don't think you should really take this class. Didn't you get the clue from the quiz?" [*Laughs.*]

At the time, I thought, *I can go and make a big deal out of this, because it's not right. Or I can just sign up for a different class.* I decided that it just wasn't worth fighting—because the class wasn't part of my major. So I just dropped it and took a different class.

I was fortunate enough to get some scholarships for college, and I always worried about grades. So I didn't do a lot of the partying. I was involved in student clubs and things. I was happy with my social life. It was my own choice not to do the partying. After I'd watched a few of my dorm mates come home drunk, I didn't need to be doing that.

When I got back to school, one of the professors was questioning me and giving me a hard time about having extended time for tests. He kept telling me that you only need extended time for tests if you haven't studied. [*Laughs.*] It was not the point. I needed the extended time for tests because somebody had to read it to me and I had to tell them my answers, and then they had to write them down.

So do I get angry? Or do I just explain? In this case there was a month left of the class and I was probably never gonna take a class with this professor again. So it really didn't matter. I decided not to do anything about it.

Everybody kind of has to figure out for themselves: *How do I wanna be? What do I wanna do with my anger?* There's a time to fight and a time not to. You may make different decisions depending on what's going on at different times. One thing I always think about is *What are the consequences really gonna be? Am I really gonna have to deal with the person that might be causing this problem in the future? Or is it gonna be finished? And just not worth fighting for?*

Difficult to Even Get a Foot in the Door

After college, I went to grad school. And then after grad school I got a quote/unquote "real" job in a nonprofit agency. I worked in that job for fifteen years, and then I was laid off. Almost half the staff of the nonprofit was laid off at the same time because of the budget crisis in Illinois. But then, interestingly enough, all the staff except for me and one other disabled gentleman were called back. I'm not that silly! The firing had nothing to do with the budget. I don't think so, at least.

So I ended up back in school. I have been job-hunting, but I haven't had a lot of luck. It's fairly difficult to find jobs. When I go in to apply for a job, somebody's gonna take one look at my white cane and go, "Oh, you can't do that."

Even if I can . . . Even if I can maybe do 90 percent of it and there's just one little part where I need accommodation or some help. They might decide that they just don't wanna hassle with that. And they might hire the person behind me who isn't as qualified, just so they don't have to deal with me.

I definitely had these experiences. I also used to always worry when I was teaching youth or when I was helping out with the employment readiness class at work. How do we not discourage them yet be honest with them about what it's really gonna be like to try to find a job out there? I would struggle to make that balance between *You should be hopeful and think you have a future* and *You also have to be real about what you might encounter on your way to the future.*

I've kind of wished that somebody had sat me down a long time ago and told me what was gonna happen when I went into the real world. To have a better understanding of how I was gonna cope with it. How I was gonna deal with it. I don't hear people talk about this a lot. I hear a lot of people just pretend that discrimination doesn't happen anymore. "We have the ADA. Everything's fine now."

I've found it harder than I thought to actually get a job interview. I find it difficult to even get a foot in the door. I found a lot of jobs that have parts of them that I really can't do. There's so much in jobs now that's automated. There are so many different pieces of computer software. And if one of those pieces isn't accessible, you can't do part of the job. There are so many new things like touch screens that aren't accessible.

I've been without a job for one and a half years now. I don't like it. It's kind of scary. When I was laid off, I called the Bureau of Blind Services in the county. I asked if I could reopen my case because I was looking for a job. The officer then told me, "I don't know if you should go back to school. You probably don't need to do that. And you should go ahead and apply for SSDI [Social Security Disability Insurance] because it takes a year and a half to get it."

And I hung up the phone and I started laughing. I said, "What's wrong with this picture? That's the exact opposite of what they should be telling me to do!" [*Laughs.*]

I went to college. I did graduate school. I worked for fifteen years. And this is what they tell me to do! It just seemed completely ridiculous to me, so I wrote them off. I was like, *OK, I'm not gonna get the services from there.*

How Angry Do You Wanna Get?

So I went back to school. I'm working on my certificate in paralegal studies. I probably have about another year to go. But I worry about the future. Am I gonna be able to find a job? Or am I gonna run into challenges with technology that's not accessible? Am I gonna be able to convince an employer that it's worth hiring me? That I'm really gonna be able to do this job? And do the job well enough that it's gonna make up for whatever challenges there might be with assistive technology?

I have applied for jobs. I haven't been to any interviews. I worry that they will not even give me a chance.

But I try not to think about it too much and just focus on school for now. Just keep looking for jobs. There actually was one job that I didn't apply for because the ad was insulting. It wasn't what I wanted to do forever, but it was a job, and I could work part-time and go to school. I looked at their clerical jobs, and at the very end of this really long job description, it said, "Vision is required for data entry."

I was like, "Really!" [*Laughs.*] So I thought, *Should I apply for this job anyway and see what happens? Or should I not bother? Because do I really want to go work for a place that's so dumb that they think that they can put something like that out in a job ad?*

I maybe let these things go too often. It's a hard thing to decide. How often do you wanna fight? How angry do you wanna get? I don't wanna be this angry, bitter, obnoxious person who's always complaining and fighting.

I JUST WANT JUSTICE

MARY ROSENBERG

I met Mary in her apartment in Ravenswood on the North Side of Chicago. Rain was pounding. It was loud—even indoors. Mary and I had a glass of wine and sat on the couch with her proud cat. A couple of months earlier, I had been working with Mary in the legal department at Access Living. I was used to Mary's sharp legal insights and felt privileged that she was willing to share her personal stories too.

I Was Kind of a Misfit

I grew up in Chicago, on the North Side. I'm the oldest of three kids. I have muscular dystrophy. I think it's supposed to be genetic. So it must have been recessive because no one in my family had had it before. When I was born, the Apgar score was very low. I wasn't breathing. So they did a lot of tests and found out that I had muscular dystrophy. I'm kind of unique because they found out so early. My sister also had it when she was born four years later.

I don't know that we talked about it all that much when I was a child. Which was weird. I guess my parents treated me like a perfectly normal kid. It was like there was nothing that I couldn't do, even though I had a disability. One thing that's funny is that mom always said that she was happy my sister also had muscular dystrophy. Because we had each other . . . you know, to have someone to share similar experiences with. Which was funny. [*Laughs.*]

The only time that I ever talked to others who had a disability was every summer when I went to camp with children who had muscular dystrophy. It was a great camp. Everybody there had muscular dystrophy. It was one of my favorite things of the year. It was kind of relaxing to not have to talk about disability because everybody had a disability. It was helpful to know that there was really a community of people. I think that's been helpful for me.

But even at camp, it was hard for me as a kid because most people who have muscular dystrophy end up having to use a wheelchair when they're ten or fifteen years or something. I'm not saying that I'm having it hard because I don't have to use a wheelchair; that would be ridiculous. But I didn't really fit in either world. Because I'm abled bodied enough to most of the time not have to deal with the fact that I have a disability.

So as a kid, I didn't fit in. Especially in sports or going on a school field trip, where I would get left behind. I couldn't keep up with my classmates. As a little child, in second or third grade, I was thinking, *Well, if my class really does leave me behind at the museum, I'll call my parents. I know the phone number, and they can come find me at the museum.* You know? That little stuff. I planned it. I couldn't keep up. That's so weird for a little kid to have to think like that.

In school, I was picked on a lot. Especially through eighth grade in junior high. All kids go through a process in junior high and high school, developing who they are. I think having a disability makes it harder because it's harder to find people that are similar to you. I know my mom said that my sister and I could share that. But we didn't really talk about disability, the two of us, until the last five years. I think my sister got more benefit from it as a kid than I did because I'm the older. I think it helped her more than me.

I've always been pretty introverted. I think in junior high I would call myself shy, though I wouldn't call myself shy now. I think the picking reinforced me being shy. Because I was kind of a misfit. It was hard on my self-esteem. Everybody struggles with that in junior high probably, but I think it was harder for me to come out of that time. I was very depressed. I remember feeling very alone. It was terrible. Thankfully, high school was better. The only time I ever considered committing suicide was in junior high. It was never serious, serious. But it crossed my mind.

I didn't have a lot of friends. I went to a Catholic private school with fifty kids in the class. They were all from this neighborhood that I grew up in. The girls were very cliquish and it was like normal junior high stuff. I feel that having a disability made it easy for them to exclude me, you know what I mean. Like stupid stuff. In class, I would keep to myself. If we had a break, I would read, and they would pick on me for that. They put tape on my back. You know, little stupid shit kids do. At the time it was hurtful. As a kid, I felt helpless.

I think feeling that low affects you for longer than you're probably even aware of. For example, in friendships and relationships, it took me a long time to feel like people would want to be my friends. I felt that I had to be grateful that anybody wanted to be my friend because junior high showed me that I wasn't worthy of friendships. I don't know that I've often had those thoughts consciously, but I definitely felt that for a long time. It sits with you for a long time. And I think you have to make efforts to move on from it. It takes a long time. For me, it's from having good relationships and friendships that I've kind of gotten over it. But it took a very long time. I would say college, or even after college.

We Just Don't Think You're Qualified to Be a Teacher

The first real discriminatory thing that happened to me happened after college. I was kind of lucky in a way. I feel like if I were poor or a person of color, maybe my experiences would have been different. I think I'm lucky in some ways.

After college, I did a Teach for America program in New York City. I signed up in January. After a month of student teaching, you're supposed to get a job in a public school. Everybody else in my cohort was getting jobs, and I didn't. I didn't know why at first. But then principals would start saying things to me like "You can't control the kids because you have a disability." Pretty much in those words. "We would like to hire you. But what happens if there's a fire in the building and you can't get out of the building because you can't climb the stairs?"

So because I wasn't getting jobs, I started to do substitute teaching while I was looking for a job. The worst experience I had was . . . Well, I was substituting in a special education class and in the middle of the day I got a phone call. The secretary of the school said, "If you're offered another substitute position here, don't accept it because you need a barrier-free school. You need a school that's accessible. And we're not totally accessible."

I was so angry. I said OK and hung up. I was so shocked. I was in the middle of teaching and thinking, *Well, I cannot even deal with this just now.*

So I went to the office after the end of the day. I was really young, like twenty-two or twenty-three. I went in and said, "Who made that decision?"

"Oh, the principal."

And then I was like, "Well, then I need to speak to the principal."

I don't know that I was even aware of a lot of my rights, but I was pretty sure that it wasn't legal to say that. Long story short, I ended up talking to the assistant principal, and he said to me, "Well, to be a teacher, you have to have a lot of energy to be able to run around. You have to be able to climb the stairs. So we just don't think you're qualified to be a teacher."

I remember saying, "Have you heard about the Americans with Disabilities Act? You can't just make that decision."

It basically ended there. I remember thinking also how ironic it was that the principal didn't think I was qualified to teach special education. You know what I mean; a person with a disability wasn't qualified to teach children with special needs! I was angry. But I'm a doer. I was like, *I'm sure there are laws protecting me against this.*

I was sure that people would be outraged to find out that someone treated me like this. I knew little about the disability rights movement, but I just had this experience. I was like, *People will be outraged to find out. That I'm not hired because of my disability. And that I'm not capable of teaching other disabled people. How ironic is that!*

I was sure that there was a way to resolve the situation. I just had to find out how. I was super naive. I remember saying, "I don't want money. I just want justice." And I really meant it. [*Laughs.*] But I ended up not pursuing the case.

I Get Stared at a Lot

I get stared at a lot. I don't think that it's always mean spirited. It's rude, but it's not necessarily mean spirited. There's a difference between that and discriminatory issues. I just ignore it. Sometimes people ask me at the market or someplace, "Did you break your leg?"

I think that's kind of a stupid question. [*Laughs.*] Well, I don't have a cast on. But that's just ignorance! It's not necessarily malice or discrimination. It's stupidity. A nicer word would maybe be *curiosity* or *showing concern*.

[When kids stare or point at me and their parents make them look away,] that feels bad too. It's almost like I'm not there. Or I'm so repulsive that I can't be discussed. I feel it's fine for a kid to ask about a disability. If a kid points and says, "Oh, look at that person. He's walking in a weird way . . ." I think the parent should just say, "Well, I think that person probably has some kind of disability. That's why he walks that way." Just that it's not weird or ridiculed.

I'd rather they ask the question than be uncomfortable. One thing you have to get used to with having a disability is having to put other people at ease. I don't mind answering questions. But it comes a lot. It's exhausting to explain stuff all the time. But I'd still rather have people asking me than being uncomfortable. Or deciding for me what I need. Because that's really infuriating!

Physical barriers can be exhausting. Attitudinal barriers can be exhausting too—people constantly staring at you. I don't get as offended by it anymore. I don't have the energy to get super upset about it, as much as I did when I was younger. I just find it exhausting a lot of the time.

I'll tell you my favorite story. People often assume that if you have a physical disability, you have an intellectual disability too. Now I find it kind of funny, but before it was annoying. One example is that maybe five years ago I broke my foot. I can't use crutches, so I had to use a wheelchair. My mom came to visit me, and we went out for brunch. The brand for the wheelchair was Nova. And it said Nova on the back of the wheelchair. [*Laughs.*] We're at the brunch place and sit down. The waitress comes over and asks if we want coffee. Then she turns to my mom and says, "Is her name Nova?" [*Laughs.*]

And I was so caught off guard that I was like, *What? I have two graduate degrees!*

My mom just answered, "No. Her name is not Nova." My mom isn't very confrontational about stuff.

I would say being treated differently is a constant part of my life. But I wouldn't say discrimination is. Being kind of different is pretty internalized for me. And being treated differently in terms of social stuff and being looked at is internalized for me. But not being discriminated against.

I kind of expect it. I can see how people who experience more discrimination would do the same thing. I'm not shocked when someone's staring at me or asks a question. I expect that stuff to happen. In terms of how I internalize being different, I think it can be very exhausting.

I also have to plan everything. It's so hard for me to describe. I've had conversations about this with other people with disability. Planning is a thing. It's essentially making sure that you can do what you want to do every day. You know . . . that there won't be accessibility-related obstacles. Everybody plans his or her day. But because the world isn't accessible to me in certain ways, I have to plan much more. So disability is a constant in my mind. Because I have to plan everything all the time. Like in the winter, if it's icy, I have to plan. It's a real part of me. I think about a lot of things that other people don't even think about.

How Am I Supposed to Feel If She Wants to Hide Her Disability?

I think when I was in school my coping mechanism or the way that I dealt with being different was essentially by ignoring it. I never talked about it. I tried, to the extent possible, not to be inconvenient to other people. I still do. But at that time, I felt that I was in the way. I wanted to fit in. I didn't talk about disability. Not until this job at Access Living have I talked about having a disability. Before, I would rarely bring it up unless my situation really forced me to. I really didn't talk about it.

My sister doesn't want to talk about disability. My sister's disability is a lot less apparent than mine is. So we've had very different experiences. She thinks that I talk disability too much. That it becomes worse from talking about it. I think she basically wants to hide the fact that she has a disability. I can't really fault her for it because it makes her life a lot easier. But on the other hand, it's good to have people who have professional achievements and have done a lot who are open about the fact that they have a disability. It's such a double-edged sword. I'm like the loudmouth of the family.

I feel like we've always had this tension. It's hard. My sister not only doesn't want to talk about it, but she really is . . . I don't know what the word is. It's not *embarrassed*. But she doesn't want the inconvenience of everyday dealings with disability. Or like the trouble of being open about having a disability. When she was dating people she used to tell first dates she didn't want to go upstairs: "If I can avoid stairs, they'll not notice that I'm different."

I get that. I haven't really had the experience that I can hide that I have a disability. So in a way, I think it's a blessing because I don't have to lie to people. Still, when she says stuff like that . . . Well, I wouldn't say that it makes me feel bad. But it's like, *How am I supposed to feel if she wants to hide her disability? I can't hide it.*

8 | OUT IN PUBLIC

PEOPLE WITH DISABILITIES GET attention in public spaces every day. Often it is negative. Most cultures see disability as awful and sad. Sometimes the attitudes are blatantly pejorative. Individuals with disabilities get stared at, called names, and photographed. In this chapter, Gary Arnold observes, "You feel like you're a museum piece or in a zoo. And you're there for the public curiosity, for public entertainment."

Fred Friedman describes in this chapter how he was a member of a social club, and how the owners asked him not to tell others that he had a mental illness "because this is like their home and they might not want to be around mentally ill people." Fred had not behaved badly. The only thing he had done was tell other members of the club that he had a mental illness.

Other times, bias is implicit, and the attitudes are more subtle expressions of pity. Whether these messages are put directly or indirectly, they are all concrete expressions of the assumed inferiority of persons with disabilities. And they are constantly leaking from the dominant cultures. They create social barriers in the public sphere for persons with disabilities and cultivate societies where discrimination and social prejudice against people with disabilities becomes a norm. Such societies are dominated by what is termed ableism.

In his book *Nothing About Us Without Us*, James Charlton points out how shame and pity form attitudes about disability: "Pity, like its source, paternalism, presupposes superiority. It is projected onto people. People with disabilities are primarily subjects of pity. The lives of people with disabilities are [considered] less, because their bodies and minds are [considered] less. To pity is to actually look at and feel bad for them. Pity is an emotion that is rooted in sight. It does not take any other factor into account. A person who cannot see or is using a wheelchair for mobility may be a happy, prosperous, well-adjusted person, but most people encountering him or her immediately feel pity."*

Negative messages descend over people with disabilities and sometimes make them stay indoors, feeling their life shrinking. Other times, people with disabilities fight back and educate their fellow citizens. Judy explains in this chapter how disruptive it is being a person with a visual impairment in the public sphere and constantly being questioned about the legitimacy of her guide dog. She describes how angering it is: "It's almost like I'm guilty until proven innocent! I have to prove myself all the time."

The fact that individuals in the majority population have preconceived ideas does not necessarily mean that they will act discriminatorily toward people with disabilities. But stigma and negative attitudes do form the underlying basis of much oppression.

* James I. Charlton, *Nothing About Us Without Us: Disability Oppression and Empowerment* (Berkeley: University of California Press, 2000), 55.

I WOULDN'T TELL ANYONE

FRED FRIEDMAN

I met with Fred several times. Fred works to secure the rights of people with experiences of mental illnesses in Chicago. He founded the not-for-profit Next Steps fifteen years ago and still works under the motto "No decisions about us without us."* We had long conversations about stereotypes, stigma, being dysfunctional, and reinventions of self. We also talked about positive things to think about.

We Never Talked About It

I first attempted suicide when I was thirteen years old. And that was a long time ago. I'm fairly old. I had a project to do, and I couldn't make myself do it. It occurred to me that if I were dead, I wouldn't have to do the project. So I walked upstairs to the bathroom and took all the meds that were in the medicine cabinet. It turned out that in my parents' medicine cabinet there was nothing particularly dangerous. They found me, and the doctor came. He said, "Your son's gonna be OK."

My father went with me to see a friend who was a police officer. The friend said to me, "Your father's a very strong man. But he cried when he told me what you did." So I knew that what I had done was very bad, and I decided not to talk about it anymore. I reinvented myself. That was how I dealt with

---

* Next Steps works to ensure that people with lived experience of homelessness, mental illness, substance use, or addiction lead the development and implementation of health care, housing, and social policies at the state and local levels.

my symptoms. I'd get sick. I'd get dysfunctional. I'd withdraw from my friends. I'd reinvent myself and go on. And that pattern has continued all of my life.

My family was working class. My father was a plumber by trade. My family is also Jewish. My father always felt uncomfortable about being working class. He felt that he should have gone to college. That he should have a profession— a white-collar job.

I was not a very happy person as a child. And I remember my mother used to say, "Put on a happy mask, and when you take the mask off, you'll discover that you're in fact happy." It's an interesting theory. It never really worked for me. But I had no doubt that my parents loved me fiercely.

My sister, who was six years older than me, also suffered from depression, and in some ways perhaps worse than I. They sent her away to an institution. This is what they used to do in America in those days . . . and that was where she was for most of my childhood, until she entered high school. This also, by the way, put financial restraints on my parents. It cost a fortune to send her to this school. I was sort of jealous of that. There would have been more money to spend on me. She hated it, so she didn't appreciate it. My parents were just sort of screwed. They were trying to do the right thing, and no one was giving them appreciation for it. Again, I told you my father's reaction to me getting sick—just sort of confusion.

After my first suicide attempt, I dropped out of sports and became active in public speech. I became active in politics and just sort of found a whole new set of friends. And again, no one ever talked about it . . . We never talked about it. There was recognition. My parents took me to a counselor. They took me to a therapist. But other than that, they didn't know what to do. And I didn't know what to do. The assumption was that I would get better—and perhaps I did.

My parents loved me. But again, the stigma of mental illness was just so large. They called it mental illness. But they had no answers. They had no way of fixing it or alleviating it. All they knew was that I was in terrific pain and they had no solution. We never talked about it.

I Just Reinvented Myself

I then went on to college. And again, I had a project, and I couldn't make myself do it. So I attempted suicide again. I came home and reinvented myself . . . again. Dropped out of political science and went into economics. Got a whole new set of friends. So that was the pattern. I would function for a while. I would do fine. Then I would gradually become more and more dysfunctional, and again the stigma was so large that rather than try to confront it, I just reinvented myself and wouldn't tell anyone about it.

I followed the same pattern. I became a lawyer. I attempted suicide again. I reinvented myself. So I decided that I couldn't practice law for someone else— either couldn't or I wasn't willing to go back and talk to them. So I started my own practice. Eventually, I built that practice into a nationwide practice. My wife and I felt that we had knocked it out of the park. I then had a project to do, and I couldn't make myself do it . . . and the cycle continued. This was seventeen years ago, and I got very, very sick. I had promised my wife that I wasn't gonna kill myself. What was I gonna do? This time—twenty-four years of marriage had passed and my wife was tired, and so she divorced me. She put me into a nursing home and assumed that I would get better in six months and reinvent myself. But instead, I spent a year and a half in a nursing home, a year and a half in my living room, a year and a half in a nursing home, and ten months in a homeless shelter. When I didn't have her providing a home for me, I just didn't get better.

We Just Mind That You Tell People You're Mentally Ill

When I was in the nursing home, I got a phone call from my uncle telling me that my father and sister were dying and that I needed to go to Florida. I said, "I can't!"

And my uncle said, "What do you mean? I just told you that your father and sister are dying. You have to come to Florida."

Again, the stigma of mental illness was such—and my relationship with relatives was such—that he had no idea where I was. He didn't know that it was a nursing home he had called, and he didn't know that I was dysfunctional. So when I said, "I can't go," he was confused.

"One, I don't have the money."

"But I'll pay for it."

And I said, "I can't. I'm at a nursing home."

And he said, "What do you mean you're at a nursing home? And what do you mean that you can't leave when you want to leave?"

And I said, "They just don't wanna let me go."

The stigma was so incredibly intense that no one had told him that I was sick. He just assumed that I'd sort of faded away and was doing fine. Just not in touch with the family. My wife, I remember, during our marriage desperately tried to reach out to other people. But again, the stigma was so huge that there were no good answers.

But I got permission to leave the nursing home, and I went to Florida. I got there on a Friday night, and my dad died that night.

I finally got out of the nursing home and went to the homeless shelter. Compared to the nursing home, it was like nirvana. One of the reasons that I didn't like the nursing home was that they only gave you really crappy food. And you couldn't have seconds. So I was always hungry. In the homeless shelter we had three meals a day. We would have to eat what they would serve you, but at least they would give you seconds if there were seconds. And certain foods were unlimited. There were unlimited amounts of salad and at least some fresh fruit. None of that was in the nursing home. For me that seemed like nirvana. I was there for a while, and then gradually I decided that I would start going to meetings. So I started attending meetings, which is pretty much what I still do. Eventually, I also got out of the homeless shelter.

I used to belong to a social club. I would pay forty dollars a month, and then I would go and have a place to hang out. The people who ran the club knew that I was poor, and they sort of waived my fee. They were very, very nice to me. But at one point we got into a discussion and they said, "Fred, you can't tell people that you're mentally ill because this is like their home and they might not want to be around mentally ill people. Now, you're fine. We don't mind that you're mentally ill. We just mind that you tell people you're mentally ill."

If they had said that about any other group—women, trans, racial minorities—think about how outrageous that sentence would be: "This is their home, and they might not like being around you people."

What was interesting was that it wasn't like I'd behaved badly. It was just that I said that I belonged to this group of people. So I quit the club and lost my second home. I guess that's an example of discrimination.

I'm One of Those People

The meaning of the word *stigma* is not particularly clear to me. And communication about stigma is fairly difficult. One of the reasons that I wear this T-shirt [that says, I'M ONE OF THOSE PEOPLE!] is a psychiatrist professor who spoke at one of the first meetings that I attended. His work indicated that the way to fight stigma is to confront people with it. He defined stigma as "an unpleasant belief system about somebody." It's one step removed from discrimination. It's not the same. Having preconceived ideas doesn't necessarily mean that you will in fact treat people differently. His theory was that you're perfectly entitled to have whatever ideas you want, as long as you treat people the same.

He was lecturing people that the thing to do was to come out . . . to tell people about your illness. Based on his studies and based on my proactivity, that's what I did. I would go to meetings, and I would introduce myself by saying, "My name is Fred Friedman. I'm very sick and very poor. I suffer from a severe, chronic, persistent mental illness. A few years ago when my symptoms were particularly acute, I lost everything that's important to me—my wife of twenty-four years, my profession of twenty years, my home of ten years, and most of my possessions. I had a year and a half in a nursing home. A year and a half in my living room. Another year and a half in a nursing home. And ten months in a homeless shelter."

This was not what they expected someone to say at a meeting. But that's what I said. And then inevitably people would come up to me afterward and say . . . two things that I always thought were interesting. One was "You didn't have to say that. No one would have known." And I would say, "OK. You sort of missed the point." And two, "Me too. I'm also!" which I thought actually was the point.

That model works as long as I'm not symptomatic. So I also present what I am: a middle-aged Jewish lawyer who is pretty bright. And that forms a contradiction, a cognitive dissonance in most people's minds. Most people, when they think of a mentally ill homeless person, they don't think of a middle-aged Jewish lawyer. The trouble is, of course, that when I'm symptomatic, I don't contradict the stereotypes. I in fact support those stereotypes.

Again, if the story is "I was sick and I got better . . ." it's a great story. If the story is [*laughs*] "I'm sick. I was sick. And I'm not all that well now," it's not nearly as good a story.

That's part of the struggle that I'm working though now. [*Sighs deeply.*] Over the last fifteen years there have been periods of mine being very, very sick and periods of mine not being so sick. When I am well, I get to do interesting, important things. When I'm not so well, I tend not to do anything. [*Sighs.*]

The overall arc of these last fifteen years has not been nearly as good as I would like. I don't have a job that pays me a living wage. I don't have an independent relationship with someone else. I don't even really feel part of a larger tomorrow. And I don't feel part of a larger group. They all seem to be well, and I'm the only one who's not. And I don't seem to feel that tomorrow will be better, in fact. I have every reason to believe that tomorrow will be worse than today. [*Sighs.*] That creates the contradiction of my life, and I'm struggling to find the answers. There's a contradiction between my mental disability and the fact that I've outlived my expected life span. So in some ways the problem should have resolved itself. I just should have been dead. Then, depending on whether or not there's a God, my problems would either be all over or just beginning. But there isn't. But I haven't. And I'm not. So I don't know what to do. [*Sighs deeply.*]

On and off during the last fifteen years, I've been building Next Steps. Not as successfully as I would like and now literally without a message that I find compelling. So I don't know. I just don't know.

I believe that if I was well, stigma wouldn't matter. Then I could figure out a way to overcome any stigma that's related to me. But I'm not well. So I can't overcome it. And it's not an unfounded belief among others. It's true! It's an actual belief that I'm just not worthy of being loved, of having positions of responsibility. I'm just too sick to have those things. So the point is that, although me and my friends believe that stigma is very important, I don't think stigma has been very important in my own life. I don't think people treated me badly because I was labeled with a mental illness. I think people treated me badly because they learned that they can't trust me or that I am toxic to them . . . that I am bad for them. I don't think my wife left me because she didn't like the word *mentally ill*. She left me because being around a mentally ill person and having sole responsibility for my care was simply too much for her. I don't believe that I haven't been able to find a significant other since then because I tell people that I have a mental illness. It's because, unless I can control it—and I can't control it for long—I'm toxic to be around. I don't believe that I haven't built Next Steps because there's a stigma against a person with lived experiences running an organization like Next Steps. It's because I get sick and I mess up. [*Sighs.*] Again, that's not a story that's nearly as good to tell or is easy to fix.

I don't think it's the name of mental illness. I don't think it's the fact that I have this title that prevents people from liking me or giving me responsibility. I think it's my symptoms. And this, interestingly enough, is a sign of either my illness or a sign of my moral upbringing. Most people are pretty darn convinced that they are OK: "It's not me, it's you." And that helps them navigate an unsafe and confusing world. I don't have that measure. I don't know if that's a sign of my illness and sense of helplessness, a sense of my forty years of treatment that hasn't worked, or a sense of my moral responsibilities explicitly taught by my parents. They always taught me that I'm responsible for my own actions. I don't know. And I guess the answer is that it's all those things. It's some amalgam that doesn't mesh well.

People Can Still Love Me

As much as I don't have hope, the idea that there is hope, that people can lead and always have led lives of purpose and value, is good, I think. Education is important. One of the most brilliant economists and mathematicians, John Nash, believed very bizarre things, and simultaneously he was the most consequential mathematician of the previous generation. That's very important. It's very important to understand that. He did his work—not when he was well but while he was sick. I guess that's the story that I'm telling myself.

Thank you for this opportunity to talk myself into it. That's the story! I don't have to be well. I can still do consequential and important work, and people can still love me. And there is always hope! [*Sighs.*] Even if it doesn't work for me, it may work for someone else. And we're all different! And you actually have to figure out whether or not this makes a difference. In most cases . . . most of the time, it doesn't.

IT'S ALMOST LIKE I'M GUILTY UNTIL PROVEN INNOCENT

JUDY

I went to visit Judy on an October afternoon. She lives in a suburb about an hour north of Chicago. On the way, trees were enchanting in their orange and brown colors. Like the other houses in the neighborhood, Judy's house had a large lawn in the front.

That always strikes me as so different from Denmark, where hedges and picket fences surround the homes. Danes want their privacy and closeness. In American suburbs, yards are open, and I get the sense that I'm invited to peek. Falsely, I know. But Judy invited me into her warm kitchen, and we just started talking.

I Know I'm Different

I grew up in Skokie. My parents moved there in 1957. We were the first Asian family. At the time—in the '60s—it had a big Jewish population. I was ridiculed walking to school every day. Every day, boys would taunt my younger sister and me:

"Chinky chinky chinaman . . ." You know, I had a lot of that.

So I grew up in grammar school being the only Asian. I actually never felt that I was Asian, because of that neighborhood. I always felt Caucasian. So as a little girl, I wanted to assimilate. I was made fun of so much that I tried to . . . This is kind of funny, but not funny. I would try to . . . ah . . . pull my nose and try to change it. Because our noses are a little flatter. Not that I could do anything about my eyes. Even in grammar school, I would stand in the bathroom and try to do like that [*pulls her nose*]. I knew that it affected me, you know. It was like, *I'm not like them. I wish I was like them. I know I'm different. And I'm being treated differently.*

That was early grammar school. When I got into fourth or fifth grade, I stood up for myself. That's when I beat up the boys at recess. I just jumped on their backs and fought them down. And then I would run off. [*Laughs.*] I was like a tomboy.

As a kid, I remember hearing my parents saying they wouldn't rent the extra apartment to blacks. I was thinking, *What! Here we're being discriminated against. Why're you doing this?* At that time, I couldn't voice my sense. It just felt wrong.

I Would Modify

I have what's called retinitis pigmentosa—RP for short. It runs in my family on my mother's side. That's my disability. I started losing my night vision at age five. I had scarlet fever, and it brought the disease up to the surface early. All other relatives started losing their vision in their twenties. Now I can see less than ten degrees. It's a small hole, and everything in that hole is blurry.

Because you're close to me, I know that you have glasses on. If you were ten feet from me, I wouldn't see your face at all. So people are like faceless dolls. I no longer can read most print. I can't tell a man from a woman, or a mailbox from a person if it's far off. [*Laughs.*] I'm also losing color. RP is a degenerative disease, so my mom is totally blind now. She's eighty-six. Yeah. That's where I'm headed. I know the outcome. I know where I'll be. I'm OK with it, though.

I was the child in the family with the disability. But I didn't feel too strange or different. My dad always tried to enforce that I lived life as full as I could. So I rode my bike at night, and I shouldn't have. I followed the streetlights and just modified to get by. And he didn't stop me. He knew I was out there after 9:00 PM riding my bike with my girlfriends. But he didn't hold me back in any way. I lived a very full childhood. I didn't let my disability stop me from living.

I would modify. But my vision didn't affect my school unless they turned the lights off. So at school my eyesight didn't really affect me. I had tremendous friends, and they pulled me through. They were so kind to just intuitively guide me. They knew when we would take a bus to a movie theater I'd be OK on the bus and OK walking to the front door. But as soon as we would get into the theater, they just knew to take my arm. They were very intuitive.

I've always had wonderful friends with compassion and understanding. Yeah. [*Sighs.*] I've had more support from friends than family! My family actually discriminated against me because I married a Caucasian guy. [*Laughs.*]

When Are You Gonna Go Completely Blind?

My day vision didn't start crumbling before I got into my thirties. I had to give up driving in my midthirties.

I worked in a laboratory for twenty-four years. My vision got worse, and worse, and worse. I was still able to do my job in the laboratory. My vision was closing in, but my central hole was very clear at the time. People would notice that I wouldn't know if they passed by me. They were picking up on my vision getting worse. So the biggest kicker with discrimination was my immediate boss. In one of my reviews, he said, "When are you gonna go completely blind?" That was the writing on the wall.

The day I left work, I cried like a baby because I loved what I did. I knew that if I had better sight, I would still be doing that. But it was a choice. Knowing that I didn't have support from my boss, I just knew it was time. I cried. They all gave me kisses and everything when I left. They kept in contact with me for years after. I've been gone for fourteen years now. When I left, I knew that I wouldn't be working again.

It's All Dog

It's all about the dog. It's all dog. We would need a month. [*Laughs.*] There are so many stories. I can't tell you how many instances I've had. Since I found out about meeting with you, I've had at least five instances. [*Laughs.*] Like two weeks ago . . . I've been going to this grocery store every week since it opened. For seventeen years, I've had a guide dog. For seventeen years, once a week, I've been in this store with one of my guide dogs. Two weeks ago, I was checking out groceries with my husband. My dog was next to me. A manager came up to me. I was paying, and my husband was at the end, bagging and stuff. She said, "Is that a service dog?"

And my husband turned to her. "You're joking, right?"

She said, "No. It doesn't have a vest. We're told to always ask for a vest."

And that's when I said, "Ma'am, this is a guide dog. It has a harness—leather-coated steel harness that I hang on to as it guides me. This is far above a vest. And by the way, the ADA law states that you can only ask me two questions. And they are 'Is that a service dog?' and 'What tasks does it perform?' Not 'Does it have a vest?'"

So I stood my ground. And she stood her ground. She ended up causing a scene in front of all the customers. But I stood my ground. And she walked away grudgingly. Because I told her, "What you just did was wrong!"

By the next day I had a letter off to the head store manager, the customer service office, and the public relations office. I sent three letters and cc'd everybody.

A couple of weeks ago, I probably had three instances in one week. It never used to be like that. There might be more people passing on their pet dog as a service dog these days. We've learned that people can actually buy vests online stating SERVICE DOG. It's a scam.

Maybe a week and a half ago, I was walking my dog in the mall. It's a great exercise because you need to get around a lot of obstacles. So I'm waiting for my paratransit bus to take me home afterward. I'm sitting on a bench. And here comes a lady who just finished shopping. She has a little white dog tied to her cart, and the dog starts violently barking at my dog. Going, "*Ark, ark, ark*" [*squeaky voice*]. "*Ark, ark, ark.*"

And this crazy lady stops and says, "I told you. [*High-pitched voice:*] You're not to bark. You don't do that in the store."

A service dog shouldn't make a noise. In the ADA law you can be removed if the dog shows actions such as what that dog was showing. So I know people are trying to pass on their pet dogs as service dogs. Some get away with it. And businesses are just cracking down overall. Businesses in general are getting more intolerant.

Yeah . . . I'm very used to people wanting to pet my dog. And, you know, if they're kind, I will respect that. I will say, "I'm sorry. You know, he's working. He's my eyes. He can't be distracted."

They most often will say, "Oh, I'm sorry. I didn't know . . . But why not?"

And then I'll say, "Well, actually, if you do pet guide dogs, they're not focused on what they're doing. I need this dog to get me across intersections.

If they're petted too much, they'll solicit petting, when they really need to focus on getting me across the street. We can both get hurt and hit by a car because they'll just be looking at people saying, 'Pet me, pet me, pet me,' and not focusing on getting us across the street."

People don't know. For the most part, the average person doesn't know. It's a learning thing.

You Educate Them!

[Discrimination stays with me a long time.] I mean, until I get a letter off or a phone call made. [*Laughs.*] Until I feel I've done my job enforcing and educating. So because of the instances that I've had over the last weeks, I always carry the ADA law with me. And I'll just hand it over to people. [*Laughs.*] I can't believe I'm taking this step now. It's gotten so bad that it just feels better having the law with me.

It's disruptive to my day. I can't do what I want to do being stopped all the time and being questioned all the time. It . . . You know . . . It's stopping the flow of my day. It's almost like I'm guilty until proven innocent! I have to prove myself all the time.

I've done presentations in grade schools. I've done senior homes. Cab drivers. Whoever wants to hear more. I'm hoping that people will learn. You know? . . . So this doesn't happen to anybody else.

It's a drive. I mean . . . Because if I don't do this . . . If I don't take that step, it can happen to ten others. And I understand that people just don't know about blindness, about the law, whatever it is . . . They're ignorant about the situation. So how do you remedy that? You educate them! [*Laughs.*] So they're no longer ignorant.

I almost always find the energy to follow up and educate. But initially . . . I'm angered. I am. When I follow up, the anger leaves me. It does. It doesn't stay. I just start wondering when it will happen next.

YOU DON'T HAVE DWARF PHOBIA. YOU'RE JUST A BIGOT!

GARY ARNOLD

I sat in the cubicle next to Gary when I worked at Access Living. From Gary I learned about the best coffee place in the area. I also learned that it is really OK to have an introverted personality. Every once in a while we would have meaningful conversations over lunch. Gary's chuckling always made me smile.

I Guess He's Not Going to Be a Basketball Player

I grew up in Madison, Wisconsin. I'm a Caucasian male little person. No one else in my family is a little person. For my type of dwarfism, it's most common to be born into a family with no other trace of dwarfism. It's hereditary about 20 percent of the time, and it's what they call a mutated gene 80 percent of the time. I have two brothers. I'm in the middle. My older brother's two years older than me. And my other brother's six years younger. So when I grew up, I was the only little person. My parents . . . I don't wanna say they were accepting of my difference or my dwarfism, but they really just went about life. Like they would normally do.

When my mother became pregnant with my younger brother, people would ask her, even close friends of hers would ask her, "Are you concerned that you might have another little person?" I don't know what the information was at the time. This was in the mid-1970s. But you know, the chances of her having another little person were one in twenty thousand or one in thirty thousand, basically. Just the same chance as for anyone else.

But this was her answer [*laughs*]: "You know, if I have another Gary, that's fine with me." So I always appreciated that.

It's good timing for this interview because I recently took a family vacation. I've been married for seven years now, and my wife has been a part of the family for about ten years. So at this family vacation, she asked my mother and my father all these questions that I never asked. [*Laughs.*] I never thought to ask, "Well, how did you find out? When was the diagnosis made?"

It wasn't prenatal. It was after the birth. My first pediatrician didn't want to make the diagnosis, but he thought that it was something my parents should get checked out. They had to wait a good amount of time to set up an appointment with a specialist who could make that diagnosis. He told them, "Your son has dwarfism."

I was only a couple of weeks old. This conversation with my wife was forty-some years later, but my parents said that their reaction was "Well, I guess he's not going to be a basketball player." [*Laughs.*]

Basically, growing up they let me do things. They didn't encourage me to overcompensate. They also didn't hold me back from stuff. I wanted to do what my older brother did. He played soccer. He played basketball. He played baseball. So I played soccer. In high school, I played baseball for as long as I could until I started getting cut from teams. I didn't play basketball. I play it now, ironically. I meet with this group weekly to play pickup games. As a child, I did all kinds of sports and active stuff.

Gary's a Minority. He's Midget.

For the most part, school was really OK. Madison's a small town. Everybody knew me, and I was treated all right. But I remember a couple of experiences that stand out.

In sixth grade I had this crush on an eighth grader. We went to a middle school where you go to classes with seventh and eighth graders. So it was my first exposure to interaction with older students. And this eighth-grade girl would just say hi to me, you know. [*Laughs.*] I was blown away by that. She would always say hi to me. So I developed this crush on her. People eventually found out about it. And this group of kids one day went up to the girl.

They got on their knees and were walking around pretending to be me. They would go up to her and say to her, "Chris, do you want to go out with me?" "Do you like me?"

When I found out about it, I was just devastated. [*Laughs.*] I didn't know how to handle it. I broke down. I remember, my friend told me about it, as we were about to go back to class after lunch. I was trying to hold it together. I would sit back in class. And then my teacher had to tell me something— a totally unrelated thing. She could tell something was bothering me. And when she asked what was bothering me, I kind of lost it. I just had to leave the classroom.

But then these two other kids from my class who kind of knew what was going on, they followed me out. That was a nice moment. I was in the bathroom. I was crying and I was telling them what was happening. They had no idea what to do, but they were just listening. [*Laughs.*] So that was nice. But it was never really dealt with. And it was never the same with that girl. She got embarrassed about it. She ignored me for months.

Over the years, my school became more diverse because of desegregation and busing. I have this vivid memory of being in class in eighth grade and this announcement came over the loudspeaker: "All minorities please report to blah-blah-blah." It wasn't this empowering thing like, *Great, we're gonna go to this empowering group.* It was more, *Oh, we're being singled out. We're clearly different from the majority of people and this classroom. And we gotta go now.*

Everyone's thinking that and watching the two or three students leave the classroom. But then, as this was going on and they were leaving, this one kid—a sixth grader—[*laughs*] said, "Gary, you should be going with them! Right?"

Some other kids were looking at him. "What are you talking about?"

"Well, Gary's a minority. He's midget." [*Laughs.*]

That was the end of it. Nothing happened. But I felt singled out. Isolated. Different.

Dwarfism Doesn't Define Me

It's hard for me to trace when I started to identify as a person with a disability. I was obviously aware of my difference. I tried to fit in. But I never really could deny that I was different. [*Laughs.*] There was no denying that. But there was never any way for me to label the fact that I was treated differently. And because there was no label for it, I think there was pressure, whether it'd be internal or external, to just kind of deal with it. You couldn't say, "It's discrimination so you should just fight back against it." Because what kind of discrimination was it? I didn't have a group of people that was fighting against it with me. I was kind of on my own.

I was in college in the late '80s when there was a big diversity and inclusion movement. Through that movement, there were a lot of active groups on campus celebrating diversity. There were support groups for different groups like African Americans and Latinos. I didn't really identify with disability at that time. I obviously knew that I was different, but I wasn't recognized as part of the diversity. So I kind of felt the need there. I was part of these movements. I was active, but I still didn't have a place.

So when I was a junior in college I went back to a National Conference of the Little People of America for the first time since I was probably nine or ten years old. I went on my own for a couple of days. I didn't do much, but it was kind of good for me to get exposure.

My senior year, I had this epiphany. I had thought that if I went to a Little People of America conference and was around all these other little people, I would blossom into this person that I always wanted to be or that I hadn't developed into because I was different in this average-size world. But I realized after three or four days at the conference . . . At that time, I had reconnected with the friends that I had met the year before, and I had met new friends, so I was feeling comfortable, and I was embraced within a group. So basically, I thought that I would . . . that I would all of a sudden be active—that I would be outgoing and really social and stuff, which I had never really been. But then I realized, *No, I'm the same person here that I am in other places.*

So that was really important for me. I realized that there are all these positive things about Little People of America, about spending time with other people in the dwarfism community. But I also finally understood that dwarfism doesn't define me. Many more things, stronger things, define me. It was all these other things that made up who I was. That explained why I was the same person wherever I went. So I think that was really important for me. And that allowed me to say, *OK. I am who I am. And my dwarfism isn't really holding me back. It isn't really holding me back from doing things when I'm in the world at large in Chicago, in Madison, wherever I am.*

A Little People of America conference, it's a juxtaposition. I definitely feel that when you go to a dwarfism conference there's this kind of shared experience that creates a common bond among almost everybody. Even though people can be completely different than you. It's like you don't have to explain yourself. You can be who you are. And you're not going to be grouped into a category because of your dwarfism. You do share so much. There are these strong bonds that connect everyone. But it's not something that needs to be spoken about. You can be yourself. And you can be really different there without worrying about being defined by dwarfism. That's the importance of the Little People of America conference. To some extent, the strength of the little people community transcends the conference. You know that you're not alone. You know there are plenty of other people out there that have similar experiences. And you know that you're not to blame for the negative stuff that happens.

You Feel Like You're a Museum Piece or in a Zoo

What do I think discrimination or being treated differently looks like now? That's being out in public as a person with dwarfism. When you look really different, almost every time you go out, you get attention. Sometimes attention manifests itself in stares. Sometimes it manifests itself in people calling you names. But in this day and age, where everybody has a phone and every phone has a camera, it most likely manifests itself in people taking your picture, surreptitiously or sometimes up front.

Trains are the hardest for me. Crowded trains. People don't necessarily take your picture. But another thing that I find probably more difficult than the pictures is people reacting as if they're scared of you. I get that more often than I ever would have imagined. It's more of a recent thing where people claim to have this dwarf phobia thing. And in the extreme case, people look to appear to be having a panic attack!

This happened probably three times in the streets around the office with the same young woman. She was always walking with someone that I think is her boyfriend. The first time it happened, she saw me. And she just ran away. She just ran away! She kind of screamed and ran away. It's hard to think that it's a real thing, a legit fear. Usually people are with a group of people when it happens. So the other people that they're with think it's funny and laugh.

Because it's comical, and also there's a hint that they kind of think that it's ridiculous also. That was the first time with this woman. The second time, it was just the woman and her boyfriend approaching on the street. She just kind of stopped. Her boyfriend recognized what was happening. He came up to me and he said, "Can you come and talk to her?"

I didn't really want to, but I was appreciative of the fact that he came up to me and asked. But before we had a chance to go talk to her, she ran away. Again. [*Laughs.*] So that was the second time. Then the third time, again on the street, again somewhere near here. And she ran away. Again. This time the boyfriend and I kind of acknowledged each other, made eye contact [*laughs*] and I said something like "She's still working out her fears [*laughs*] with dwarfism?" And he just kind of rolled his eyes. I think he thought it was ridiculous also.

I always struggle with trying to give people the benefit of the doubt. Like maybe there's something going on that they have to work through versus—like, this is ridiculous. It's just a form of bigotry. It's like me running away and saying that I'm afraid of a specific type of minority. That would not be a legit phobia. That would just be bigotry. That's just discrimination. It's hard for me to work that out in my head.

I did confront somebody on the train once with that. It was a woman and a guy. They were young. I got on the train. The woman was kind of like . . . goes like that [*hides his head under his right arm*]. Sometimes I just go right in their face. I did in this case. I sat down across the aisle. And then I said, "Don't worry. You don't have any phobia. You're just a bigot!" [*Laughs.*] I said that. The girl didn't say anything. She just kind of kept hiding. But the boyfriend didn't like that. He started calling me a racist.

One of the most recent incidents I remember was on the train again. It was this woman. She had a couple of little kids with her. She got on the train after I was already seated. She sat down, and she was talking to the kids. And then all of a sudden, she saw me, and she went into this panic attack mode. It was funny because this time [*laughs*] this guy was sitting next to her. And he was like, "What is going on?"

Then he looked at me. I was kind of, "Well, it's me. Sorry." [*Laughs.*]

So those experiences are hard to deal with. I find nothing that really works there in terms of how to deal with it. I like confronting people about it, because I do think it's ridiculous—that people have this so-called phobia. It's harder to deal with than people taking my picture because people maybe believe that they have some kind of fear like a fear of spiders and that it's a sickness and that they can't control it. When taking pictures, it's something that everyone knows that they shouldn't be doing. There is no hiding that.

I was biking down State Street in River North, and this car was pulling past me. From the backseat of the car, a passenger extended her arm with a digital camera out the window. I didn't see her face. It was just this arm. But it was clear what was happening. She took my photo. They hit a red light right away, and I knew I could confront them. I knew I could block them without blocking other cars. They couldn't get around without running me over. So I did it. I blocked them for three red light cycles. I said stuff. But I tried to say as little as possible in order to stay calm. I just kept telling them, "I need your camera!"

Usually, my goal is to get them as agitated as they agitated me by doing what they did. I want to piss them off.

I feel people do this to little persons for a number of reasons. One is that people feel a stronger sense of power over persons with dwarfism because of physical stature. There's a power dealing with size. That also has a lot to do with why people would say anything to a little person. They'll ask you any question. They feel safe. Whatever boundaries there are between typical strangers, those boundaries are gone when it comes to a little person. They'll ask you personal questions. They'll ask you inappropriate questions. They'll say stupid things that they wouldn't say to other people.

Another reason for that has something to do with an acquired disability versus a disability that you're born with. If you have an acquired disability, I think there's more empathy. People can relate to that and realize—maybe not consciously—that anyone can get a disability. But there is no human connection to someone with dwarfism. People know they'll never be a little person. They assume that no one that they are close to will ever be a little person. So that's something to do with why this line of personal space of little persons is just gone.

Back to the story. My goal was to piss them off. I could get some satisfaction out of that. And these people got pissed off! The woman in the backseat who took the picture kept screaming, "I deleted the photo! Let us go. Let us go!"

The dude that was driving kept swearing at me. "Get out of the fucking way!"

There was a second woman in the passenger front seat who was threatening to call the police. And I just kept saying, "I want your camera. I need to see your camera."

Eventually, a police officer drove by. He asked what was going on. I said, "They took my picture. I want their camera."

"But there is no law against that. You can't do anything."

He was in his car at the time. So I just repeated, "But I want the camera."

He then threatened to get out of his car. And I was like, *All right, that's enough for me.* I went away. [*Laughs.*]

When someone takes my picture, it feels like . . . It's similar to when people just point at you. And this is the worst. When, like, a mother points out to her child, "Look at him." That's just devastating. You feel like you're a museum piece or in a zoo. And you're there for the public curiosity, for public entertainment. You're on display, and people talk about you right in front of you without regard to how they would feel if it was them. Cameras are like that. Only there's also this fear: Where is the picture gonna show up later? On the Internet? In social media? I once found this YouTube video of a little person moving into an apartment unloading stuff out of a moving van. Somebody across the street was filming it and posting it: "Here's a midget moving in across the street."

Sometimes I worry about having internalized these experiences. I worry that there's stuff under the surface. Like, so many people come and work at Access Living and move on. They move on. It's not common these days for people to spend a long time in one place. I've been working with Access Living for seventeen years now—a long time. Sometimes I worry, *Am I here still because I'm afraid to go out? I'm afraid that I wouldn't be able to find another job elsewhere? Is there something going on that I'm not aware of?* I wonder about that. Sometimes.

But by and large I feel pretty confident and comfortable.

9 | INDEPENDENCE

We drank coffee all the time, strong coffee with milk—that is, when we weren't going for long walks with Torben's dog or taking the minivan to go shopping or explore the city of Århus. I was working as a personal assistant for Torben during a gap year from law school. He needed assistance twenty-four hours a day, and I would usually work seventy-two-hour shifts. I would suggest different activities during our long days together. But Torben was the one to decide. He was a young man who had severe disabilities, but he had choices—he was in control, and he lived an independent life.

TORBEN'S EXPERIENCE IS NOT the case for most people with disabilities. All over the world—all throughout history—persons with disabilities have risked living in isolation, in institutions, far away from family, excluded from local communities, without control of their own lives, without individualized support.

People with disabilities are often forced to choose between remaining at home with their families or moving into institutions or nursing homes to get the services, treatment, or support that they need.* Often, the choice between living in an institution and living independently is not genuine. While institutionalization can differ from one context to another, certain common elements define it: isolation and segregation from community life, lack of control over day-to-day decisions, rigidity of routine, identical activities in the same place,

---

* Arlene S. Kanter, *The Development of Disability Rights Under International Law: From Charity to Human Rights* (London: Routledge, 2015), 65.

a paternalistic approach in the provision of services, and disproportion in the number of persons with disabilities living in the same environment.*

Living in an institutional setting has grave effects on people. People with disabilities often experience institutionalism, which is a condition marked by withdrawal, loss of interest, submissiveness, lack of initiative, impaired judgment, and eventually a reluctance to leave the institutional setting.†

Outside institutions, the barriers of society make independent living challenging. There are physical barriers to places of work, shops, health care facilities, housing, transportation, and public buildings. There are negative attitudes and stigma about the ability of persons with disabilities to live where and with whom they choose and about their ability to make decisions for themselves.

Most people simply want to live regular, independent lives. This is no different for people with disabilities. In this chapter, Michelle Garcia explains how angry her mother got when Michelle decided that she wanted to move out and live by herself: "It was basically more about her needs than mine. She wanted me to be close to her."

Most people want to be included in their local community and have personal control of their lives. Nobody really wants to be warehoused and live in isolation. Individuals in the Cambiando Vidas group explain in this chapter that they feel excluded in their own Latino community. They describe how they are looked upon as nonproductive individuals: "We should be staying at home being taken care of."

For people with disabilities, independent living is about having the same range of choices as persons without disabilities. It is about controlling where they live and whom they live with. It is about getting individualized support and controlling everyday life decisions about sleep, food, clothing, school, work, and participation in culture.‡ It is about having meaningful interactions with their surroundings and developing personal relationships.

---

* Office of the UN High Commissioner for Human Rights, Thematic study on the right of persons with disabilities to live independently and be included in the community, UN Doc. A/HRC/28/37 (December 12, 2014), ¶ 21.

† Andrew Solomon, *Far from the Tree: Parents, Children, and the Search for Identity* (New York: Scribner, 2012), 26.

‡ Office of the UN High Commissioner for Human Rights, UN Doc. A/HRC/28/37 (December 12, 2014), ¶ 22.

From a socioeconomic perspective, it is only rational to promote independent living.* Self-determination of people with disability is associated with a variety of positive outcomes, including better employment, greater inclusion in general education settings, improved well-being, and greater independence.† Michael Grice explains in this chapter how he constantly tells politicians and other people in power: "Don't you want to save money? It's cheaper to have us in the community. Much, much cheaper."

---

* Jim Mansell, Martin Knapp, Julie Beadle-Brown, and Jeni Beecham, *Deinstitutionalization and Community Living—Outcomes and Costs: Report of a European Study* (Canterbury: Tizard Centre, University of Kent, 2007).
† Tamar Heller and Sarah Parker Harris, *Disability Through the Life Course* (London: Sage, 2012), 27.

JUST LIKE A PERSON

MICHAEL GRICE

Michael waited for me in the small lobby of a high-rise in Lakeview. New management was renovating the whole building, and Michael was one of the few tenants still living there—he was waiting for his new place to be made accessible. In spite of the age difference, he reminded me of Torben back in Denmark. Michael had the same mild and captivating smile as Torben.

We Didn't Know

I'm a quadriplegic with cerebral palsy due to several accidents. So I acquired my disability. I had my first accident when I was seventeen. It was a severe motorcycle accident. Six years later, I had a diving accident. So I broke my neck in the left side and I severed my spinal cord.

I grew up in L.A. When I had my first accident in the '70s, we didn't know about a lot of resources. Luckily, I ran into another person with a disability, and he told me about a rehab center in Berkeley, California. I was there for the first eight months. After eight months, I got transferred to a rehabilitation institute in Chicago. And I was there for about a year and a half before I went home. Mind you, my parents' home was not wheelchair accessible, and I needed a wheelchair. My mother left her work, and she took care of me. She was my sole caretaker while my stepfather worked to take care of our family. At that particular time, I had a respirator and a ventilator. I couldn't do anything for myself. I needed twenty-four-hour care. My mother didn't want me to go to an institution. So she stayed home and continued to do my care for almost two years. Then I developed complications from my first accident—breathing problems, pressure sores. So I had to go back to the rehabilitation center.

That was a very tough time for me . . . because I was young and I hadn't fully realized what had happened to me. You know, I was still in a state of shock. But I told myself that I was gonna pull through it.

I couldn't go home again because the house wasn't accessible, and my mother needed to work. So the only choice that I had was to go to a nursing home. And I really didn't want to go. But I did. Mind you, it was hard to find good care. My family members were very supportive, but we didn't know what to expect.

I was in and out of nursing homes for years. I thought I would never get out for real.

There Is No Life in a Nursing Home

It's . . . You have no life. There is no life in a nursing home. You know, the CNAs [certified nursing assistants] get you up if they have the time. They're so overwhelmed with so many residents . . . to take care of them all. So any given day you may or may not get out of your bed. It really depends on how many CNAs are working that particular floor that day. It also depends on how the nurse in charge is making the schedule. There were many days in the last nursing home where I didn't get up until two or three o'clock in the afternoon. I had appointments that I couldn't make because of the shortage of CNAs. Or my visitors would come and say, "Mike, what are you still doing in bed at this hour of the day?"

But residents don't have control. And as far as sticking to a diet, it's very rare that the nursing homes do that. For me, I'm lactose intolerant, and I would tell them, time and time again, "I can't have dairy products." And they would constantly make foods that I couldn't eat.

You basically can't make any decisions yourself. And nursing homes dislike residents like myself because I had a good circle of friends and I had different organizations that I could reach out to. Mind you, a lot of other residents don't have those connections. But I was able to advocate and say to the nursing home, "This food that you're giving me is garbage. It's making me sick. And I'm not gonna continue to accept it. I'm just gonna do what I need to do."

And that's what I did. I had great support from different organizations. Most nursing home residents are intimidated by the nursing home administration. But I wasn't intimidated!

I got dropped several times being transferred. Because a number of CNAs wouldn't listen to me when I asked them to go get another CNA. I broke bones several times.

Most nursing homes have a wide age range. The age range of residents can be anywhere from twenty to one hundred. A lot of residents have been in a particular nursing home for so long that they die complacent. It's . . . It's "I'm here. I'm stuck. No one comes to see me. Nobody calls me. Nobody writes me. So what am I to do? I have no money. The only money I have is the thirty dollars I get per month. And it's only thirty dollars. Once I spend that, I have to wait for the next month. Unless friends or one of my lost relatives decides to come and visit me. Otherwise I'm stuck."

Living in a nursing home takes your self-esteem. Your whole desire is stripped. I just said to myself, *Mike, I don't wanna die here. Don't wanna die in a nursing home. That's the last thing I wanna do. So I'm gonna concentrate on working on my health. Getting it to be the best I can get it to be. And then I'm gonna get the hell out of here. I don't wanna stay. Because if I stay here any longer, God knows what's gonna happen.*

Because I'd seen too many people die in a nursing home. I'd seen too many people, at twenty, thirty, forty, fifty, or sixty die in a nursing home. And I didn't wanna be a victim. I didn't wanna go out that way. It wasn't my time yet. It's still not my time. So I made up my mind. *No, that's not gonna happen to you. You're gonna make your body strong. You're gonna do whatever you need to do to get out. And you're gonna stay out!*

That's what I did the last two years I was in the nursing home. I just focused on my health and nothing else. And I did everything that Access Living told me to do, step by step. They made me stronger mentally. And then it began to happen physically. But it had to happen up here first, mentally [*points to his head*]. I got the tools to believe in it, and I used the tools to my advantage. That's what I teach others today: "It's a work in progress. But you gotta do it every single day. You gotta be persistent. You can't do it today and then put it on the shelf for two weeks. You gotta work the program every single day."

It's like being an addict. An addict has to work the program every single day. It's the same thing when you're getting out of a nursing home: work that program every single day! And then you get out.

I Can Go Where I Want at the Spur of the Moment

I've been in this apartment for three years now, and I have four marvelous PAs [personal assistants]. I have PAs for eight and a half hours a day. And I will do everything within my power to stay in the community.

I can make my own choices: when I get up, what I eat, what I wear, when I go, where I go. I don't have to sign in and out. I don't have to get a pass on the weekend if I want to go visit family or friends or go to a movie. I can just go. This community is great because to me it's really accessible. It has good transportation. Right outside my building there's a bus stop. The El station isn't too far away. I use public transportation. Now they also have wheelchair-accessible cabs. So I can go wherever I need to go.

Living independently gives me a sense of reassurance because I can go where I want at the spur of the moment. I don't have to take permission from a social worker. I don't have to get a doctor's order to go out. I can just go. I can call Pace paratransit if I choose to. I can go wherever I want. So it's the freedom. For me it's the freedom to go be with friends, family, colleagues, meet new friends, go to different events, different functions, be a part of different communities. Be a person.

And most of all, it's my right. People with disabilities have human rights. Sometimes we don't voice our rights as well as we should. But we all have human rights to live like everyone else. Just like a person. And that's the way I want it.

To live independently means that I have choice. I can make choices. In a nursing home you can't choose what you want. Because the menu is always the same for the entire nursing home. You can't really choose anything.

My day-to-day work is to be an advocate for my brothers and sisters. I take it very seriously. Especially when it comes to advocating for my brothers and sisters in nursing homes and fighting for accessible and integrated affordable housing. We're constantly saying, "Don't you want to save money? It's cheaper to have us in the community. Much, much cheaper."

I WANT TO SPREAD MY WINGS TOO

MICHELLE GARCIA

It was a hot summer day in the office. It was vacation time, and most cubicles were empty. The only sounds were quiet telephone conversations in the background. Michelle ordered coffee, and the local coffee guy delivered it to our desk. We spoke in peace for hours; later, Michelle's husband came by to say hello.

But I'm Not Sick

I'm originally from El Paso, Texas. I grew up in a mixed-race family. My father was from New York. He passed away when I was a little girl. My mother is from Mexico City. I lived part of my childhood in Mexico and part of it in El Paso, Texas.

I was born with cerebral palsy. The left side of my brain is completely paralyzed. But it doesn't mean that the whole side of my body is paralyzed. I can still use my left hand. Both my legs are paralyzed, and my right arm is paralyzed. When I was younger I couldn't move at all. But through therapy and surgery I became able to move as I do now. However, because of age, I've started losing my movement—the little that I did have when I was younger. [*Laughs.*] Age doesn't work—more so for a person with a disability.

My father was very conservative. He didn't like me going to the doctors. It doesn't mean that he didn't love me. He was more like, "Let's not take her to the doctor. I don't want them to hurt her." He was very overprotective. He thought that the doctors were going to hurt me. He didn't like to see me cry. He passed away when I was seven years old. He saw me when I couldn't move or do anything.

After he passed away, my mother investigated what more could be done to help me. I started going toward more surgeries and therapy. Up until I was fifteen or sixteen, I went through a lot of surgeries, and I lived more in hospitals than at home.

My family has always been overprotective. Even now, my mother and my sisters call me almost every day to see how I'm doing. I live here in Chicago, and I'm married. And they still call me to ask, "Did you eat? Are you OK? Are you at home?" [*Laughs.*] So the overprotectiveness is still there.

With my family, I often think, *Why don't they support me more in what I do?* Like now that I've been quite ill because I'm aging, my family keeps telling me that I should come back so that they can take care of me. They tell me that I should stop working. But *no!* I cannot do that. I have to work. But they don't see it that way. They don't see it like me. They keep saying that I'm sick and that I should stop working. But I'm not sick. I'm disabled. That's part of me. It's not just my family. It's the way society in general sees disability: *Oh, poor you, you're sick and you cannot do this.*

I hate that pity stuff. I can't deal with people who feel pity for myself or for my husband and me. Help us out, but don't feel pity. Don't do it out of pity. Help because you want to do it . . . not because you feel sorry for us. Does the pity make me feel sad? Yes, it does. I feel frustrated, and it makes me feel disempowered. But then I'm like . . . I'm not going to let that bring me down. They don't deserve me being all sad and crying and frustrated. I have to come out of this and turn it around to make something positive. I try not to carry these things around with me. I don't linger. I don't drag them with me.

You're Going to Make Us Look Bad

School was homeschooling for me. When I was little, I couldn't speak. Now I can speak my head off. I had a speech therapist and started speaking when I was around six or seven years old. I didn't go to an actual elementary school before third grade. I remember I went to school a little bit in second grade, but I had a stutter and I couldn't walk myself. So it didn't work. They didn't give me a wheelchair. My mother said, "No, you can do this with a walker." [*Laughs.*]

They thought that I could do more than I could. I didn't use a wheelchair until I was in middle school heading into high school. So the overprotectiveness was also because I was always at home.

When I started school in El Paso, there were kids who were cruel. But there were also some kids that were nice. I used to sing in choir. I loved singing. There were some kids who were excited to help me out. And there were kids who would make fun of me. Even the choir teachers . . . They wanted me to be in the bleachers where you stand up to sing. And I was like, "I cannot do that. I cannot stand. I have to be on a flat surface."

They would say, "Have two of your friends stand next to you and hold you." But I couldn't do that.

The teachers told me, "You're going to make us look bad if you don't do that."

After that, I didn't want to do anything. I just wanted to be by myself. I didn't want to get involved. No choir. No activities. No friends. I withdrew. I kept to myself.

I also needed help to write notes in school. I would ask for help, and people would just say, "I cannot help you right now."

I needed help going to the restroom, and I sometimes didn't get help in time. I would end up just going on myself.

I ended up not wanting to go to school anymore. I was twelve or thirteen years by then.

After that, we went to live in Mexico. It was totally different. I had friends. People thought I was cool. I had friends coming over to our house after school. We'd be out on the street selling candy. But I couldn't get around. There was no accessibility.

So we came back to El Paso when I was sixteen and starting high school. It was challenging. The high school that I wanted to go to wasn't accessible. I wanted to go to this school because it was close to our house. I didn't want to take the little yellow bus that they put us in. They told me to go to the other school. It was farther away, and I didn't want to go to that one. It was for people with disabilities. It was a special school. My mom was like, "But it's for people like you."

And I told her, "That's why! You keep putting me in this box. You keep saying that my daughter is a person with a disability."

She still does—to this day. She still says, "My daughter—the one in the wheelchair." She doesn't say Michelle. She introduces me as her daughter in the wheelchair.

"That's why I don't want to go to that school. I'm not your daughter in the wheelchair. I'm Michelle."

I told my mom that if she wasn't letting me go to the other school, I wasn't going to school at all. [*Laughs.*] So they put elevators in that school. Just for me. That was how I got into fighting for accessibility. I wrote an essay about what it would mean to me to go to that school. I really wanted to go to school because I wanted to be mainstreamed. I didn't want to do resource room. I was smart enough to be in school. I wanted to show that I could do this. It took them the summer to put in elevators.

In the beginning the other kids in high school looked at me as if I was some alien. The elevators went out a couple of times, and there were stairs all over the place. They would hang robes and take me down with the robes. [*Laughs.*] It was so scary.

I had one professor in high school. She had it in her brain that I didn't write the right way. She was like, "No, people who are left handed write like this." She insisted that I have the paper straight in front of me rather than turned.

I told her, "I cannot write like that. I'm left handed yes, but I turn the paper so that I can write."

She said, "No. You need to put your paper forward. If you don't turn your paper forward I'm going to give you an F."

But I couldn't do that. So she sat me in the middle of the room. She told me that she wanted me to write the same sentence twenty times: "I'm going to write with my paper facing forward blah-blah-blah." And she wanted me to do it with the paper facing forward. I refused to do it. So she sent me out of the room.

I walked out. Or I rolled out, and I went to the principal's office. I didn't go because she sent me. I went there, and I complained. Two days later, there was a meeting with the principal, the professor, my mother, my counselor, and me. I told them that I didn't want to be in her class. It was an English literature class. She said that I refused to do the work that she assigned me to do. But that wasn't even true. She wanted me to do stuff that I wasn't able to do, physically. I couldn't do it. She also wanted me to write with my right hand. But I couldn't do that. She insisted and said that I could.

First I felt embarrassed and wanted to cry. But then I was like, *I'm not going to show this person that she got to me.* It was just outrageous. She was really, really stupid and ignorant of the fact that I had a disability and couldn't do what she asked me to do. It was mean. She tried to force me even though I showed her that I could—not—do—it.

We had the meeting. My mother was crying. She doesn't know English. She knows just Spanish. She kept asking, "What are they saying? I feel so bad that you're going through this."

I was trying to calm my mother down. I was so mad at this lady. But I couldn't switch to another teacher. She was the only professor who taught this particular class that I had to take for credit. So I toughed it out. We went back to the classroom. She looked at me with these evil eyes. I knew it. She gave the class an assignment. She gave me extra work to do for that assignment. From then on, she gave me extra stuff.

Another incident was when the professor gave an assignment for Thanksgiving about the pilgrims. The assignment was to go to her home. She lived on a hobby farm. She had pigs and cows and lived in a trailer. I couldn't get in to a trailer home. I had a wheelchair. There were animals all over the place. There was grass and dirt . . . all the things that I cannot go through with my wheelchair. My mother asked, "Why did she have you come all the way out here? Why didn't she give you another assignment? She knows that you cannot do this."

I asked the professor nicely if I could leave because I couldn't do all this. She said, "If you leave, you will get an F for the project."

So I stayed. We had to report on what we saw in the fields. We had to report on the food that we ate. The others decided to go on a hunt. But I couldn't go hunting. The professor told me, "Just stay here with my husband and my kids. But stay outside with the chicken and the ducks and the cows and the pigs." [Laughs.] I was so mad. It was so humiliating.

I felt frustrated that nothing was being done about it. My mother felt frustrated because of the language barrier. She didn't know what to do. My mother's status wasn't the greatest. She wasn't a legal resident of the US at the time. Now she is. She was afraid. That also played a role for me. I was frustrated that my mother couldn't do anything about it. But I was also frustrated that the school system didn't do anything. So what was I supposed to do? I didn't know how to defend myself.

In college, I also had professors who were rude because I had a disability. I was allowed to tape my classes because the professors were speaking so quickly. I had a history class and I had asked if I could put my tape recorder on the table while the professor spoke. He said no. The next day I got him a little microphone to stick on his shirt. I had the tape recorder on my table. I asked him nicely again. He said, "No, it's going to ruin my lecture." [*Laughs.*]

After that, I went to the dean of the college and said, "I'm a student here, and I'm trying to do my best. I want to get my degree like everybody else. I need the professor to do what he needs to do."

They talked to him and he didn't want to allow the recording, but he ended up doing it anyway. How did that experience make me feel? Empowered. After this, I was like, *See! . . . Stuff can be done!*

I had one job counselor in college who said, "For people like you, maybe working in a factory is the best thing." I could quote/unquote "work" in the lines to assemble stuff.

I told him, "I'll have a degree in linguistics and interpretation and you want to keep me in the box of working in a factory. I don't want to do that." [*Laughs.*] He expected nothing from me because I have a disability.

You're Not Going to Be Able to Do It on Your Own

When I was in high school, my mother and I had a car accident. We flipped in the road. My mom ended up in the hospital. They told her that she might not ever be able to walk again. She was in the hospital for six months. She wasn't able to move . . . That put a dent in all of our lives. My sisters were sent to my grandmom. I was sent to my aunt, who was able to care for me. It kind of switched a bulb in my head: *What will you do? You have to do something yourself. Your mom obviously isn't going to be there forever.*

After the accident and having my mother in the hospital, I learned how to dress myself. I learned how to put my shoes on. I learned how to take a shower by myself. That was another thing. Before, I would ask my mom or my sisters to help me into the shower. And they would take forever to help me. And I hate waiting. I can wait for a little bit, but not for an hour or two. It is humiliating, sitting there waiting. So I said, "Screw this."

I wanted to learn to do it myself. I fell. I hurt my legs. I busted my head. But I learned how to transfer myself from the chair to the toilet and back to the chair. I learned it because of perseverance and because I don't have so much patience. I learned it because of my mom. I didn't want to rely on her and others. And because of not wanting people to do it for me if they don't want to. I got angry. I also got frustrated and sad at the same time of looking at people who were thinking, *Now she's asking for help again.*

Years later when I was moving out of my mother's house to live on my own, my sisters and my mother were like, "You're not going to be able to do it on your own."

Instead of being supportive, my mother got mad when I said that I wanted to buy a house. She didn't talk to me for two months. I asked her why she was mad at me instead of being supportive. She said, "Because you had told me that you and I were going to be together forever—that we would live together and grow old together."

"Mom, my two sisters are married and have kids. Why are you so stuck on me being here? We can visit each other. I want to spread my wings too. I want to have a life."

I was in my early thirties. It was basically more about her needs than mine. She wanted me to be close to her.

All my life my mother has helped me out. She would always help, and we would always get into frictions: "Don't put this on. You want to show too much. What about this shirt? Not this color." We always had frictions. So when I moved to live by myself, I was really looking forward to it. *I can do whatever I want. If I want to eat this, I can. [Laughs.] If I want to dress like this, I can. Whatever I want!*

But then she asked me if she could be my personal assistant. I didn't think it would be a good idea. But I also wanted to save money, and I wanted to help my mom. I knew her situation. So I decided to try it out. But it wasn't a good idea. She wanted to come to my house at whatever time she wanted to. I told her when I had to go to a specific place at a specific time. And then she would argue why I was going out so early. She wanted to know where I was going and what time I was coming back. If it was nighttime, she wanted to know why I was going out so late: "Why are you wearing that? When are you coming back?"

It was too much. I told her that it wasn't going to work: "Mom, I love you and I understand your situation, but this isn't going to work."

She cried when I told her that I didn't want her as my personal assistant anymore. She cried when I told her that I was going to hire somebody else. She sobbed and sobbed and sobbed. She told my sisters that I had fired her as a mother and that I had fired her as a personal assistant. I never said that.

That wasn't the case. I just didn't want us to be fighting and arguing about what I was doing and where I was going.

So family can make you feel bad in the moment. But family also makes you stronger. That's what happened to me. What made me a lot stronger and empowered was that I don't like to be told that I cannot do something. People have told me, "You're not going to be able to move out. You are going to come back and not make it on your own."

I haven't been back to live in my mom's house since I moved out. When I told my mother that I was moving to Chicago, she flipped—"You're not going to be able to go out by yourself."

But I'm married. I live here. I have a job. [*Laughs.*] So don't tell me I can't do stuff.

That will push me to action. These things made me stronger. I use my anger to empower myself and to empower others. When I'm angry . . .

Why Date Somebody with a Disability?

One time I was at my house with a person. We were watching a movie. My mother came in because she had a key to my house. We weren't doing anything. We were just watching a movie and holding hands. She closed the door quickly. She called me from outside the house with her cell phone. "Why didn't you tell me you had company?"

I was like, "You didn't tell me that you were coming, so how could I tell you that I had company? Second, you just walk in and waltz out and shut the door like a crazy. [*Laughs.*] We weren't doing anything. But if we were, you would have scared the shit out of us."

She told my sister that I was indecent. But it was my house within my own four walls, and I wasn't even doing anything. [*Laughs.*] I was with somebody who was my partner at the time. So that's where the overprotectiveness plays in. She also said, "And he's a person with a disability too!"

I'm married to someone with a disability. I've always dated persons with disabilities. My family has always asked, "Why date somebody with a disability? Are you guys going to be able to do anything?"

That has nothing to do with it. As long as your partner loves you and cares about you, whatever we do or don't do doesn't matter. But for my family, I don't know. [*Laughs.*] It's just weird.

They See the Wheelchair

When I was looking for employment myself, I would apply for a job and be called for an interview. So I would show up for the interview. First thing they see . . . They don't even see me. They see the wheelchair. "Oh, we didn't know that you're in a wheelchair."

I don't mention the wheelchair when I apply for a job. I don't say that I'm a person with a disability: "You asked for my qualifications for the job, right? I don't have to tell you that I have a disability."

It automatically disqualified me. I felt like being in a sport where I had done something wrong and I was disqualified. Well, me having a disability, is that wrong?

I once went for an interview for a job in the reception of a doctor's office. Answering a phone isn't a problem for me; I can do it. He said no as soon as he saw the chair. He looked at me and said, "Oh, we were looking for somebody who could be behind the counter and move around."

I said, "I can move around, and I can be behind the counter."

"No, you will be a liability because if something happens, you won't be able to move away from the counter fast enough." [*Laughs.*]

That was so stupid. I felt that I was being disqualified because of the supposed risk that they would take hiring me . . . because of the liability that I was for them. I left. I felt angry.

I Don't Want to Give Them a Door to My Vulnerability

I'm more cautious with new people. Especially in friendships, I'm very cautious. On the whole, I very much keep to myself. I'm a very quiet person. This conversation . . . it's just because you're asking me these questions. I normally don't talk unless I've known the person forever. I'm very cautious about how I say things and what I say. I don't want people to hurt me or say things that . . . I guess I don't want to give them a door to my vulnerability. [*Sighs.*] That's how I feel. I'm cautious, so I just keep to myself.

BUT WE DO NOT LIKE PITY!

EDWIN, LUISA, ALFREDO, ALBERTO, JOSE, AND MICHELLE

I met the Cambiando Vidas (Changing Lives) group at Access Living. It's a group of Latinos with disabilities that organize for community support and disability education in the Latino community in Chicago. There were around ten of us in the room. I apologized for not being able to communicate in Spanish. They repeated that it wasn't a problem; Michelle acted as the interpreter. It was hot and humid, but there was no shortage of kind words, water, and cookies. It was like family.

I Was Always Behind

Edwin

I went to a high school where I was the only Latino. It was an all-white school. There was definitely discrimination against me. I was bullied. I was called names. Constantly. The students called me names that normally were directed toward Latinos, like "Pork Chops."

I also felt discrimination that I couldn't put my finger on, by the teachers. They were subtle. I felt basically ignored. During high school years, I was also blind, and I think that added to the degree of discrimination. It felt really bad. I was being ignored and left behind. This is another topic; I'm a Braille reader and sometimes I wouldn't get my books in Braille until months into the school year. So actually, I *was* always behind!

I Was Trying to Be Tough for My Daughter

Luisa

I feel discrimination when I get on the bus. Because of the fact that I'm disabled and I don't speak English. I feel that the drivers discriminate against me. I'm in a wheelchair and they don't tie me down when I get on the bus. They don't pay attention to me when I ask for help.

I was once traveling with my young daughter. The driver didn't tie me down. So my daughter started crying when she realized. The driver didn't do anything. My daughter got really scared and started crying, "Why do you do that? My mom is in a wheelchair, and she needs assistance."

And the driver still didn't do anything about it.

So I was telling my daughter, "Don't worry. I'm OK. Just come over here, and I'll take care of it. Just come near me."

I was trying to take care of my daughter and make her stop crying. I tried to be tough and show her that everything was fine. I tried to show her that everything was gonna be OK. I was trying to be tough for my daughter. But I really didn't feel it was right. I felt that it was a wrongdoing of the driver. It was humiliating.

I don't know what to do about it. I know it's discrimination. I know it's wrong. But I don't know what to do about it. How do I defend myself?

You Don't Have Nothing to Tell About, So Just Go Home

Alfredo

For a long time, I've been looking for a job. I got a call last month to go to the suburbs for a job interview at a supermarket. I got there ten minutes early before my job interview. But this person asked me, "Do you have any job experience?"

I told her, "No, but here's my résumé, and I have a lot of training."

When the time was up, she told me, "I have other persons who do have job experience. You don't have nothing to tell about, so just go home. I'll get to you later."

I didn't get the interview.

I feel it's because I'm not really that tall. Sometimes they just look at me and they bend their head to the side and do this face: "Oh . . ."

I think it's because I'm Hispanic. I also think it's because of my disability and my size.

One Day I Found a Rope
Alberto

I was born different, with a disability. When I was a little kid, I was treated really badly by my family members. In school they said, "You're a dumb person." They called me names: "dumb special ed person," "retard Mexican."

One day I found a rope. I tied the rope to the ceiling, and I stood on a chair. I was thinking twice in my head. Like, *I hate myself.* But then I changed my mind and took away the rope. I was like eight or nine years old.

When I was a teenager, I turned toward bullying. So I hurt people who were different. So I beat them up. I looked like a gang member.

I feel bad. Because I used to be really nice. As a kid, I was a really sweet person. But I changed. As a teenager I changed to anger. I became an aggressive person. I'm sorry. I feel sorry.

The Wheelchairs Are Coming
Jose

I use CTA [Chicago Transit Authority] a lot. Just a couple of days ago, I used CTA. I have a prosthetic leg. It's difficult for me to walk long distances, and I use a cane. I was on the bus. I was sitting in a seat that's for people with disabilities. And then a person behind me said, "Sir, you're gonna need to move. Sir, you're gonna need to move."

She patted me twice on my back and asked me to move. And I was like, "Why?"

"Because there's a baby carriage that needs to get on the bus."

And I was like, "No, I'm not going to move. I'm a person with a disability."

"Sir, you're gonna need to move."

And I had to tell her again that I'm a person with a disability. "Do I have to lift up my pant so that you can see that I have a prosthetic leg?"

Besides, those seats are not for strollers. They're for people with disabilities and the elderly. There is a huge sign that says that.

Me and my wife and Michelle and her husband live around the same area. So when we're all together, we take the bus at the same stop. When the bus stops, we hear people start saying, "Oh, here come the people in the wheelchairs."

And then we still want to get on. But the driver doesn't say one word. He doesn't ask the people to move. So we're forced to wait for another bus. It's uncomfortable for us because we have to wait. But it's also uncomfortable to hear people saying these things. The fact is that we're not even considered as people. We're just "the wheelchairs are coming."

It makes me feel bad because I feel that people put barriers on us. Society puts barriers on us. But we're people like everybody else. We wanna be productive like everybody else. But society really limits us so we can't be out and about and do our things.

It's the Pity

Michelle

There are not just these stories. There are tons of other stories. Within our Latino community there are a lot of stories that are repetitive.

We're always kept at home. Our community thinks we don't wanna go out. Why would we go through the hassle of being on a bus? What are people gonna say?

Within our Latino community, that's very common. Very, very common. It's because of family. It's because of society. We're regarded as nonproductive individuals because we have a disability. We should be staying at home being taken care of.

In the Latino community there's a phrase about this that we all know. We hear it all the time. It's something like, "Oh. Oh. Poor you." It's the pity. But we do not like pity!

10 | I AM NOT INSPIRING

"I'M NOT YOUR INSPIRATION, thank you very much." These were the words used by the Australian comedian, journalist, and disability rights activist Stella Young. She described how exhausted she was being seen and treated as exceptional.* It is not that people with disabilities do not have challenges in their everyday life. But these challenges stem more from physical and attitudinal barriers in society than from the individual bodies of people with disabilities.

Most majority people mean it in a positive way when they tell a person with a disability that she is inspiring. They feel that they mean well when they give out compliments. One of the reasons is that most majority people do not experience people with disabilities as professionals, as their doctors and craftsmen. Teachers and accountants typically do not use wheelchairs. Persons with disabilities are typically not seen as so-called ordinary people. Instead, most majority people have learned that people with disabilities are exceptional, especially if they are doing well. People with disabilities are basically in this world to be pitied or to inspire.

As James Charlton writes, "If a person with a disability is 'successful,' or seems to have a good life, he or she is seen as brave and courageous or special or brilliant. Given the intrinsic abnormality or awfulness of disability, anyone living a 'normal' or ordinary life must be extraordinary."†

---

* Stella Young, "I Am Not Your Inspiration, Thank You Very Much," TED video, April 2014, https://youtu.be/8K9Gg164Bsw, 9:16.
† James I. Charlton, *Nothing About Us Without Us: Disability Oppression and Empowerment* (Berkeley: University of California Press, 2000), 52.

But most people with disabilities do not want to be pitied or admired; they simply want to get on with their lives without being stared at.

Majority people have often learned that disability is a bad thing and that living with a disability is sad. As Stella Young describes, society has objectified people with disabilities in a way that benefits people without disabilities. Majority people get to think that, however bad their lives are, it could be worse. It could be those lives that people with disabilities live.

But living with a disability is not a sad and bad thing. And a disability does not make the person exceptional. As Andrew Solomon writes, "Being anomalous does not deprive anyone of the right or ability to be typical."* Being extraordinary and being ordinary are not incompatible goals.

Jacky Dorantes describes in chapter 1 how people come up to her and tell her that she inspires them. Her reaction is that it does not feel like a compliment because she is seen as someone who is supposed to have a shitty life: "I don't fucking know you. I don't know you. You don't know me. How the hell's that inspiring? [. . .] So really what you're telling me is that you expect me to do a lot less because I'm disabled. The mere fact that I'm doing what everyone else is doing impresses you."

The reality is that those compliments of inspiration can be flat-out degrading. Because nobody wants to be admired for simply doing ordinary tasks. It is just not inspiring to live a typical life. It is not inspiring to get up in the morning, go to work, have lunch with colleagues, go home, walk the dog, make dinner and eat, see friends, or watch TV. These are just ordinary things that are not particularly admirable. In this chapter, Keianna Parker explains how people tell her that she is amazing because she goes to the mall by herself. Keianna finds it sad. "I'm not . . . I'm just a regular person who happens to not see. I'm living my life, just like you do. I'm not a hero. I'm just regular."

Efforts may be inspiring, but as Birdy Holzmueller says in this chapter, "You don't wanna be inspirational just because you exist!"

---

* Andrew Solomon, *Far from the Tree: Parents, Children, and the Search for Identity* (New York: Scribner, 2012), 688.

I'M GOING TO GIVE THEM A SHOW

AMBER SMOCK

Amber is the director of advocacy at Access Living and was the first person I met at Access Living in 2014. I am truly grateful to Amber for introducing me to committed people in the Chicagoan disability community. I later worked at Access Living and got used to hearing Amber's loud, contagious laughter in the hallways. We finally sat down for an interview for this book in 2018, and it was a privilege to learn from Amber's sharp wit and experience and to witness her strong energy close up.

I'm Identifying Myself as Deaf

When I was three and a half years old, my parents noticed that I wasn't speaking correctly. I was able to talk, but it didn't sound right. The first doctor they took me to said that I had mental retardation. My parents felt like that was not correct. They knew what the developmental milestones were and that I was meeting or exceeding those milestones. The only thing that was different with me was not talking correctly. So they took me to a second doctor who made a referral for a hearing test. That doctor had a little bit more of a clue. [*Laughs.*] Anyway, the audiologist told my parents that I had a severe hearing loss.

The spectrum of hearing loss is mild, moderate, severe, and profound. I am right on the cusp of profound, but I have enough hearing that I can make use of hearing aids. My parents wanted to know what kinds of support I needed. The audiologist said, "Well, she is going to need to get hearing aids. But lip-reading should not be too hard for her because she's already doing it." My parents asked how the doctor knew that. The doctor said, "I'll show you."

Without using his voice, he looked at me and asked, "What are you gonna do today?" And I said, "We're gonna go buy some ice cream." So basically, it was decided that I was getting hearing aids on both ears. I would also have speech therapy to work on speaking correctly. In school, I would rely on lip-reading, and I would have to sit in the front of the classroom. Basically, for the next twelve years we would coach the teachers to make sure they didn't turn their backs on me. Because I was reading their lips! So I can hear some, but I really, really need to see peoples' faces, and there is quite a bit that I will miss.

I used to identify myself as a person with a hearing loss . . . as a person who wore hearing aids. After I became more accustomed to the deaf community and the deaf perspective, I would more often identify myself as deaf. The trick is that deaf people come in a lot of flavors. Some deaf people can hear a little bit. Some deaf people don't hear at all. Some deaf people talk. Some deaf people really don't do that. Some deaf people read lips. Some deaf people really can't. There's a lot of diversity within people who self-identify as deaf. When you self-identify, you talk about a cultural perspective, right? You are not talking about your medical diagnosis; you're talking about the fact that you primarily live life through a visual lens. If, for example, I am cooking, I cook by watching. I don't cook by listening to the food bubble in the pan.

An important part of a deaf culture perspective is valuing sign language. Using it, valuing it, seeing it as equal with spoken language, that is also a cultural value to have. And that's how today I'm identifying myself as deaf.

I Rejected Inspiration Porn by Gut Instinct

I have a story to tell you. When I was sixteen I belonged to a high school club. This club involved volunteering different things in the communities. So we would clean up somebody's yard or clean up somebody's house. At the end of the year, we were invited to lunch at the local civic club. So we were at the lunch, and we were all sitting there eating the food. My high school history teacher came running over to me and asked me if I would like to stand up and say a few words. And I said, "What do you mean stand up and say a few words? About what?" And she said, "I think that it would be really great if you could stand up and say a few words about how important it is to volunteer even when you can't hear. Because I think that they would really like that." And I said, "What does that have to do with volunteering?" And she said,

"Just say a few words about how important volunteering is and how anybody can do it, even if they have a disability and stuff." I was just like—but when you're sixteen, you are still figuring things out—*OK, I feel there is something wrong about this situation, but I don't know what to do about it. So for today, I'm gonna go along with it.* So I got up and said something awful, you know, like, "I really love volunteering with the club. We went to Miss Jones's house, and anybody can do this kind of thing even though they have a hearing loss." And I swear, it got all this applause.

I thought about it afterward. I sat down and I thought, *I'm never doing that kind of thing again. That's ridiculous!* I think that was the beginning of me feeling, *So, OK, if people are going to look at me because I have a disability, then I'm going to give them a show! If I walk into a room and I have one interpreter, two interpreters, etc., it's fine if they're looking at me. I have their attention.*

On a general level, inspiration porn is basically people with disabilities being placed in the public view and other people telling stories about them that inspire feelings of awe or pity for doing something ordinary. Inspiration porn tends to be something that catches on and goes viral. It can be as simple as one incident, but more often it tends to be repeated, like the sharing of a story as super inspirational.

For deaf people, inspiration porn has specific shadings . . . What happens is that hearing people will be overawed by deaf people doing something normal: "Deaf people can drive! Can you believe it? That deaf person is driving. I just can't believe that a deaf person can drive a car."

I felt very early on that people are weird about disability. I rejected inspiration porn by gut instinct. But I also understood that the ability to command attention gives you some power. Today there are things that I want to be done. There are things that I'm trying to do, and I need people to work with me on it. I'm OK with having attention, but I'm not going to let it go into the inspiration porn zone. Being able to set boundaries is like a muscle, you know. Being able to control what people say around you is hard. Once in a while, I will come upon a person, and it's like everything he or she knows about disability will suddenly be attached to me. But it helps when you are able to set more boundaries and when you insist on being seen for what you choose to be seen for.

To find the borderline between inspiration porn and being praised for something that you have done well, first ask, "Do you know the people praising you?" Second, "Do you know what you have done? Do you know for a fact that what you're doing is ordinary or exceptional?" So self-knowledge is part of it. There is a balance in figuring it out. I also think that segregated settings perpetuate the inspiration porn practice. If people are segregated and shut away and then suddenly let out to fly away like butterflies, that tends to elevate the specialness of it all.

Deaf Doesn't Mean That You Don't Have a Sense of What Is Right or Wrong

In school, I know that my teachers made an effort to make sure that I could understand them. The vast majority of them did pretty well with it. But the interesting thing about having a disability related to communication is that you are not totally sure about what you miss.

I was there . . . [*long pause*] in terms of social interaction. But I really preferred one-on-one conversations so that I could easily understand people. If I were in a group, more often I would not understand but just kind of ride along. I constantly had to make a decision: *Do I wanna be here or do I not wanna be here? Am I able to stick it out so that I can maybe have a one-on-one conversation? Is that worth it, or not?*

Did I feel left out? Sometimes. Yes, sometimes. But I didn't think about it a lot. Sleepovers were tough. Because they were overnight, and there were extended conversations. School was OK because the classes broke up the school day. I do remember incidents of definitely being bullied by friends or being used as part of a joke because I couldn't hear well. Like a friend would tell me about a bad thing that had happened. I would totally believe it and didn't realize that everybody had set it up as a joke. Being who I am, I let them know that it wasn't OK! I mean, just because you have a disability or you're deaf doesn't mean that you don't have a sense of what is right or wrong. And I think you have to figure out the internal resources to stand up for yourself. Fortunately, I had people around me that were very good at showing me how to do that. But, you know, I wonder sometimes if there were examples of being left out that I just had no idea about. Because I can't eavesdrop! I don't know what people say, you know . . .

I always felt that they were the ones who were wrong. That it was not my problem. [*Laughs.*] Some people get very down on themselves and feel like it must be their fault. I was very fortunate to have parents that would tell me, "You're smart. You're talented. You can do a bunch of stuff. Now go clean up your room." So they were encouraging, but they were also very realistic that I had to work hard. But they didn't make it disability specific. They just said, "You have to be a hard worker. You have to help clean up the yard. You need to go to school on time. You need to do your homework." It was the same expectation that they would have for any kid. But they would also encourage me and say, "You have a pretty dress on, and I like your hair." So I had a lot to think about myself that was positive. And when somebody would try to make me feel bad, I would feel bad. But I would also be like, *It's your problem. It's not mine.*

I Never Internalized Ableism

Ableism is basically discrimination and social prejudice against people with disabilities. I am not sure why it is that some people with disabilities are more prone to internalize ableism than others. I don't know if it has to do with support. I don't know if it has to do with having family members that are supportive of you and believe in you. I don't know if it has to do with race or poverty. But for whatever reason, some folks are definitely struggling with internalizing ableism.

My folks never blamed me for my disability. They never referred to me as a person with special needs. They referred to me by saying, "Our daughter wears hearing aids" or "Our daughter has a hearing loss." But more often, they'd say, "Our daughter has straight As. Our daughter does this thing. Our daughter is very creative. She enjoys animals." They talked about all the other things that I did. And they would sit down with me and communicate these things with me—face to face. My mother, in particular, made it a point to say exactly what she thought was positive about me. I think that if you're in a situation in your life where you have to guess the feelings of the people around you, it's very difficult. It is much more empowering if somebody interacts with you and says, "I believe in you. I think you are important. I think you are amazing. You're kind and you're nice." Being direct about those things is essential, and I never internalized ableism. I sometimes felt bad about things that people said. But I always felt like it was their problem.

You Also Have to Talk About Anti-oppression

When you talk about oppression, you also have to talk about anti-oppression. Anti-oppressive practices in the disability world mean taking people as they are. It means not fixating on diagnoses. It means listening to people. It means seeing the value that people bring. It means communicating clearly with them that they are of value and importance to you. It means vouching for each other. It also means being visible if you have a large public platform. Senator Tammy Duckworth, for example, has a large public platform. She's also disabled, and she uses her disability to beat back oppression from different kinds of people.

I'M JUST A REGULAR PERSON DOING REGULAR THINGS

KEIANNA PARKER

I visited Keianna on a late Saturday morning. It was a sunny November week-end in the predominantly African American neighborhood of Austin. Keianna's home was a typical Chicagoan two-family house. Her mother said a quick hello and then took a nap while we talked in the dark living room. The curtains kept the sun out. When I left, Keianna was going out to treat herself—it was her day off, and she had decided to get her nails done.

You Have to Learn How to Do It Yourself

I grew up in this area. We've been here since I was three. So a *looong* time.

I'm blind. I have what's called Leber's congenital amaurosis. It's an eye condition. Visually, it means that I have no peripheral vision. I've never had any. But as a child I still had quite a lot of central vision. I wore glasses, but I could see and run around with friends. I could read and all that. They knew that this condition is degenerative and that I was going to lose more vision. So I learned to read Braille at age ten.

When I was like eight, I lost some vision. After high school, I lost some more vision. In 2000 I lost a little more. And basically, today I don't have any vision left. But I had enough to know what the world looks like. I know what colors are.

I am the middle child. Both my younger sister and I have the condition. My sister's is not as severe as mine.

231

As children, we were raised to be as quote/unquote "normal" as possible. I knew I couldn't see as well as everybody else. But that was never shown to me to be something to be ashamed of. We were not coddled children at all. It was momma's greatest philosophy [*laughs*]: "I'm gonna show you how to do it . . . help you learn how to do it. Because I'm not always gonna be here to do things for you. You have to learn how to do it yourself."

That attitude has been instilled in me, and it's helped me become strong. It helped me know that life is going to kick you. It just happens to everyone. That's what happens. You have to get up and shake it off. Because when all is said and done, no one is going to come take care of you. My momma always said, "No, I don't have any babies. I have grown kids because I've raised you and given you the tools to be grown and independent."

I'm sure, at some point, I must have internalized things. But I only had those momentary depressions. For me, it's the support system that I've had— my friends and, for sure, my family. I remember when I was like six and in first grade. I think I was frustrated with something that I couldn't see. I was in the little adaptive room, and my teacher was trying to help me. I had a tantrum and an outburst: "I hate this. I hate this not being able to fully see. If I can't see it all, then I don't wanna see at all."

Well, who knew that my teacher would call my mom and tell her all about it? So when I got home, my mom was like, "So you said you wanna not see at all, if you can't see everything. Ha. Well, try it!"

So she made me wear . . . she made me wear a little blindfold and go around the house for like an hour. Just to give me some sense of what your world would be if you had no vision at all.

It was to help me be grateful for who and what I was. And of course, I bumped into stuff and ended up crying in my room . . . But Mom came and talked to me. "Do you see what I'm trying to tell you? That you should be grateful for what you have?" [*Pauses. Swallows hard.*] It still brings up emotions now . . .

We've talked about it later. My mom's said to me, "You know, I was so mad because I had to fight for you to even go to regular school. They wanted to put you into one of those programs just for the blind. I had to fight for you to go to regular school, and I was just so mad."

You're the Blind Girl

In school I definitely noticed that I was different than them. But no one made me feel bad about being different. I didn't notice that my difference was supposed to be a bad thing. I don't remember . . . ever being bullied. I don't remember feeling marginalized. There were things that I didn't do that everybody else did. But then again, I didn't want to. [*Laughs.*] My friends would say, "Let's go to homecoming."

And I was like, "I have no desire to do that."

In college . . . I should have been more popular. I was popular in class, in that, you know, I was smart. I knew things. But I was still different enough that they didn't think to include me in things or talk to me outside class, because "you're the blind girl."

I guess it was a little lonely.

You Inspire Me

People are uncomfortable with what they don't know. That's why there's discrimination, period. That's why there's bigotry. We are afraid of what we don't know. I think one of the biggest fears that a quote/unquote "regular" person has . . . is being blind: "Holy crap, how do you even do anything?" A lot of times, that's the first question people ask. I'm on the bus and someone goes, "Oh my gosh, you're out. You're out here by yourself."

And I'm like, "Well. Yes. How is my life gonna . . . I mean, I don't live in my basement. I have to go out and live my life."

In some form—one way or another—that question is always there: "If it were me, I would be sitting at home waiting for someone to do things for me."

And I'm like, "No. You wouldn't. Because life has to go on."

I love, love, love shopping. It's my thing. It makes me happy. [*Laughs.*] When life is crappy, I need a little retail therapy. Even if it's just to go to the mall and touch some things, try some stuff on, and leave everything behind. I still feel better after having done it. [*Laughs.*] For me, it's totally normal. Because I was raised in a household where [*laughs*] "we're not gonna do it for you. You have to learn how to do it yourself."

But I meet people in the mall who are like, "You're here by yourself. You went shopping by yourself."

And I'm like, "Uh huh. Yeah. Didn't you come here by yourself?"

"Yes. But . . ." You can just hear them stop themselves before they say, "But I'm not blind."

And I'm like, "Yes, but my life is not over because I'm blind."

My life is not limited to my blindness. And it's sad that people don't understand that.

I think, looking at it and talking to you, that it's discrimination. They have separated me into this group. I'm supposed to be in this little box. That box is disabled. Like, I need to be somewhere and taken care of. But I don't. I don't live in that box. I've never felt that I needed to be that person. So when people [*laughs*] say to me, "Oh, you came here by yourself."

"Well, yes, I did."

"Oh, you're so, so amazing. I just feel like you're my hero."

"I'm not . . . I'm just a regular person who happens to not see. I'm living my life, just like you do. I'm not a hero. I'm just regular."

But sadly, they don't see it in that way: "It is heroic. It is amazing that you get out and do things."

I just think, *It's sad that you don't see that I'm normal. I'm trying to be as normal as I can. I wanna blend in, just like you do. I can't really, because I'm walking around with a sixty-pound furry thing. But I'm still as quote/unquote "normal" as I can be for me. And normal for me is getting out and doing things.*

People say all the time, "You inspire me. You're my hero. I'm just so amazed by you."

I'm not amazing. [*Laughs.*] I'm not amazing. I'm not heroic. I'm not inspiring. I'm just a regular person doing regular things.

It really frustrates me. Don't put my blindness in the category of physical ailment. I'm not sick. I just can't see!

Mostly, I feel discrimination comes because people see my difference more than they want to see my similarities. People want to separate me, put me in this category . . . more than they want to see me as a person who has something extra.

They Don't See Me

Looking back on it, I think I never really dated in high school. And I think it's for the same reason that people don't understand my blindness. So they'll talk to me [*sighs*] in a social situation. But they don't really want to get to know me or sit down to try to know me because "You're different. And I'm uncomfortable."

There definitely were times where I was like, *I have to be the problem. Everybody else has a boyfriend. All my friends are having sex. How come I'm not having sex?*

I've had a lot of friends but never anybody in my life. [*Sighs.*] I'm forty this year, and still there's just me and my dog. Usually, it's . . . You know, if the same things keep happening, you've gotta think, *Is it you?*

And it's me in that I'm different. Sadly, it's them in that they won't see that my differences don't make me completely separate from them. I definitely know by now: It's not me. It's them. I'm the best me I can be!

People would say, "After work we're gonna go to this place."

And I'm like, "I wanna go. Where is it?"

"Well . . . We'll let you know . . ." [*Laughs.*]

And you know? When it's time to go, I look up and they're gone.

"Uh huh. Well, OK . . . I guess me and my dog are going home again." [*Laughs.*]

So people are like, "I don't know how to see you as a person . . . as a person first, . . . rather than your disability first."

I want somebody in my life to be my partner . . . not my keeper . . . not my crutch . . . I think that's intimidating to a lot of people. Not just men . . . but people in general: "You're different and you're disabled. You're supposed to need me to do things for you. If you don't need me to do things for you, then I don't know how to relate to you." Which is sad.

Friends ask me, "Aren't you lonely?"

"Yeah. Did I plan to be forty years old and still not married? No."

I know the issue. It's partly me in that I'm not willing to live in the basement . . . I'm not willing to conceal myself and pretend to be somebody that I'm not. But sadly, a bigger part of the issue is that people around me do not see me as a person first, instead of seeing my disability. People see the disability. They don't see me.

[*Guide dog comes over to Keianna and puts head in her lap.*]

Are you here to comfort me? [*Sighs deeply.*]

A lot of men are intimidated by strong women. And then, of course, a strong black woman with a disability is even harder for them to understand.

Because, you know, my disability is supposed to make me weaker. It's supposed to make me more dependent on them. They're supposed to need to take care of me. And I'm like, "But I don't need you to take care of me. I need you to be my partner, to be my friend. You know? Go through life with me . . . I don't need you to carry me through it."

That's something that's an eternal struggle for me: "You don't see me as someone who could be your equal!"

HIS EXISTENCE IS NOT INSPIRATIONAL

AARON AND BIRDY HOLZMUELLER

I met with Birdy at a café in Evanston. It was early June and we sat outdoors with our coffee and delicious scones. The traffic was occasionally noisy, and the wind a bit gusty. But coming from Denmark, I love being outside whenever weather permits. I was happy that Birdy enjoyed taking in the light as much as I did.

A month later, I met Birdy and her son Aaron in their home. Aaron had just finished his junior year at Evanston Township High School. When I arrived, he was completely absorbed in the Tour de France bicycle race on TV. Once it was over, we talked in the living room, which was full of books and sports equipment. Birdy was in the room next door, and once in a while Aaron called out for his mom. He just wanted to make sure that he was allowed to share certain things with me.

You Just Wanna Be a Mom in a Park

Birdy

My son was born with a diffuse and catastrophic brain injury as a result of a very bad birth process that no one fully understands. Shortly after birth, he had seizures, and it was clear that there was some pretty bad brain damage to him as a very young infant. There was a lot of assessment and testing and different sorts of early interventions with him. The result being—he's now seventeen and he has a form of cerebral palsy. He has a very poor core body, and he has a lot of spasticity in all four of his limbs. But he does walk, and he's actually very active in sports and different things. And he has epilepsy. That combination is something that if you read about it, as I did when he was very young, it looks very dire and stark. Many if not most children with that combination have a lot of challenges. In the end, he's affected . . . but not as catastrophically, I would say. I don't think of his narrative as particularly catastrophic.

Aaron spoke very early and was very verbal and very social. So by the time he was three or four, it became clear that he was going to be a boy with an average or above-average intelligence, which met one set of trajectories for him. But his physical milestones were delayed. He didn't walk before he was two and a half.

When he was probably twenty months old, he would scoot on his left side and be motoring around. We were outside one time, and this woman came up to me. She said, "I'm a physical therapist, and I have to tell you that I think there's something wrong with your son."

I was just in the right mood, so I said to her, "*No*, really? Do you really think so?"

And she did this whole thing: "Yes, I really do. Because he's not using his blah-blah-blah . . ."

"Really. You think so? Oh my goodness! I guess I'll have to check it out."

There was a lot of that kind of stuff when he was little. When you're in a playground and other mothers talk to you. "Oh, how old is he?"

"He's two."

And then the whole dynamic changed when he was scooting around on his left butt. And at a certain point, I'd just say, "He has cerebral palsy. He had a massive brain injury when he was born."

That would shut people up. [*Laughs.*]

That was back when he was so young and little was known. We just didn't know so many things. I think the main feeling or thought that I had at the time was *You have no idea. I wouldn't wish this on anyone else. But you're not in my shoes. You don't know what this is. Don't . . .*

And I have mixed feelings about this reaction of mine. Because yes, of course I want to educate people. It's good for my son. It's good for other kids coming along. But sometimes you just wanna be a mom in a park enjoying your kid. And not focus on it. So I guess it's . . . I don't know what that feeling is. Discomfort. Feeling like you're being watched or judged in a certain way.

I think a lot of well-intended, good people just don't even know. And I think a lot about the term *microaggression*. You know? Just like little insults that are based on a physical or some other sort of status. The term gets used a lot around race. With my son . . . because he's physically different . . . if he walks into a room, everyone notices he walks differently. His gait is different. People make assumptions based on that that might or might not be true. But a lot of the assumptions they make are around his intelligence.

I Guess I Just Have to Adjust

Aaron

I haven't really experienced much discrimination at my school. But it's because I go to Evanston Township High School, and it's so progressive. For the most part, we're known to be a progressive school.

Being a person with a disability in Evanston, I feel kind of sheltered. But if I go somewhere else . . . I know there's discrimination out there. And it's going to be something that I'm gonna experience. Like when I go to college, there'll be people from all over the state. Perhaps, depending on where I go, from all over the country. And some may not have seen someone with CP before. And they might . . . You never know . . .

Here, I know that I'm not likely to experience discrimination. But depending on where I go to college, I might experience a fair amount. I guess I just have to—*hmm* . . . adjust.

Show Them How Much You're like Them

Birdy

I don't know if you would call that discrimination . . . but it was probably the first challenge that Aaron faced in school. He's quadriplegic, and he had trouble going to the bathroom. So he went to kindergarten with a full-time paraprofessional. The school thought they would be great by putting a teacher that he'd had in pre-K class into that program with him. But unfortunately, that teacher just really didn't wanna change dirty pull-ups. It was really a difficult kindergarten year from that perspective. It was an awful experience for us. He didn't need much support except for that. We were trying to get him to learn to use the bathroom. He would do things like come up to this woman an hour before school was out and say, "I think I'm dirty. Could you help me change my pull-up?"

And she would say, "Oh, your mommy will do it when you're at home."

And it was like, "So you're basically making the decision to leave my child dirty because you're uncomfortable with this?"

Ultimately what I ended up doing . . . and this is a strategy that I've used on and off. I'm lucky enough and blessed that I have a flexible job, and I'm able to do this type of thing. I ended up moving into the classroom. And I said to the principal, "Unless you can guarantee that someone is going to be here who's gonna help him with this, I'll just be in the classroom."

I moved in. And the teacher was fine. We got along just fine. It took about a week and a half before they made the commitment and hired someone with the ability to take care of this.

There's another story. This is from the beginning of middle school. There was a kid who was new to the school who budged Aaron in the PE line. And one of the kids who had been in school with Aaron since kindergarten, who actually had his own behavioral issues at school, turned to this other child: "Did you just budge Aaron?"

He said, "No."

And Aaron said, "Yes, he did."

And this boy said, "I don't know where you're from. But here we don't budge people with cerebral palsy just because we can. That's not nice. We just don't do that!" [Laughs.]

There was a lot of that kind of stuff. It was a very nice group of kids in school. Aaron had friends all though middle school.

I think high school has been interesting. Aaron is very active in sports. He runs cross-country. He swims. And then he runs track. I think he has friends or people that he's friendly with. But a lot less social activity outside school. It's not really clear to me whether that's because he's been excluded or because he's actually being included but he's just tired at the end of the day with all the school stuff and sports. That he doesn't really have it in him to do these other things. Or he just doesn't quite feel comfortable.

But I do think in general he feels included in school. I also think he feels a growing sense of awareness that he is partly a person that's gonna teach people about things they don't know. When he was younger . . . I remember when he was probably in third grade; he was so upset one night: "I'll never be able to do this. I'll never be able to do that."

And I said to him, and I've said it a number of times, "You know, you're a pioneer. You know what a pioneer is, right? [*Laughs.*] You're a pioneer. Most people have never met anyone quite like you. So part of what you can do is to show them how much you're like them and what's different for you."

My Friends Are on the Sports Teams

Aaron

I'm a three-sport athlete. And that takes up almost my entire year. I have cross-country and then I get a week off. After that, I start swimming. And then really right after that, I start track practice. I even do track in the summer.

My teaching assistant in school is an assistant coach on the basketball team. So I also know a lot of the kids there.

Even though my graduating class is gonna be over eight hundred people, being involved in all the sports makes the school feel a lot smaller . . . because it's easier to get to know people.

A lot of my friends are on the sports teams.

Coach Is a Genius

Birdy

The high school cross-country and track coach knew our family because our older son also runs. So when Aaron was young, before he was even in high school, I'd told the coach about Aaron, who's fairly competitive for his disability class. When Aaron started high school as a freshman, the athletic trainer came and gave a little talk about the seizure rescue medication . . . God forbid he has a seizure at the pool or at the track. And the coach had Aaron talk about it too. My older son came home and said, "Coach is a genius, mom."

Because apparently the coach had said to the kids, "You know, we might be out somewhere at a meet or something. And in cross-country we're like a family. Somebody might try to make fun of Aaron. Somebody might look at him and see he's different and try to start something. And I know you're all gonna want to kick that person in the ass. I'm gonna wanna kick that person in the ass. But that's not what we're gonna do. We're gonna find a better way. We're gonna figure out how we can help that person."

So my oldest son came home and said, "Not only is everybody now gonna be looking out for Aaron in sports, but no one is gonna let anybody mess with him at our school either. Because coach just set this standard. He just said, 'We're family. We protect each other.'"

You can nominate coaches for an award, and Aaron wrote a nomination for this coach. He said in his nomination what a huge thing it was that the coach had talked about the seizures in front of the whole team. Not just the coaches, not just the captains, but in front of the whole team. He said, "It made me feel that it's OK. I can be here. I'm part of this team, and it's not a big, scary thing."

I would say that out of all the stigmatizing things . . . the physicals, it is what it is. You look different. People think whatever they think. But seizures are really scary. They're very stigmatized in this culture, I would say. But that little action from the coach made a huge difference for him. For Aaron it was just this way of acknowledging that he was part of the team. That it was no big deal.

Just Because I Had a Disability, It Didn't Mean That I Was Different
Aaron

I've noticed some people will look at me. But I don't really pay attention to it that much.

I was running in a cross-country meet. As I was finishing, a kid from another team was asking . . . and he was standing right by my mom, "Why is that kid's arm swinging like that?"

When I run, I swing my arms kind of awkwardly. I swing my arms forward like this . . . across my body. This kid said it in front of my mom, and she said something like, "Well, he has a physical disability. And yet he is able to outrun you too!"

From the very first day of my freshman year, my coaches made sure that everyone knew that just because I had a disability, it didn't mean that I was different. They said that to the whole team. It probably also helped a lot that I had an older brother who ran.

I'm the only one with a physical disability running on the track team and swimming on the swim team. I think I'm the only one at school with a physical disability who's doing sports.

All my coaches have been helpful to me. Like, my sophomore year . . . [*Shouting:*] Mom, do you remember this? My sophomore year, one of the freshmen asked the coach why he kept putting me in the races. I think he also wanted to run in the meet. I don't know what the boy said exactly. Because it didn't happen in front of me. But afterward the coach went in front of the entire team and basically said, "Well, Aaron might be the slow person on our team because he has CP. But in his classifications, he's one of the fastest people in the United States. That's why he runs in the races."

You Don't Wanna Be Inspirational Just Because You Exist!

Birdy

What I think is more the case for me is the narrative of inspiration porn. You know, "Aaron is just so wonderful. He's so lucky to have you. You're a saint." Saint Birdy. Wow. "It must be so hard."

Like I can't feel the same joy that you do. When in fact my guess is that when my son walked, my joy was quite a bit greater than yours.

People say to me, "I could never do what you do. Aaron is so lucky to have you."

And depending on the mood I'm in [*laughs*], I might shoot back, "What are you talking about? *Lucky* would be if this didn't happen. *Lucky* would be he got to have the same stressors that your children have. That's lucky. To get born with your brain uninjured would be lucky." Or I'll say something like, "You know, you only have two choices really. You can go to bed and give up. Or you can do what you do for your kid. What are your other choices? Of course you would do what I do. You might not do it the same way, but you would do it."

One of the things that I think about a lot because of the political situation is what it is about us that makes us want to make these distinctions. These us-and-them kind of distinctions. Like, *If I'd gotten a kid like that, it would have been much worse. Because you're a saint, and I'm not. It's fair that it happened to your kid. It's right. Good for you.*

As opposed to *Between us there is more in common than is distinct*. It always feels like they're putting me over here.

The whole inspiration business is really mixed and problematic. I don't have a problem if you're finding it inspirational that my son can run a mile in six and a half minutes on a track. Or I don't mind finding the efforts inspirational. But his existence is not inspirational . . . I mean, not more than mine or anyone else's is. That's where I think it gets complicated.

You don't wanna be inspirational just because you exist!

It Was Inspiring

Aaron

I went to the Paralympic trials in North Carolina in 2016. That was an incredible experience. [*Soft voice:*] I could see people who would be on the Paralympic team.

After the trials were over, I got to go in the room where they announced who would be on the team. I didn't think I would be on the team. No. I was just hoping to get like a PR [personal record], to perform my best there. I'm aiming for 2020.

At the trials I got to see people of every disability doing high-level sports. It was inspiring. It was also incredible to know that I was there. That I was competing in such a huge event.

11 | IF NOBODY THINKS I'M WORTHY, MAYBE I'M NOT

When I was a child, I would proudly show my report card to my parents. Most often, my father would ask me why I did not get the highest score possible. He would smile. But my results were never really good enough. I was never good enough. I still catch myself trying to live up to the ideal of perfection. But even more so, I practice accepting that I am just fine.

PEOPLE WITH DISABILITIES ARE often blocked by ongoing experiences of being excluded and frequent instances of discrimination. As explained by Rene Moses in chapter 1: "It's hard to take back those kinds of moments in someone's growing-up time. It becomes very profoundly shaping."

If a group in society is seen as inferior, when generation after generation of people with disabilities have been treated as if they are subhuman and have no value, it intrinsically affects the way the group perceives itself. Kathiana describes in this chapter how she internalized that she was not good enough, which is "the burden that society in general puts on people with disabilities." Kathiana shares, "You're not valued and you have centuries of being devalued. [. . .] After a while, you go, 'Screw it.'"

Psychological internalization is a component of disability oppression. In James Charlton's words, "It creates a (false) consciousness and alienation that divides people and isolates individuals. Most people with disabilities actually come to believe that they are less normal, less capable than others."* They are getting beaten down and come to believe that they are less.

---

* James I. Charlton, *Nothing About Us Without Us: Disability Oppression and Empowerment* (Berkeley: University of California Press, 2000), 27.

245

As poet Kenny Fries writes in his memoir, "I have internalized everything the world threw my way about my different body to the point where the feelings seemed my own."*

Some people with disabilities refuse to accept perceptions of inferiority. Like Mike Ervin, who explains in this chapter how vigorously he is against people with disabilities internalizing that they are less than: "I can't think of one reason why anybody should ever do that. I think that's the worst we do. And I think that's the biggest mistake we make." But the reality for many individuals is more difficult, more complex.

Chimamanda Ngozi Adichie says, "We are all social beings. We internalize ideas from our socialization."†

Many people with disabilities clearly see that the way they are treated has more to do with their surroundings than with their individual impairments and capabilities. The problem is the attitudinal, structural, and physical barriers in society. It is not the fault of persons with disabilities that they are excluded and discriminated against. It is something bigger than that. It is the social. It is the other.

So genuine equality will not emerge from changing or building up the self-confidence of the individual person with a disability. Genuine equality is more about educating others and tearing down barriers in society. Andrew Solomon warns, "Self-acceptance is part of the ideal, but without familial and societal acceptance, it cannot ameliorate the relentless injustices to which many horizontal identity groups are subject and will not bring about adequate reform."‡

---

* Kenny Fries, *In the Province of the Gods* (Madison: University of Wisconsin Press, 2017), 16.

† Chimamanda Ngozi Adichie, *We Should All Be Feminists* (New York: Anchor Books, 2014), 30.

‡ Andrew Solomon, *Far from the Tree: Parents, Children, and the Search for Identity* (New York: Scribner, 2012), 6.

YOU'RE NOT IMPORTANT ENOUGH

MIKE ERVIN

Thirty years ago, public transportation in Chicago was all but impossible to use if you were in a wheelchair. This was the issue that brought together the Chicago chapter of ADAPT. Change was needed, and this group was ready to act. ADAPT is a grassroots national community that organizes nonviolent direct actions to assure the human rights of people with disabilities. I met with Mike, who has been a member of Chicago ADAPT since the beginning.

She Just Assumed That We Were Smart Kids

I have what I believe to be spinal muscular dystrophy. I was born in 1956. When I was a kid in the sixties, they called everything muscular dystrophy. They would just take a guess. Personally, I never really cared. I wasn't really diagnosis oriented. I mean, what difference did it make?

I'm the third of three children. My sister also had muscular dystrophy, and she lived until 2011 . . . died at the age of fifty-seven. And I had a brother with muscular dystrophy who was born in 1946 and lived until 1954.

So I was born on an army base in Germany because my father was in the army. We moved back to the South Side of Chicago after that. As my father was in the army, he wasn't around very much. I pretty much feel that I was raised by a single mom. Even though that's not technically true, that was basically the reality. In my childhood the person who was doing all the heavy lifting with the parent stuff was my mom. And my dad was pretty much the guy who went out to raise money.

I don't think my mom had an ideology or an agenda raising my sister and me. I think she was naive in a good way. Maybe naive isn't the word, but a lot of other parents would have thought, *Oh God. Another kid . . . And especially the third one . . . One has died already from this disability. Let's put him in bubble wrap and make him safe.*

But she just assumed that we were smart kids. Like every other kid around us, we were going to college. We would do something. And I never really thought otherwise. It was kind of surprising to me, when I was around ten or eleven years old, to realize that other people would have other ideas about that. But at that time it was too late—I wasn't going to internalize all that stuff. My mother's attitude had a lot to do with that.

Still today, I am vigorously against internalizing that we're less than. That's the worst. Plus I don't think there is any reason to ever do that. I can't think of one reason why anybody should ever do that. I think that's the worst we do. And I think that's the biggest mistake we make. If there's one thing I want to get across to people, it's to say, "Stop." Just say, "Bullshit. Bullshit. Bullshit. Bullshit. Bullshit. Bullshit. Bullshit. Bullshit." Whenever people tell you stuff about being less . . . Because it never serves you well.

I think it came from the assumptions that my mom had. She took us places. We went places. I never really felt like I didn't deserve to go. That I didn't belong.

All Kinds of Freaks Were Put Together

My sister and I went to segregated schools until we started college. For high school we went to the Illinois Children's Hospital School. At that time, it was a boarding school for kids with disabilities. So it was super segregated, essentially. We lived at the school during the week. It was a little different for us being at the state school because the school was mostly intended for kids who were wards of the state and didn't have families. So there weren't a lot of us going home every weekend and for summers like my sister and I did. We were kind of out of place. But we were at the school because my father wasn't around, and my mother was going to a secretarial school to get a better job.

I can't say that I hated school. But I also didn't like the state school I was sent to. It was different. And after a while, I began to wonder, *Why am I being sent here? Why are all these kids being sent here?* I didn't necessarily resent it, but I wondered about it.

At the state school, all kinds of freaks were put together. That was the main qualification for sending children there. If you look at the definition of disability, it should be about whether it's hard for you to perform certain activities. But there was a kid at school . . . and the only reason he was there was because his face was burned and it was all scarred. That didn't keep him from performing any activities. It just made him a freak. So they sent him there because that's where they'd send the freaks. [*Laughs.*] The criteria was mostly "Are you a freak?" "Do you not belong?" "Do you scare or upset other people at other schools?"

I did feel out of place. My school friends were totally different than my home friends. It was something that I noticed. I had good friends at home— neighbor kids and cousins. They were pretty good about figuring out ways to include me in the bunch. Even when they played baseball, I'd get in there somehow. And they didn't try to push me out. I was also in a wheelchair when I was a child.

I didn't have a name for discrimination at the time. But so much around me was inaccessible. To get into the museum, my mom had to have all these people and guards yank us all the way up the stairs. There were no curb cuts. And lots of buildings were inaccessible. So pretty much every day I was excluded in some ways. But I didn't really realize until I was older what was going on.

Socially . . . the problem wasn't individual people so much as systems. People in my neighborhood were generally pretty good about accommodating. But the systems and the cultures were in general so exclusionary that—I can see now—I was left out of many things.

All I Really Wanted to Do Was to Become a Writer

I got a better understanding of discrimination when I was looking around for colleges because I started to realize how few colleges that I could actually go to. A lot of colleges were completely inaccessible. I wanted to major in journalism.

I ended up going to Southern Illinois University. I lived in a dorm for two years. I hired people to help me. I remember insisting that my worker should be my roommate. So for the two years that I lived in the dorm, my workers were my roommates.

I was stubbornly trying to dismiss [questions like "How are you going to work in journalism if you can't run out to cover a fire?"]. But then I would be secretly thinking, *Maybe they have a point.* I was still determined. *I'll figure it out. This is what I wanna do. There must be other ways. There must be other things that I can do.* All I really wanted to do was to become a writer.

I think it probably [affected my self-esteem] more than I'd realized. But I was very stubborn at the time, and I wouldn't let it dissuade me. It might have slowed me down a little bit. Then again, it might have made me more aggressive. I don't know. It might have made me more determined to figure out a way in. But really . . . I don't know.

I and Others Were Excluded

I graduated from college in 1978. Until '84, I lived in my mother's house. I then moved into subsidized housing with a woman who I ended up marrying. She died about fifteen years later. I worked for a while at a newspaper, and then I was freelancing. I still do freelance. I wanted to get around. I was a young man, and I wanted to go places. Especially when I started freelancing, I wanted to get around more. I wanted to be out there and pursue things, and I didn't want to depend on anybody. But there were very few transportation options.

So in the early '80s they started the door-to-door paratransit. And I thought, *Wow. I can go somewhere without anybody.* But the conditions were ridiculous—like nine to five on weekends. And then there was the whole drill of waiting. So I very quickly felt the opposite. I started to feel insulted. I wasn't used to having curfews. Like, it was five o'clock on a Saturday and I would have to say, "I have to go home now."

So I went from feeling liberated to feeling insulted. At the same time, ADAPT started up in Chicago. This was in 1983.

I began reading *Rules for Radicals* by Saul D. Alinsky. And what was going on all really clicked in my mind. I remember feeling really stupid. For all these years, I'd been living in my mother's house, there was a bus that ran right down her street every day. And it wasn't until this moment of reading this book that I realized that I never once thought that the bus was for me. I was just so used to not being a part of it that I didn't even consider it to be an option. I remember thinking, *Oh my God. Look at what you have been doing to yourself all these years.*

That was when I really started to not only think about things in terms of myself but in terms of the bigger picture. About how systemically and systematically I and others were excluded. That was when it all really started to click for me. Before that, I was very good at negotiating my own space on the lifeboat. I could save myself and stand up for myself. But then I realized that the reason that I had to do that and that I had to fight so hard every time was because of this larger problem. And the answer is really more long term, more brutal and harder. So the more permanent answer for me was to join all these other folks and attack the problems as root causes. I became an activist.

It Felt Empowering, and That's Good

Shortly after this, I got involved in ADAPT. A group of us had a series of kitchen meetings. We put together our first action. Chicago had zero accessible buses at the time. It was even more insulting when I started to learn that all these other cities in the US had accessible buses. We said that any new buses had to be accessible. Our first action was that we simply showed up at the offices of the CTA [Chicago Transit Authority] board. We learned that this was the pressure point because there were seven people on that board. So that was the place to go and direct the action. We'd also go to people who had influence on the board, like the governor, who appoints three members, and the mayor, who appoints four. So that was where we put pressure.

We did various actions and we would go to those board meetings and disrupt them—we were noisemakers. The good thing about it was that there was always press there for the meetings anyway. So we could just [*laughs*] . . . They would always write about us. We also brought a lawsuit. This is what ADAPT people call the pitchfork approach . . . Lawsuits. Political pressure. Street pressure. Just whatever you can pile on. Don't stick with just one particular route. Get them from all angles. So that was essentially what we did. We did street actions. We brought a lawsuit. And we had meetings with the governor. Eventually the board switched, and we won.

I enjoyed it because I remember one time—and this was with the woman that I was married to at the time—I was waiting for a ride home from the city, and right in front of Marshall Field's pulled up the No. 11 bus, which would have taken us to, like, half a block from where we lived. And I remember thinking, *Damn. I'm sitting here waiting for this paratransit, and there is a bus right there.* But then we had an action coming up, and I remember thinking, *That's alright. We're gonna get you folks!* And then I felt better. I didn't feel the hopelessness. I felt like I had some control over it. So I enjoyed it in that respect. It felt empowering, and that's good.

You're So Unimportant That We Don't Even Think About You

In general, I think people have a very severe distaste for disability and for people with disabilities. At least some do. And I think the systems in society are rooted in that distaste. The thinking is, *You're so unimportant that we don't even think about you.*

You have to prove that you're human. You're wasting all this time trying to prove that you're human. Other people don't have to do that. It's like a Monopoly game. In order to be in the game, you have to start off showing that you're human—and all these other folks, they just got in and started playing . . . When you've proven that you're human too, then you can finally start playing the game. But by that time, all these other people have gotten this huge head start on you. [*Laughs.*] Just because you're in it doesn't mean that you're necessarily playing alongside everybody else.

I think transportation is an example. Once I got a grip on it . . . Why wasn't the bus accessible? Because someone thought that I'm not important. People wouldn't say that directly. But they would say stuff like "Are we gonna spend all that money on a lift, when there's only five of you?" and "You're not important enough!" They wouldn't say it directly, but this is what they meant.

I'M FREE FROM THAT NOW

KATHIANA

I visited Kathiana in River Forest, just west of Oak Park. Her apartment was full of sunlight and dominated by blue colors. We sat at her polished wooden dining table. We drank juice and just talked. After the interview, Kathiana asked me to help her with a document on her computer. After all that she had given me during our several hours of conversation, it felt wrong that I didn't know how to fix her problem. But I didn't.

They Never Made Me Feel Like I Was Different, or Special

I'm a twin. I was born in 1954, with my brother. We were premature. So we were placed into incubators. I stayed in the incubator for about a month. My brother was able to gain weight and leave the incubator sooner, and he does not have any disabilities. They discovered that there was too much oxygen in the incubator, so I developed what was called retinopathy of prematurity. What it meant was that the oxygen in the incubator settled in my eyes and caused me to become visually impaired. I'm legally blind. I do have some vision, but it's limited.

I grew up in Chicago, in the inner city in a neighborhood called Englewood. It's getting a lot of bad publicity now. When we first moved there as kids, it was racially mixed. But eventually it became predominately African American. I grew up with my parents and my brother, and we were African Americans.

I'm really grateful for the way my family treated me with my disability. I mean, they were realistic about what I could do and couldn't do. They didn't treat me differently than my brother. For example, when my brother got his first bike with training wheels, I got my first bike with training wheels. When we played softball, I got to go out and play softball too. My dad would often play with us, and they would slow it down so I could hit the ball. But there was no special treatment—like "She can't do this because she's visually impaired." They never thought that way. It was more "You do the best you can." I was grateful for that. Because they never made me feel like I was different, or special. That was really good.

When I was about sixteen years old, I started taking skiing lessons. That was the best thing that ever happened to me. I just adored it. It was amazing. It was also interesting because of my family's reaction. We were from the inner city, so people didn't know anything about skiing. That wasn't part of what people were doing. I would go outside the city to this area in Wisconsin or other places where they had little hills, relatively small hills. But I learned how to ski. And my family, they really had a hard time. That's the first time that they ever said anything about being concerned about my well-being. Because they just didn't get it. "How can you go out there and ski? It's dangerous for you." But they realized that I loved it.

I would say, "My brother, he plays football. That's dangerous. You guys let him do that. This is what I like to do." And they just kind of shook their heads and said OK.

They Said *Nigger* Like You'd Say *Potato Chips* or *Toast*

Because I was visually impaired, I was sent to schools in the city that had special programs for children with visual impairments. When I first started kindergarten, they thought I had no vision, and they taught me a little Braille. What happened was that they noticed I would take a piece of paper and try to hold it up to my eyes. They realized that I had a little bit of sight. So then I was put into classes where they had large prints. I was able to read large-print materials, but only on a limited basis. I still had the resource room.

School was pretty tough, to be honest with you. That was hard. I went to predominantly white schools. We were bused. The bus would pick me up in my neighborhood and take me to school. My bus-mates were black, white, Asian, Hispanic. But when we got to the school, it was predominantly white. So in kindergarten or first grade, that wasn't a big deal. But as we got older, kids would call us racial slurs and some really horrible names. You know? I didn't understand it. It was really hurtful. At that time, the teachers didn't say anything about it. Most of it happened when we were at the playground. I don't know if the teachers knew and just ignored it. But there was no conversation about it.

When I got to junior high, I transferred to another school. The school was in an area of Chicago called Marquette Park. During that time, it was one of the most racist parts of the city. So when I went to Marquette Park School, people would have swastika signs up. Their kids would have swastika signs up. They didn't like Jews, and they didn't like blacks, and they were brutal.

There was only myself and two other black kids in the school at the time I was there. I remember that in some of the classrooms the kids would move out of their seats because they didn't want to sit next to me. They called us the N-word. They said *nigger* like you'd say *potato chips* or *toast*. It just rolled off their tongues as if it was nothing. They said that we had diseases. And a couple of times I knew the teachers knew and just ignored it. They ignored it. We would go out to the playground, and these big white bullies would come up to us and say that they were gonna beat us up. We were little kids. I was afraid. It hurt because I didn't understand it. Primarily because that wasn't the way I was taught in my home. We had people of different races who'd visit and come in and out of our house over the years.

I remember one day I was in my homeroom class and somebody—a white boy—said, "What are chitlins? Or chitterlings?" What it is, if you don't know, is a dish that African Americans, primarily, have eaten over the years. Not my cup of tea anyway. But somebody was asking the teacher.

And this teacher said—and I was standing right next to her at the time— "That's what the nigger children eat."

I was standing right next to this teacher. And she said this. It always stayed in my head. This teacher, who was supposed to be my teacher in the homeroom for all of us who were visually impaired. That was when I realized . . . I didn't know the word *racist* at all. It wasn't part of my vocabulary. But I realized that she had prejudice. And I must have been eleven or twelve years old.

The other thing that happened when I was in this school was that Martin Luther King Junior died. I remember it was a school day. We were still coming out of Marquette Park School and getting on the bus. Some of these white kids came taunting us and said, "Your leader is dead! Your leader is dead! What are you niggers gonna do now? Your—leader—is—dead!" As we were leaving the neighborhood, they were throwing bricks at the bus.

So I graduated from Marquette Park School and went on to high school. One of my friends, who had albinism, said that she would never get over the treatment that she'd experienced in that school. She said that she would never have anything to do with anybody white because she just hated the way that she had been treated. But I had friends of all races, and my parents did too. So I understood that this group of mean-spirited and racist people did not represent all people. That helped me.

Even though my brother and I were twins, we were sent to different schools. The schools that I went to were in predominantly white communities. They had the resources to support me as a visually impaired person. They didn't have that available to the same degree in the neighborhood that I lived in. So I went through grade school, from kindergarten through eighth grade, in special classes. My brother stayed in neighborhood schools.

When we went to high school, there was a special needs room in the high school that my brother was going to. But my parents didn't send me to that high school because, by the time we got to high school, the level of education that I'd received—I hate to say this, but in all honesty—it was a higher level of education than my twin brother had received in the schools closer to our house. So it was decided by the board of education and my parents that I would continue going to a different school rather than move back into a place where it wouldn't have been as challenging for me. As I look back on it now, it seems strange. Now that I understand more about discrimination and who gets resources and who doesn't get resources, I can see the discrimination that my brother experienced at that point.

It Was Like Double Hell

In school . . . Was it race? Was it disability? That's the thing, you don't know. You really don't know. That's part of the struggle. The fact was that I was in special needs classes in school. I was put into that environment because I had a disability. Some people said stuff: "You're blind." "You can't see." I heard those taunts too. I had both. I—heard—both.

The other thing that I heard was people in my own community saying to me, "Why do your eyes always do this?" My eyes move around more than most people's do. I wore glasses, and they would call me four-eyes.

So I got both. And I got both in both communities. Not so much taunting in my neighborhood. It was more people asking questions all the time. But in school, in addition to the race-baiting, I also did get the stuff on disability. So it was like double hell. It's like you're getting slammed because you're visually impaired, which you can't do anything about, and you're getting slammed because you're black, which you can't do anything about. It wasn't like one over the other. It was both.

Teachers used to say to us visually impaired kids, "Because you're visually impaired, you have to work harder than all the other kids. You have to work doubly or triply harder than they do just to prove yourself and make sure that you can get a job so you can move ahead."

Saying that to a kid really was complicated, because I felt like I had to always do more. It pushed me to be a perfectionist. In terms of my own self-esteem, I was hard on myself. Because I wanted to be accepted like every other kid. And the only way that I could be accepted was by working hard. I didn't wanna be treated differently. I didn't wanna have different expectations. It was already pounded into my mind: "In order for you to succeed, you have to work harder than everybody else."

I think it affected my whole work ethic. It's only as an older adult now that I'm finally able to say, "That's crazy. I don't have to do that." But I spent a lifetime doing it. And as I look back on it, it was exhausting . . . Exhausting. Because what I began to do was internalize that I wasn't good enough . . . I wasn't good enough. No matter what I would do, it was never gonna be enough. So that's the burden I began to put on myself. And I think, in some ways, it's the burden that society in general puts on people with disabilities.

Part of what I did was program myself to just keep going. To just keep doing. Just go. Just go. Just go. It's amazing what we'll get our bodies and brains to do. It's not always good for us, but sheer will does a lot. I'm not saying that it's necessarily a good thing. You just get on a roll. And you just do it. Do it. Do it. That's what I did.

We Don't Want a Black, Blind Pastor

After I finished college, I went to graduate school to get a master's degree in Christian education. I was almost finished with that degree, and I got a nudging to become a pastor. And I said, "I don't wanna be a pastor. I go skiing on Sundays. Get somebody else. I'm not the one. I ski. No."

But obviously there came a point that I knew that it was my way. It was a calling. I knew I had to go. That meant two more years of graduate school to get what we call a United Methodist Church master of divinity. I was already stressed about school, but still I made the commitment. That was a faith commitment to me.

My first job was in a local predominantly black church. It was maybe a ten-minute train ride away from Oak Park, where I lived. The guy that I worked with was a prominent African American pastor. It was a big church, and I was the associate pastor. I learned a lot. But another discrimination happened. I was working on my ordination. I was just about ready to become ordained. And this pastor made a pass at me. All this stuff about Donald Trump that they're talking about brought up a whole lot to me. Because I was in the pastor's office, and this man walks up to me . . . and he kisses me. I was totally unprepared. And startled. So my basic response was to take my hand and wipe my mouth and walk out of his office. And say what these women say today, "That didn't just happen, did it? It was some horrible dream."

To make a very complicated story short, this guy was on the board of ordination, and he tried to stop my ordination after that. He said, "She's not fit. She's not a good pastor. I worked with her. She doesn't have the tools that she needs to be a pastor."

I went before the board of ordination. They're supposed to ask you a lot of theological questions. But the interesting thing was that when I went before the board, they spent most of the time asking me questions about how I would get around. It was all about me being visually impaired. I was like, *Oh man. Here's this guy being on the board of ordination, and I'm getting all these questions . . . if I'm really fit because I don't drive.*

"How will you get around? You can't drive." "How will you do your sermons when you can't see?" So we spent a lot of time on that. I was just like, *After all this time, I'm probably not even gonna get ordained.* So here's more stress. More stress.

I told a woman pastor who was also on the board what the guy had done. There was a big deal about it. They had to make a choice to either believe him or me. Luckily, this woman was really strong and stood up for me becoming a pastor. So I was finally ordained in 1980 and began to work in local churches.

I moved to another church in Oak Park. This was in the '80s. And race came into play again. The bishop appointed me to that church. But there were people saying when they found out that I was gonna be the pastor—even before they knew me—"If she's a pastor, we're not coming." Some said, "We don't want a blind pastor." Some said, "We don't want a black pastor." Some said, "We don't want a black, blind pastor." So, *bam* [*laughs*], they stopped coming. They hadn't even met me.

It was on my first night in the parish. I was unpacking with an old college friend. The doorbell rang, and six people came to the house. "We wanna talk to you."

These were all white people from the church. We went in and sat in the dining room. I asked what they wanted. And they said, "Hey look, we don't want you to take offense at this, but we don't want you as our pastor."

I was thinking, *Oh my God, what am I gonna do?* So I said, "What's the bottom line?"

They said, "We want you to leave."

And I said, "My bottom line is, I'm not leaving. But you certainly are welcome to."

Ultimately, they did. We had about eight prominent families leave the church. They never saw me in the church before telling me that they didn't want me in their church. That was race. Yeah. That was predominantly race. I mean, they didn't want a person with a disability either. [*Laughs.*] You just juggle the cards which one you want it to be. Depends on who you talk to. So they left. [*Sighs.*] And I stayed. The good thing that happened was that people who would have given me hell left. The rest were so embarrassed that it turned out to be a great church. But it was painful.

That Horrible Perception

I had experienced racism before. And I had decided at this point in my life that these people in church didn't know me. That they were working from their own lack of knowledge, not mine. So I had to separate myself from them, because they didn't know me. They made assumptions that affected their lives. It affected me too. But they were the ones who left the church they loved.

That's why the election of Trump is so painful for me. Because of all the race-baiting and all the prejudice that has come out about people with disabilities and the womanizing stuff. All of those things hit me at my core. It has such a potential to diminish another person's life, unless the person has the fortitude and the clarity about who he or she is as a person. For me . . . It's taken me years to get there. I mean, that's why words that people speak can have a powerful effect on the outcome of other people's lives. On the lives of people that they'll never meet.

I have been very fortunate to have people who care about me, I have a strong faith, and I try not to let people's ignorance stop me from moving ahead in my life. Of course it saddens me. But now that I'm older, it saddens me more for them. Because it's their lack of knowledge of themselves and of humanity as a whole that keeps them at a lower level of happiness. I really feel that people who have all these issues with a person who's visually impaired, or who has a disability or is black or whatever, they're the ones who are diminished. I am not. It's taken me a long time to figure that out. But I have figured it out. So it just makes me sad. But I don't take it on anymore. It's like, *That's your problem! I've been there. I know what that's like. I don't have to do that. I'm free from that now.* But it's taken a lot of unearthing and just having good people in my life.

Some of the violence that's happening in predominantly black communities today—and people asking why they're doing this—my theory is that if a group is seen as inferior for generation after generation after generation . . . If you take the whole concept of slavery in this country, which nobody wants to talk about. People were enslaved. Some got out of slavery, but the stereotypical attitude toward black men has still not changed to the point of acceptance. If generation after generation after generation is treated as if they are subhuman, treated as if they have no value, I think it intrinsically will affect how a group perceives itself. If you say I don't have any value, then I stop valuing myself after a point. Screw it. Why should I? If nobody thinks I'm worthy of it, maybe I'm not!

If a society treats you all the time like you have to prove your worth. If you're not valued and you have centuries of being devalued—you can say the same about people with disabilities. Why aren't more of them working? Because there are so many barriers. People are saying that you're not capable. You almost have to be superman or superwoman, or that's what they make you think—not true—to feel that you can even compete. After a while, you go, "Screw it, I'm not gonna do it! I'm not gonna compete! I don't care. I'm just gonna live my life and have lower expectations of my own abilities."

We as a society get cheated. People who could give an amazing gift of their own abilities to the world don't get to do it. Because they give up. I really do understand when people say, "I'm done with that." It does take a toll on you.

I retired early—in my fifties. And once I did, I realized I was exhausted . . . Exhausted. Because I had spent all these years just revving it up. Doing it. Doing it. Doing it. And I think I did an OK job of it, probably a pretty good job of it. [*Sighs.*] But I got exhausted. Because I'd given and given and given. And I'm happy with what I gave. But there comes a point where you go, "I've given you all I have. Done."

I think that's what happens to people if they are experiencing ongoing stress and strain—or just diminishment. In the case of people with disabilities, the lack of inclusion in terms of jobs, it's ridiculous. Same thing with race. People who feel that they are treated as if they have no worth take on that horrible perception after a while. And they begin to act the way people expect them to act. I'm by no means saying that's the full case . . . but I do think that generations of maltreatment or inappropriate thinking has an effect on a group. So I think what you're doing is important. I think the only way around that is for people in these groups to say, "Here are some role models. Here are people that are making it. This is something that I can do too."

In addition to clearing away barriers in society . . . if we want people with disabilities to feel that they're valued, then opportunities to be valued have to be put in place.

EPILOGUE

Intersectionality

The phenomenon of disability oppression has many parallels in class, gender, sex, and race oppression.* People with disabilities are objectified in ways that are very similar to the experiences of other oppressed groups.

People with disabilities are more than "just" persons with disabilities. Apart from disability, every individual contains an intersection of multiple vertical and horizontal identities: gender, race, sex, religion, class, and more. The voices in this book primarily focus on disability identity and talk about their experiences of exclusion and discrimination because of disability. Yet a number of them also talk about situations where they experienced oppression stemming not only from disability but also from race and gender. Most often, disability oppression itself is only a partial experience of oppression.

Kathiana describes her appointment as a new pastor to a church where some parishioners, whom she had never met, left the church upon her arrival. They didn't want a blind, black pastor.

Andre explains how she was caught in the middle. She grew up in Chinatown with her Chinese father and African American mother. She had a strong Chinese identity but realized early on that this was not the way she was perceived by others. She was rejected from participating in a summer camp. Andre was called names like "nigger chink." She did not understand why or what was going on: "For some reason, it made me angry. But I didn't understand my anger." When Andre was around twelve years old, she moved with her mother to an African American neighborhood in South Chicago. In Chinatown she had never thought of herself as different because she was blind. But in her

---

* James I. Charlton, *Nothing About Us Without Us: Disability Oppression and Empowerment* (Berkeley: University of California Press, 2000), 75, 164.

new neighborhood people would stare at her and ask her questions: "Can my kids catch what you have?" At the time, Andre did not really understand the reference line. She did not think she had anything: "As far as I was concerned, I didn't have a disease."

All over the world, a great number of people with disabilities live in poverty. Poverty exposes people to conditions that result in disability. And people with disabilities who are poor often live in neighborhoods where attitudinal and physical barriers are even greater than in wealthier neighborhoods. Disability can be both the cause and the consequence of class and poverty.

Candace Coleman explains how she feels imprisoned mentally, physically, and emotionally. Candace has a physical disability and experiences discrimination on a daily basis because of the physical barriers in her surroundings. She also describes the poverty in her neighborhood that results in a lack of reasonable accommodations. Finally, she constantly experiences racial discrimination in all layers of society. She says, "It's like a three-layer whammy."

The reality is that ableism, racism, classism, sexism, and other prejudices are usually inextricable from one another. Forms of oppression interrelate and entangle. They create systems of exclusion and injustice that reflect the intersection of multiple forms of discrimination. James Charlton describes how the barriers that he is up against as a white, middle-class, spinal cord–injured man are not the same as a poor African American woman with a mental illness. He concludes, "When you're looking at discrimination and intersectionality, it's very hard to parse out whether persons are being discriminated against because they're black or because they're disabled or because they're poor. They're probably getting discriminated against on the basis of all of the above. You'd never really know."

In short, the different kinds of oppression feed one another. And this understanding is the foundation for the theory of intersectionality, recognizing that ableism cannot be eliminated without addressing racism, classism, and other forms of discrimination in concert. In order to significantly advance social change, the struggle for genuine equality for people with disabilities must be linked to other peoples' movements.

Human Diversity

Some of the people I have interviewed for this book may live on the fringes, but they are productive members of society. And although they face challenges (most of them environmental), they value the opportunity to contribute their unique experiences to the diversity of the world.

People with disabilities might want to improve their condition, but fundamentally, they don't want to change. Andrew Solomon proposes that only by allowing people with horizontal identities "*not* to change does one allow them to get better. Any of us can be a better version of himself, but none of us can be someone else."* Heather Gabel explains how she sees "disability as an aspect of human variation more than anything." People with disabilities are simply part of human diversity and should be accepted as such.

Coping Strategies

Looking at the bigger picture, the exclusion of persons with disabilities is systemic and systematic. And the impact on the group as well as on the individual with a disability is huge. Exclusion is interwoven in many layers of everyday life and is sometimes difficult to see. However, for the excluded group of people with disabilities, it is an ever-present specter haunting most spheres of their lives. As a group, persons with disabilities are left out and frequently told to just stay at home. For the individual person with a disability, the general experiences of exclusion are often exacerbated by concrete instances of discrimination.

Rather than simply outlining how persons with disabilities live with their individual impairments, this book illustrates how people with disabilities experience their surroundings. The book is about the social, the barriers of the world:

- The constant exclusion
- The physical, organizational, and structural walls and fences
- The preconceived ideas and negative attitudes
- The stares
- The degrading words
- The frequent discrimination

---

* Andrew Solomon, *Far from the Tree: Parents, Children, and the Search for Identity* (New York: Scribner, 2012), 687.

So how do people with disabilities respond to this oppressive world? How do they belong and live? What are the coping strategies for the individual person?

Judy describes how she deals with discrimination by educating others: "I almost always find the energy to follow up and educate. But initially . . . I'm angered. I am. When I follow up, the anger leaves me. It does. It doesn't stay. I just start wondering when it will happen next."

A blind woman, whose story is not part of this collection, once explained to me what she tries to do when people walk all over her: "Sometimes people that don't have disabilities think they can do that. They can't. And I would like to say that if you have a disability, make sure to be assertive and stand up for yourself. Speak up for yourself! Because a lot of times, nobody is gonna do it for you. You have to do it yourself."

The reality of poverty, exclusion, and degradation makes many people with disabilities angry and mad. They move toward greater self-awareness and social awareness, and they start acting and fighting for social change. But not every person with a disability responds like that. There are a number of ways that people with a disability cope with discrimination and exclusion:

- Internalization: People with disabilities come to think that they are less.
- Acceptance: People with disabilities accept a shrunken world. They make do.
- Realization: People with disabilities recognize that it's not about them. It's a problem of others.
- Anger: People with disabilities stand up and speak up. They claim their human rights and their dignity.
- Education: People with disabilities teach others. They try to make people without disabilities see and understand.
- Responsibility: People with disabilities feel the obligation to act. They take charge and organize. They become activists.
- Empowerment: People with disabilities recognize that they have power.

Though the list is by no means exhaustive, these strategies can serve as powerful tools for coping with the social—the world surrounding people with disabilities. Different people use different strategies at different times in their lives. The same person might end up adhering to all the strategies throughout his or her lifetime—and some of them at the same time. The list of coping strategies is not a linear process that every person with a disability necessarily goes through. However, thinking and acting and gaining more control are markers on a continuum toward empowerment, which is the antithesis of disability oppression.

Marca Bristo went through these different phases and became not only a resister but also a political activist. She explains how she personally experienced the paradigm shift from internalization and acceptance to realization, anger, and empowerment. She realized that she did not have to just suck it up and accept her shrunken world. She realized that it was the world that needed to change: "It was a moment of empowerment when I realized that I had something to offer that the rest of the world didn't have."

A Possible World

Disability is not miserable. But not being regarded, not being respected, being seen as less than, not being treated with dignity—all this is miserable. Barriers in the world can make living with a disability miserable. That is why people with disabilities struggle to survive. That is why people with disability fight to change the world.

I am worried, I must admit. Fear, intolerance, and ugly faces of bigotry worry me. I am worried about everyday ableism, sexism, classism, and racism. I am worried about inequality and discrimination against marginalized groups.

I dream about living in a world that is more respectful, where we care about common interests and the public good. I dream about living in a world where we listen and treat each other in a civilized manner. I dream about living in a world where being different and quirky is considered a value and not a threat. I dream about living in a world where genuine equality is a common goal that we strive for. I dream about living in a world where laws and policies and social structures promote true equality. I dream about living in a world where people with disabilities are no longer invisible.

Like the playwright Bertolt Brecht, I have sought to "understand the particular case," the individual voices of oppression, as one of the keys to advancing genuine equality.

It takes a lot of things to change the world:
Anger and tenacity. Science and indignation,
The quick initiative, the long reflection,
The cold patience and the infinite perseverance,
The understanding of the particular case and the understanding of
*   the ensemble:*
Only the lessons of reality can teach us to transform reality.

—Bertolt Brecht, "Einverständnis"

Writing is about attentiveness to life. I have listened to the voices of oppression, and I have written these voices down on paper. They have elicited empathy and identification. The voices have made it possible for me to imagine a kinder world. It is also a possible world.

ACKNOWLEDGMENTS

IT BRINGS GREAT SATISFACTION to thank an extraordinary group of people for their immeasurable contributions to making this book a reality.

I begin with the individuals I interviewed: thank you for everything. Most pages of this book are filled with your words. You invited me into your lives and you taught me greatly. Your stories will all be part of my being forever, and some of you have become dear friends. This book would not have been possible without your stories. Thank you—this one is for you.

Moving to Chicago from Denmark in 2014 was at the same time grueling and wonderful. When I missed home and was challenged by things being new and utterly different, welcoming neighborhood families and colleagues made all the difference. I thank each and every one of you for helping my family and me to feel that we belong.

My editor, Yuval Taylor, recognized the power of oral histories. I thank you, Yuval, for your patience and for always finding the right words. Thank you for understanding why this work matters. I would also like to thank Devon Freeny, Andrea Baird, and the rest of the team at Chicago Review Press. You were most helpful, kind, and inspiring.

I give special thanks to Heather O'Donnell from Thresholds, Barry Taylor from Equip for Equality, and Marca Bristo and Amber Smock from Access Living, who were the first disability rights activists I met when I moved to Chicago. Thank you for your engagement and for referring me to other inspiring organizations and individuals in Chicago. I began this project while still working in the legal department of Access Living, and I thank Ken Walden for that opportunity, for believing in my ideas, and for introducing me to my first interview subjects. In particular, I thank you, Marca Bristo, for your commitment and your ongoing support for this book. I am forever indebted to all of my former colleagues at Access Living, and I hope the book is a satisfying conclusion to this journey.

I thank my former colleagues at the Department of Disability and Human Development at the University of Illinois at Chicago, including Tamar Heller, Sarah Parker Harris, and Aly Patsavas, for inspiration and advice on this project. I am particularly appreciative of my collaborative work with Robert Gould. We developed a class on disability in world cultures and lectured together for three years at UIC. Thank you, Rob, for teaching me a great deal about American disability studies and for your continued and most compassionate encouragement on this book.

I am incredibly grateful for the title "From the Periphery," which was given to me by Jim (James) Charlton, who also read and commented on my whole manuscript several times. Thank you, Jim, for your important writings, which inspired me, and for your careful feedback and wise counsel.

I thank my brilliant Danish friend Helle Stenum, who listened for hours on the phone from Copenhagen and who cheered and mentored me. I am also grateful to my friends who read chapters in progress as well as the completed manuscript. Their thoughtful suggestions made this book possible. I thank Susan Nussbaum, Lili Duquette, Julie Peterson, Deena Hurwitz, Tish Armstrong, Melanie Hauck, Julia Cormier, Lone Amtrup, and Malou Halling. I give special thanks to Emily Whitfield, who guided me in every step of the process. Emily and her husband, Robert Fader, provided invaluable insights into the publishing world and wisely counseled me all the way from the start of the project to finding a publisher to the printing and marketing of this book. Lindsay Anderson professionally guided me in the world of social media, webpages, and marketing.

I thank the great writers who inspired me, in particular the oral historians Studs Terkel and Svetlana Alexievich. I had dinner with Andrew Solomon many years ago in Denmark. It was a truly stimulating evening, and I am grateful for the inspiration that his writings have been for me ever since.

Finally, for believing in me and empowering this work, I would like to thank my family. I am especially indebted to my partner in life, Torsten Madsen, and my children, Marius, Ida, and Alfred. Ida, in particular, I thank you for reading and commenting on different versions of this manuscript. To all of you, I am grateful for your unceasing support, your wisdom, and most of all for your love.

INDEX

ABOUT ACCESS LIVING

A PORTION OF ALL PROCEEDS from this book will go to Access Living. Established in 1980, Access Living is a change agent committed to fostering an inclusive society that enables Chicagoans with disabilities to live fully engaged and self-directed lives. It is a cross-disability organization governed and staffed by a majority of people with disabilities. Nationally recognized as a leading force in the disability advocacy community, it challenges stereotypes, protects civil rights, and champions social reform. Its staff and volunteers combine knowledge and personal experience to deliver programs and services that equip people with disabilities to advocate for themselves. The organization is at the forefront of the disability rights movement, removing barriers so people with disabilities can live the future they envision.

Access Living fosters the dignity, pride, and self-esteem of people with disabilities and enhances the options available to them so they may choose and maintain individualized and satisfying lifestyles. To this end, it offers peer-oriented independent living services; public education, awareness, and development; individualized and systemic advocacy; and enforcement of civil rights on behalf of people with disabilities.

For further information, visit www.accessliving.org.